'Many Australians say they want to know more about the history of the country and the culture they supplanted. This book would be a good place to start. The authors consulted east coast First Nations people and recorded their histories and their hopes and dreams. You will close this book feeling closer to your country and that begins the responsibility to care for her.'

BRUCE PASCOE

'A wonderful contribution to the most creative and innovative new chapter in Australian history, which merges settler stories with those of the First Nations – a must-read.'

HENRY REYNOLDS

'A must-read for every classroom. Impressive collaboration in truth-telling and history, so essential in these times.'

DR JACKIE HUGGINS, AM, FAHA, AUTHOR/HISTORIAN

'Rix and Cormick started with a supposedly "simple idea" but the result is complex, subtle, surprising and poignant. On this journey through Aboriginal memories of Cook's arrival, our tour guides lead us through many eras of Australian history. From deep time to the present, back to the signal year of 1770 and then through key moments of the subsequent colonial past, we learn afresh about the ongoing effects of European invasion on First Peoples. Blending archival research and new interviews with Indigenous knowledge-holders, *Warra Warra Wai* is a triumph of collaborative truth-telling.'

KATE FULLAGAR

'Australia has a history problem. Too few know the story of Australia's violent creation; the frontier wars, massacres, First Nations resistance, and the loss and suffering that resulted from this continent's colonial conquest by the British. *Warra Warra Wai* details the voyage of James Cook and the *Endeavour* up the east coast of Australia through the eyes of the First Nations who witnessed it. From the Gunai/Kurnai people in today's Gippsland to the Kaurareg people of the southern Torres Strait, this book reveals the oral histories from that time and contemporary reflections on what Cook's voyage meant for First Nations peoples. As the authors themselves observe, "The determination of First Nations people to have the truth told is strong, and the stories will be told." If we are to build better relationships and mature as a nation, these are the stories that Australians need to hear.'

KAREN MUNDINE, CEO, RECONCILIATION AUSTRALIA

'There are so many myths and misconceptions, as well as a great deal of historic amnesia, about the full impact of Lt. James Cook's voyage in the *Endeavour* along some 4000 kilometres of Australia's coastline in 1770.

The authors, Darren Rix and Craig Cormick, lead us on a fascinating exploration of the view from both the ship and the shore. The interplay between the oral histories of First Peoples and journal accounts written by sailors or settlers takes us on an intriguing voyage towards the truth. Where facts are uncertain or contested, this book honestly addresses the complexity of our history.

The numerous voices we hear for the first time offer delightful insights into how diverse communities see Cook and the world at large. They help explain the misunderstandings that began over 250 years ago. So much was lost in translation.

Warra Warra Wai is told with freshness, gentle humour and empathy. This is a balm for the pain of the invasion and theft of the land. As cultural storytellers along the coast explain what happened in their view of the *Endeavour*'s journey from Point Hicks to Possession Island, we are treated to the discovery of new names, places you will want to visit, and communities with so much to share.

To walk with Australia's First Peoples and listen affords the richest stories you will ever discover about the longer timelines of the history of this land. The land itself begins to sing to us all.'

JEFF MCMULLEN, JOURNALIST, AUTHOR, FILMMAKER

'In *Warra Warra Wai*, Darren and Craig engagingly capture, in a calibrating way, the paradox of perspective between the experience of Lieutenant Cook (and company) encountering the east coast of Australia in the mid-eighteenth century and the experience of mob who had been caring for country for tens of thousands of years.

Perhaps like a DNA helix, the connected yet distinct parallel stories remind us of an unfriendly history driven by overbearing entitlement and a patient, potent resilience, and will lead us (hopefully) to an increasingly holistic future.

The innate interconnectedness between people, country, lore, language and ceremony is palpable on almost every page, encouraging us to know our true history and the local elders & community connected to country – which in turn may provide us with a stronger environment to experience an Australia together.'

LIAM GLOVER, EXECUTIVE DIRECTOR, AUSTRALIANS TOGETHER

WARRA WARRA WAI

ALSO BY CRAIG CORMICK

A Darker Shade of Moonlite
What If History of Australia: Gold Rush: Going Gold Crazy
What If History of Australia: Colonial Settlement: France vs Britain
On a Barbarous Coast (with Harold Ludwick)
The Years of the Wolf
The Science of Communicating Science
Backseat Drivers
Ned Kelly Under the Microscope
Uncle Adolf
Time Vandals
In Bed with Douglas Mawson
Of One Blood
Kurikka's Dreaming
Unwritten Histories

DARREN RIX & CRAIG CORMICK

WARRA WARRA WAI

How Indigenous Australians
discovered Captain Cook
& what they tell about the coming
of the Ghost People

SCRIBNER

SCRIBNER

First published in Australia in 2024 by Scribner, an imprint of
Simon & Schuster (Australia) Pty Limited
Suite 19A, Level 1, Building C, 450 Miller Street, Cammeray, NSW 2062

Simon & Schuster: Celebrating 100 Years of Publishing in 2024.
Sydney New York London Toronto New Delhi
Visit our website at www.simonandschuster.com.au

SCRIBNER and design are registered trademarks of The Gale Group, Inc.,
used under licence by Simon & Schuster LLC.

10 9 8 7 6 5 4 3 2 1

© Darren Rix & Craig Cormick 2024

All rights reserved. No part of this publication may be reproduced, stored in a retrieval system, or transmitted in any form or by any means, electronic, mechanical, photocopying, recording or otherwise, without prior permission of the publisher.

A catalogue record for this book is available from the National Library of Australia

9781761424021 (paperback)
9781761424038 (ebook)

Cover design by John Canty
Cover painting, *Invasion Day*, by Gordon Syron
Text illustrations & map on page xi by Darren Rix
Typeset by Midland Typesetters in Adobe Caslon Pro 11.5/16.5
Printed and bound in Australia by Griffin Press

The paper this book is printed on is certified against the Forest Stewardship Council® Standards. Griffin Press holds chain of custody certification SCS-COC-001185. FSC® promotes environmentally responsible, socially beneficial and economically viable management of the world's forests.

'Not only have Aboriginal achievements been underplayed, but Aboriginal ways of telling history have always been discounted in terms of the academic white way, so the validity of oral history has been questioned. But that's the way Aboriginal people convey their history.'

VICTOR BRIGGS

'Truth-telling is the ultimate gesture of respect. It indicates a willingness to listen, to learn and to concede that the stories should be heard of those who have been victims of great wrongs.'

HENRY REYNOLDS

Contents

Cultural Warning xi
Maps xii

Introduction *1*

Munda Bubal/Tolywiarar (Point Hicks)
Gunaikurnai & Bidwell Countries *5*

Gulaga (Mount Dromedary)
Yuin Country *27*

Kembla (Red Point)
Dharawal Country *46*

Kamay (Botany Bay)
Dharawal Country *60*

Warrane (Sydney Harbour)
Dharug/Eora Country *75*

Whibayganba (Nobbys Head)
Awabakal & Worimi Countries *89*

Dooragan, Booragan & Mooragan (The Three Brothers)
Birpai, Gumbaynggirr & Dunghutti Countries *103*

Wollumbin (Mount Warning)
Bundjalung Country *121*

Beerwah & Tibrogargan (The Glass House Mountains)
Kabi Kabi & Jinibara Countries *137*

K'gari (Fraser Island)
Butchulla Country *158*

Gooragang (Bustard Bay)
Gooreng Gooreng Country *177*

Ngari (Hook Island, Whitsundays)
Ngaro Country *193*

Thul Garrie Waja (Cleveland Bay)
Bindal & Wulgurukaba Countries *204*

Munamudanamy (Hinchinbrook Island)
Bandjin & Girramay Countries *217*

Djilibirri (Cape Grafton)
Gunggandji, Mandingalbay, Yidinji & Irukandji Countries *230*

Kulki (Cape Tribulation)
Kuku Yalanji Country *247*

Whalumbal Birri (Endeavour River)
Gugu Yimidhirr Country *257*

Pajinka (Cape York Peninsula)
Gudang-Yadhaykenu Country *279*

Thuined (Possession Island)
Kaurareg Country *293*

Notes *311*
Acknowledgements *327*
Image Credits 329

Cultural Warning

It is customary for some Indigenous communities not to mention the names, or reproduce images, of the recently deceased. Members of such communities are respectfully advised that over time this text will invariably reference such people.

This book also contains words and descriptions that may be culturally sensitive, and uses terms from the past that may be considered inappropriate today.

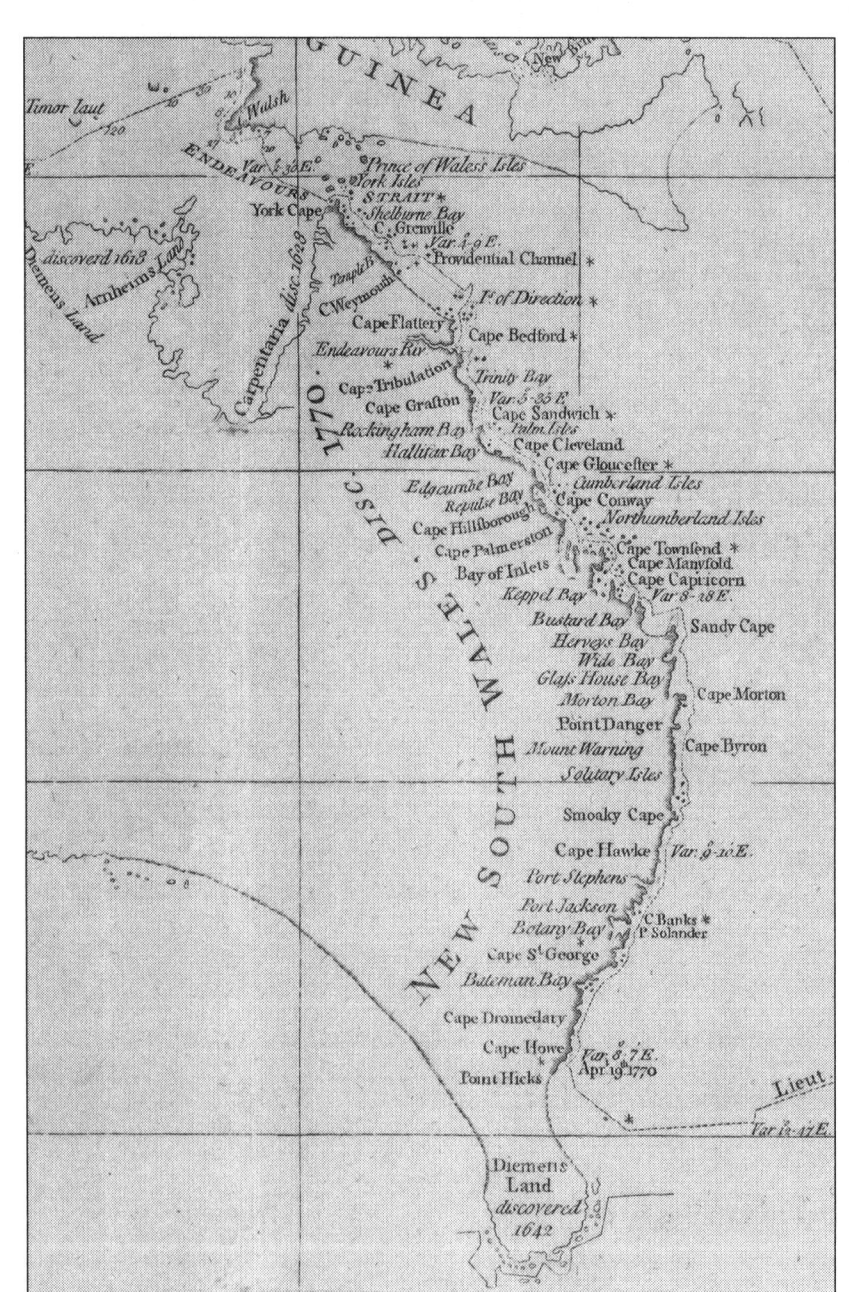

The east coast of Australia, showing the sites renamed by Cook

The east coast, showing landmarks on the right and corresponding language-group Countries on the left

Introduction

This book has been a blackfella–whitefella collaboration, because too much of our history has been written by one voice only, and we need to find more collaborative ways to tell our past, present and future. The idea behind it was a simple one: visit all the places on the east coast of Australia that were renamed by James Cook in 1770, put back the original names, and ask the First Nations people there what stories they wanted to share.

As simple as that. Just ask them.

In this collaboration, we each worked to our strengths. Craig did most of the work in the archives, and Darren did most of the oral interviews – and the people we talked to got the final say on the text. The stories we gathered belong to the individuals and communities we visited. This is their book.

There has been a big journey behind *Warra Warra Wai* – 4,000 kilometres through different nations in Victoria, New South Wales and Queensland in 2023, during which a hundred or so interviews and discussions were held. These were informed by more than 200 books and articles. We have both learned a lot about different country – from magnificent beaches to rocky headlands and offshore islands; from cool rainforests to dry scrublands; and from shallow creeks to wide rivers, deep valleys and tall mountains. We have experienced the wonder of land and sea and sky country, and we have been welcomed onto those places by so many different people. In sharing some of our experiences and encounters and learning with readers, a few things need stating:

- This book touches on the wisdom and experiences of only a handful of First Nations people along the eastern coast of Australia. There are many, many more people we could have talked to, and many more stories that could have been told, and hopefully they will find homes in other books or places. We acknowledge that some of the stories we tell here may be contested by other story holders.

- It is possible for someone to have multiple Countries/nationalities, through marriage lines of ancestors. Darren Rix, for example, is a Gunditjmara-GunaiKurnai man with Ngarigo bloodlines, who was raised on Yuin Country and now lives on Ngunnawal Country in Canberra.

- First Peoples' tribal names can be contentious, with different spellings being preferred by different communities. So know that when you see a name, it is not the only name or spelling that might be used, and we use inconsistent spellings in the text for this reason. For example, while Darren uses the spelling GunaiKurnai, elsewhere in the text the spelling Gunaikurnai is used.

- Many Australians now understand that before whitefellas arrived, the continent consisted of hundreds of different First Peoples with their own languages and cultures. Because of this, the experiences, lore and stories of one people cannot be projected across peoples from other locations.

- Some First Nations people are closely related to neighbouring tribes in language and culture, but this does not always apply. And many tribal names and borders have been defined by nineteenth-century anthropologists, which different First Peoples may or may not agree with.

- The chapters in this book are divided up into the different Countries, and the landmarks that Cook sighted, but these have been given their original names.

- Due to dispossession and the destruction of knowledge

systems, there can be disagreements as to which stories and history and lore are correct for any particular place.
* Owing to displacement resulting from the stolen generations, as well as to modern travel and work opportunities, many First People now live away from their Country – but they can still maintain a strong connection to their Country.
* Some First Nations people prefer to be called Aboriginal, and some prefer Indigenous, and some prefer neither of those.
* While this book is written in both our voices, references to experiences of mob and connection to Country are Darren's, as is the use in the narrative of 'our' and 'we'.

When yarning with people for this book we asked them all this question: What is it that whitefellas most need to know about your mob? Overwhelmingly the answer was truth-telling, and we heard many similar stories of dispossession, massacres, forced relocation, and so on – which were frankly quite difficult to hear once, let alone repeatedly. So this book is both linear and circular. It moves along the east coast and recounts similar lived experiences in different places, through different tellings.

The courage to tell the truth needs to be balanced with respectful listening. So while giving First Peoples a voice – as we have sought to do in this book – is important, it is just as important that readers have an open mind. We started out writing a book about Australia's history but have ended up with a book that tells as much about our present and perhaps our future, as the consequences of colonisation are still playing out in communities.

Wherever possible, we talked to people on their Country, but much of the background to their stories was researched and written on the lands of the Ngunnawal people. We acknowledge that, like all of the continent, none of that land was ever ceded.

Darren and Craig

Munda Bubal/Tolywiarar (Point Hicks)

Gunaikurnai & Bidwell Countries

Mulbitthunga boorum batha tuk Boolootha waty bulga; mandtha budgee budgee mul Buth moongan batha yuckan ba kani.	Long ago the pelican and the musk duck Flew over the mountains; they came here As the parents of the Kurnai people.
Mulbitthunga ba boorum batha tuk Wooraylwukan nindi thana kani. Dindan ma wuk wukkan.	Since the time of the pelican and the musk duck Gippsland has belonged to the Kurnai people. This is our land.[1]

> ... I have named it Point Hicks, because Lieutenant Hicks was the first who discover'd this Land.
>
> Cook's journal, 20 April 1770

The first the people of Gunaikurnai Country would have seen of the *Endeavour* was a strange object far out at sea. Was it a cloud? Was it a large bird? Where had it come from? It was something unknown in their many generations of stories that explained the land and sea and air, and everything they contained.

And as such it would bear close scrutiny.

For Lieutenant James Cook and his crew, the earliest signs that they were close to the east coast of this vast continent were floating seaweed and small birds, followed by a distant dark smudge on the horizon. The first person on board HMS Bark *Endeavour* to see that dark smudge was Lieutenant Zachary Hicks, the 32-year-old second-in-command. And so, Cook wrote in his journal, he 'named it Point Hicks, because Lieutenant Hicks was the first who discover'd this Land'.

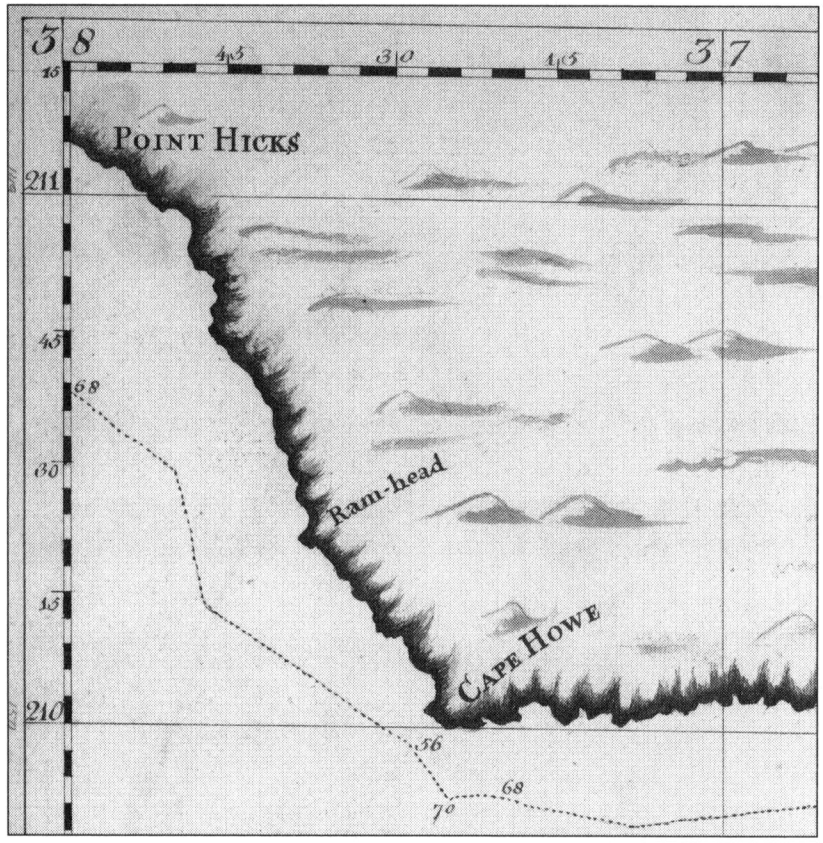

Cook's chart of Gunaikurnai and Bidwell Countries

But our people had occupied the land for over 60,000 years. And it had been sighted and mapped by at least forty voyagers prior to Cook, with over three-quarters of the continent charted and known. Cook was simply filling in the last gap on European maps, along the east coast, and giving names to places that already had names.

To the Bidwell and Gunaikurnai peoples of eastern Gippsland, the landmark that Cook named Point Hicks is Tolywiarar, or

Munda Bubul. The scrub-covered rocky outcrop reaches out wide into the Tasman Sea, shaped like a fist with the fingers and thumb half closed, defying the waves and swells that smash against it, having travelled from far out over the horizon. The strong wind here blows the clouds away one moment, leaving the point bathed in sunshine, and the next it blows low chill clouds back.

According to Uncle Clayton Harrison, a Bidwell man whose lands run up to the east, past Point Hicks, all the valleys and hills here were created by Djidjigan, the rainbow serpent, while other parts of the landscape were formed by the sea. He tells that Djidjigan was ngarandyil (very large), and as he moved over the Country he created the valleys and the hills by cutting them with his wirruk (tail). He made his way past the mountains to lay his eggs there. 'Big eggs, that are still everywhere on the landscape as big rocks. That is special Country. Djidjigan then went all the way past Wamoon (Wilsons Promontory) and when he finished, his duduk (head) was at Port Melbourne, right near the bay.'

Clayton Harrison is now in his seventies but can remember when he was younger his grandmother telling him that you had to look after the land. That is a fundamental principle of First Nations existence – knowing how to look after the land so that it can look after you, providing food, water, shelter and spiritual sustenance.

The Gunaikurnai, whose lands are to the west of Point Hicks, tell that parts of the land were formed by the sea. Narkabungdha (the sea) had become tired of playing with fish, and of rushing over rocks and rolling up and down on the sand, so it searched the coast for somewhere to rest, at last finding a quiet place with tall gum trees for shade and with soft earth to lie on. Narkabungdha lay down there to sleep and wriggled down into the soft sand, turning its body this way and that way until it was comfortable. And that place became Bung Yarnda (Lake Tyers), where Narkabungdha still rests among the trees.[2]

Munda Bubal/Tolywiarar/Point Hicks

On board the *Endeavour*, the first inkling that Cook and his crew had that the land before them might be inhabited was the following day, when they saw smoke rising from the thick green bushland.

To the Gunaikurnai, the word 'inhabited' does not adequately explain that they have been on the land since time immeasurable, or that they know the story of the first man and woman. The man was Booran the pelican, who came down to their Country from the mountains of the northwest. He was travelling alone, carrying a bark canoe on his head. As he walked he heard a constant tapping sound, but look as he may, he could not find its source. At last he reached the deep waters of an inlet near the coast and there he put his canoe down. And much to his surprise he saw there was a woman sitting in the canoe. She was Tuk the musk duck. Booran was very pleased to see her and she became his wife, and she is the mother of all the Gunaikurnai people.[3]

According to the Gunaikurnai Whole of Country Plan, developed by the community and the Gunaikurnai Land and Waters Aboriginal Corporation, Creation stories about the origins of their

Boorun's canoe

people help explain their bonds to Country, and remind them that their ancestors are still watching over the landscape today. As the plan puts it, 'It is important for us to be able to walk in their footsteps and follow their journeys from thousands of years ago – it is a powerful, spiritual aspect of our cultural heritage, and fundamental to our recognition and respect. We are guided by the spirits of our ancestors when we walk through this Country.'[4]

'The Dreaming' was a term coined by the anthropologist W.E.H. Stanner in a 1956 essay of that title, in which he said that the term was the closest analogy he could make to First Nations concepts of Creation and spirituality. Wuilli Wuilli (northwest of Brisbane) author Lisa Fuller has written that the term was an attempt to describe a limitless and complicated belief system that changes from nation to nation: 'It is hard to explain the Dreaming to non-Indigenous people, because it is not exact or in a straight timeline with one event after another.'

The Dreaming, Lisa explains, includes the Creation time of what has happened in the past, but also what is happening today and will happen in the future. 'But all at once rather than as separate times. In the Creation time, the ancestral spirits came and shaped the world – the hills, mountains, rivers, oceans, skies and stars – and created plants, animals and humans. They also created law, the rules by which we all live and behave. Spirit stories follow songlines all over the Country, the spirits marking the land as they moved. 'Each area they passed through has its own version of these stories, much like how there are different versions of the Bible – no story is more important than the other, they all make up the songlines.

'Different areas also have their own specific stories about ancestral spirits that stayed in that area, or became a part of the landscape.'[5]

So not only does the Dreaming describe how the world came to be, and explain the significance of places, but it can contain a vast cultural and legal framework, explaining the rules as to how people should behave – especially to the land. And the ancestor spirits that created the land can be felt through ceremony, song and artwork, connecting the past and the present.

Understanding songlines is important to understanding how mob think of Country. Songlines can be seen as understanding a family's heritage, through where they walked; or as telling how different mobs are connected by songline paths; or as a repository of people's knowledge, which is mapped out across the landscape; or as the basis for all language and culture.

Rob Hudson is a GunaiKurnai man with a very important job. And that job involves preserving and keeping artifacts of his people, and teaching the stories about where they have come from.

Rob is the cultural manager of the Krowathunkooloong Keeping Place in Bairnsdale (properly named Warung or Wy-yung, 'the black duck'), whose purpose is to keep Gunaikurnai culture alive. When he talks, his eyes glow with an excitement born of the importance of his position and the impacts of sharing knowledge. Pride of place in the Keeping Place is a large bark canoe, dating back to 1900 – similar to the canoe that Booran would have carried down from the mountains. It is one of only a few such canoes being preserved in keeping places like this one, and you can see how the bark has been carefully folded at each end, often sealed with clay, and with sticks used as stays for support along the body of the craft.

It is a powerful object to have amongst the hundreds of finely carved clubs, boomerangs and carefully woven nets on display in the Keeping Place, and no matter how you walk around the room it keeps drawing your eyes to it.

Rob said, 'Since the time when Booran and Tuk founded our people, the Gunaikurnai hunted the animals and gathered the fruits of a vast natural wilderness. This land fed, clothed and sheltered us. At times this land was generous, at other times cruel. To our ancestors, life was a constant test of the weapon maker's skills, the hunter's endurance and the tireless explorations of the gatherers.'

He also explained that there is often confusion around the proper spellings of different peoples in Australia today, which has led to many alternatives – like Gunnai or Kurnai, or Gunaikurnai as a compromise between the two – because the written names were recorded by anthropologists who might have come from Scotland or Germany or England and did not have a 'black ear' for different sounds. In much the same way that Cambodia and Kampuchea are attempts at English and French spellings for the same-sounding word in Khmer.

Rob Hudson

Rob Hudson said, 'You have to listen to the old fellas.'

The land that is now called East Gippsland was home to the Bidwell – around Mallacoota – and the five major clans of the Gunaikurnai. Those clans were the Bratwoloong people of South Gippsland; the Brayakooloong people around the current site of Sale and Latrobe rivers; the Brabawooloong people in the land ranging up to Bairnsdale; the Tatungooloong people around Lakes Entrance; and the Krowathunkooloong people from Point Hicks to Lakes Entrance and Lake Tyers.

'This land fostered our clans, the creation of our language, our rich mythology, our laws, social customs, and skills in craft and other artifacts. Our land was our mother,' Rob said.

And the land here has a unique feel to it, that keeps drawing people back to it. So many different environments – the woodlands and the wilderness and rock formations, and all the lake systems that feed from the rivers. Walking through Country, you feel at ease. You feel animals. You look for birds to guide you through that Country. If you see kookaburras it is the old people coming back to look after you and make sure you don't get into any trouble.

Sitting up on top of a hill, looking down at Lakes Entrance and Victoria Lakes, it makes you think how good our people had it. This land would have been so pristine, and they would have gathered so much from those waters.

And seeing the land looked after gives you a feeling in your heart, like seeing the regrowth after a burn; you can feel the spirits in the Country then.

But it's not all looked after. A lot of things are out of season. It's like the bogong moths disappearing. They shouldn't be doing that. It shows you that the land isn't what it used to be.

Mostly the clans lived in harmony with each other, and met for ceremonies that involved very complex marriage customs and rules, initiation and trading – though it was not unknown to raid another tribe to steal a wife. In Gunaikurnai culture a couple could be married by running away together – which often meant finding a wife from a nearby tribe.

Rob Hudson said that in his people's history they were often raided by the Bunarong people, from around the Mornington Peninsula, who were looking for wives, and one of the important protocols of First Nations lore was never to enter another people's land without permission. Doing so would result in conflict, and this lore led to a strong tradition of fighting to defend their land.

The people followed the patterns of nature, moving across their Country in accord with food sources, hunting the plentiful mammals, reptiles, fish and vegetation, and allowing the land to regenerate as they moved on.

Every member of a tribe had their own thundung (totem), which was generally an animal, that they were then responsible for caring for. This also meant they were forbidden from eating their own thundung. Sometimes this thundung was passed down from one's father, or it might be an animal the mother saw while giving birth.

According to Gunaikurnai law, like the law of all the people across the continent, animals could only be killed in sustainable numbers. The law also stated that nothing should ever be wasted, as almost every part of each animal had a use. Meat was shared and eaten by the family, while the fur could be used for clothing, sinews made threads, feathers were used in decorations, skins were used to make clothing and carry bags. Animal bones, as well as shark's teeth and stingray barbs, could be used for making sharp tools or weapons.

Rob Hudson said, 'No one was chief and all were equal.'

Living on abundant land meant there was a lot of leisure time, which could be devoted to family time, games, or ceremonies. The Gunaikurnai even played a form of football, where teams of players ran around with a dirlk (ball) made from either bark or the scrotum of a large kangaroo, and they would throw it in unexpected directions.[6] The game has been described as being remarkably similar to Aussie Rules – and was known as Marn Grook ('ball', 'game') in the Woiwurung language of the Kulin people.

As Cook viewed the land through the narrow lens of his telescope, he was also viewing it through the narrow lens of European expectations, looking for farms and villages as a sign of the inhabitants having tamed the land in pursuit of its wealth. But the people who lived on the land had developed a very different view of how to live with its wealth. Our life was based around achieving a careful balance with nature, that had sustained us for tens of thousands of years.

We had a strong legal structure, based on land care and respect for Country, and we had a strong reciprocal duty to the land – if we looked after the land and the waters, they would look after us. These were not concepts that the British people on board the *Endeavour* would have easily understood, as to them land was governed by private ownership – the privilege of only the wealthy – and having land was about 'improving' it and generating wealth.

Like other peoples of Australia that the *Endeavour* crew were to encounter and fail to understand over the next four months, the Gunaikurnai and Bidwell lived a lifestyle that continually enhanced their physical, mental, emotional and spiritual wellbeing – through their relationship with the land – which was emphasised in their stories.[7]

The story of Legend Rock, which lies in the shallow waters of Bancroft Bay to the west of Lakes Entrance, is an important part of Gunaikurnai culture. The story tells that one day three fishermen caught a great many fish in their nets, but did not share their catch with their mob, instead eating it around their campfire.

The women of the tribe, who were the protectors of social law, saw that the men had eaten far more than enough but had neglected to feed their dogs. And one of the dogs even spoke: 'You greedy fullas, why don't you share the fish?' Everyone heard it, but they kept on feasting.

As punishment, the whole camp was turned into stone, and now stands as a red rock on that spot by the shores of the lake, to this day.[8]

Rob Hudson said that the rock is referred to as Wallung, and like most Dreaming stories it has a moral to it. 'It's a Dreaming story of sharing and caring. It's a story about only taking what you need and looking after the animals around you. Dreaming stories aren't just stories – you need to know what they actually mean.'

To state that Dreaming stories do not accord with scientific facts is to fail to acknowledge how many European Christian beliefs do not accord with scientific facts either. There are even many aspects of the 1770 *Endeavour* voyage that have assumed their own mythologies and don't always accord with facts.

Lieutenant James Cook, for instance, was not technically Captain Cook until a few years later, and he was not even the first choice to lead the voyage. He was the third choice. It was originally going to be Alexander Dalrymple, a rather pompous Scotsman who had put forward the idea that there must be a great southland in order to balance up the land mass in the northern hemisphere. But as he insisted on having overall command of the expedition, as well as being the chief astronomer, the Admiralty vetoed the idea. Instead they proposed a naval man, Captain John Campbell. He was one of the most accomplished navigators of the time, but he was approaching fifty and didn't much fancy heading off into unexplored waters for so little reward, and he politely refused the offer.

So the Admiralty poked around, looking for someone who wouldn't be as arrogant as Dalrymple, and someone perhaps more subservient than Campbell. Someone who would follow orders and who could navigate well and draw a fair chart. And their eyes fell on Lieutenant James Cook. A competent ship's master and navigator who had come to the navy late in life, and who, to make a promotion to captain, would have to prove himself in some way.

Also, Australia was not the Great Southern Land – despite what pop songs might have you believe – as it had largely been charted. Cook had actually been looking for the mysterious land to the east of New Zealand, whose west coast had been partially charted nearly 130 years previously by Dutch navigator Abel Tasman. This was thought to be a part of a large unknown continent. On the second of Cook's three great Pacific voyages (in 1772–75), he was still searching for the Great Southern Land in the waters around Antarctica. Needless to say, he never found the imagined continent as it did not exist beyond Dalrymple's and others' imaginings.

Another Cook myth is that he specifically came to the east coast of Australia to chart it. In fact, his drive-by was almost an afterthought and very nearly didn't happen. His primary objective had been to observe the transit of Venus at Tahiti, as part of a simultaneous global observation to help determine distances across the solar system. The transit was observed on 3 June 1769, and after that Cook opened secret sealed orders to try to find the missing southern continent.

With the assistance of a Polynesian navigator he had taken on board, the Ra'iatean man Tupaia, he visited several Pacific Islands and fully charted the whole coastline of New Zealand, spending six months there. He then had to decide whether to sail back home directly to the west, below the already-charted southern coastline of New Holland, or to travel north. He wrote in his journal: 'I consulted with the Officers ... To return by the way of Cape Horn was what I most wished, because by this rout we should have been able to prove the Existance or Non-Existance of a Southern Continent, which yet remains Doubtfull; ... but the Condition of the Ship, in every respect, was not thought sufficient for such an undertaking. ... It was therefore resolved to return by way of the East Indies.'

So the *Endeavour* headed north rather than west, along the east coast of New Holland. Cook had actually been aiming to reach land on the uncharted northern side of Van Diemen's Land – which he would have given a random European name to – but a large storm blew him further north, to that point Lieutenant Zachary Hicks sighted on 20 April 1770.

Or did he?

There is some controversy over the location of Point Hicks, as the coordinates Cook gives (38°0'S, 148°53'E) are actually 20 kilometres out at sea, which supports an argument that what they saw was a cloud bank, and that the first sighting of land was further to the east. Nevertheless, Point Hicks bears a memorial that states: 'Lieutenant James Cook R.N. of the Endeavour first sighted Australia near this point which he named Point Hicks after Lieutenant Zachary Hicks who first saw the land. April 19th (ship's log date) April 20th (Calendar date) 1770.'

A quick explanation about dates here: Cook used ship's time, which counted a day from 12 noon to 12 noon the following day, while

Joseph Banks used the more familiar midnight to midnight, often causing some confusion over the actual date that things occurred. But by late morning on Cook's 19 April or Banks' 20 April, the men on the ship could clearly see land. Banks wrote: 'at 10 it was pretty plainly to be observd; it made in sloping hills, coverd in Part with trees or bushes, but interspersd with large tracts of sand'.

And while the crew of the *Endeavour* did not see any of the local people ashore, they themselves were being carefully observed. Wayne Thorpe, who identifies as Gunnai and lives in the Aboriginal trust of Bung Yarnda (formerly the Lake Tyres Mission), tells that it was his ancestor, Boondjil Noorrook, who first saw the ship and passed a warning to other people all along the coast.

Sitting in his lounge room, surrounded by First Nations art and books, Wayne said that Boondjil Noorrook had been up in the mountains doing ceremony during the bogong moth season, when he looked up at the stars and saw by their locations that it was time to come down to the coast to hunt seals at the mouth of the river.

'Early in the morning, he was out spearing seals to get some ngulli (meat) for his family when he heard a big noise out in the ocean. *Boom, boom, boom!*

'Before long he spotted something strange, he saw what looked like a big canoe with white wings on it coming in towards the coast. Well, that was the *Endeavour* with Lieutenant Cook, later known as Captain Cook. This is when the *Endeavour* was coming from New Zealand and they were heading straight for Tamboon Krauratungaloong Gunnai Country, the south-eastern parts of Australia, and doing the soundings with the ship's cannon. *Boom, Boom, Boom!*'

He said that when Boondjil Noorrook spotted something strange out there it looked like trouble. 'He went back to his Elders and told them about it, what he'd seen. They said to him, "Send a smoke signal and a song and forewarn all the people up along the coast." The south-westerlies were blowing fairly strong and the *Endeavour* was turning up along the east coast.

'Boondjil Noorrook sent off the smoke signals to communicate with all the different mobs up along the coast. Our people were communicating and sharing information with our family and friends, our neighbours, our alliance groups, to forewarn them about something out there that looked like danger.'

Wayne Thorpe said, 'Too many times people think the story starts in Sydney, or is about Cook discovering the land – but I say that Boondjil Noorrook discovered Cook.'

He also said that other peoples along the coast, having sighted the *Endeavour*, also sent smoke signal messages. And this was a form of resistance. Of looking after Country. Forewarning people that there could be danger. He said that each group would relay their own song and story within the smoke they sent: 'Keep an eye on them people out there, whoever that is out there.'

As the ship went up further along the east coast, the people lit signal fires. In Joseph Banks' and in Cook's journals they both write about the sighting of land and various landmarks and where the locations were, and where they sighted these smoke signals and fires.[9]

The people along the coast would have known the difference between different types of smoke, such as smoking ceremonies, campfires, cultural burning and signal fires. The fires that accompanied Cook all along the coast were carefully managed signal fires situated on headlands. The journals of the voyage mention smoke consistently along the coast, but the British didn't understand that what they were seeing was a warning signal, alerting others to their presence.

There are other stories telling that message sticks had travelled up the coast on walking tracks ahead of the *Endeavour*, warning people of its coming.

Uncle Clayton Harrison said that he has a story about a walking track along the coast that goes all the way up to Queensland, and the story and the track are so old that the track had previously gone south all the way to lutruwita (Tasmania), when the land was joined – over 12,000 years ago, when the first agricultural societies were just evolving in the Middle East.

A little while after sighting land, the crew of the *Endeavour* were to witness something quite astonishing. Three waterspouts rose up from the ocean between the ship and the land.

Banks described one of the spouts as 'a column which appeard to be of about the thickness of a mast or a midling tree, and reachd down from a smoak colourd cloud about two thirds of the way to the surface of the sea; under it the sea appeard to be much troubled for a considerable space and from the whole of that space arose a dark colourd thick mist which reachd to the bottom of the pipe'.

To the Bidwell people, the waterspouts were an ominous sign of trouble coming.[10]

There were just over a hundred men on the ship – a converted coal carrier – including twelve marines and nine civilians. The most prominent amongst the civilians was Joseph Banks, an amateur naturalist keen to make a name for himself. He'd paid £10,000 to participate in the voyage, effectively buying his passage, and took along his four servants, secretary and two pampered dogs.

With two botanists, an astronomer and two artists, the *Endeavour* was on one level a scientific voyage, but Cook also had those secret orders from the Admiralty to search for the great southland. Who knew what riches a new country might hold? Gold like the Spanish had found in the Americas? Spices like the Dutch found in the East Indies?

Amongst Cook's secret orders were instructions to carefully observe the land's flora and fauna and rivers, and 'in Case you find any Mines, Minerals, or valuable Stones you are to bring home Specimens of each'. He was also told that with any people he encountered he should 'cultivate a Friendship and Alliance'. And in an instruction that was to become very contentious, he was told: 'You are also with the Consent of the Natives to take Possession of Convenient Situations in the Country in the Name of the King of Great Britain …'

We will be looking at that instruction in more detail later. For when Cook reached the most northern tip of the land he was to name New South Wales, he did indeed take possession of all the 'convenient situations' in the name of the King – but without 'the consent of the natives'.

As the *Endeavour* sailed on, Cook renamed the headland Konowee as Ram Head (after a headland near Plymouth in England), although it's now named Little Rame Head. The point where the modern-day borders of Victoria and New South Wales meet he renamed Cape Howe, after the Treasurer of the Navy and First Lord of the Admiral, Earl Howe.

He did not know that he was now entering Yuin Country.

Contact

The *Endeavour* had startled the Gunaikurnai and Bidwell people when it entered their territory, but it had sailed away to the north. However, more ships were to come, bringing sealers who were violent and stole women, and this naturally led to hostility towards white settlers when they made their way onto Gunaikurnai and Bidwell lands. Stories that preceded them told that these strangers had power to draw the banks of a river together so they could pass over it, and that they could flash death with their eyes.[11]

The first real incursion into Gunaikurnai lands did not take place until relatively late – 1839 – when squatters moved south from the drought-stricken Monaro Plains, looking for new pastures. They had no idea that the people whose land they were entering and occupying had been hardened by many years of conflict, not only with other tribes, but with sealers, whalers and castaways.

Among the first settlers to the area now called Gippsland were the Isle of Skye opportunists Lachlan Macalister and Angus McMillan. In October 1840 Lachlan Macalister laid claim to about 24,000 hectares of Gunaikurnai land, and McMillan claimed 6,500 hectares. Combined, it was 350 square kilometres, about a third of the area of today's greater Melbourne.

To the squatters' outrage, the local people were hostile to their presence, and scattered their stock and attacked their workers. One settler wrote years later, 'It is absurd to blame the Aborigines for killing sheep and cattle. You might as well say it is immoral for a cat to catch mice. Hunting was their living, the land and every animal thereon was theirs. To seize their lands by force and to kill them was robbery and murder.'[12]

The early anthropologist A.W. Howitt, who for a time bore the rather ineffective title Guardian of Aboriginals in Gippsland, said that the violent response from the Gunaikurnai to incursions on their territory was the same as that meted out to their tribal enemies.[13] One of the first reported attacks was on Lachlan Macalister's run in 1841, with an estimated 600 warriors taking part. It would have been a fearsome sight to see, and the Gunaikurnai were fearsome warriors. And unlike some of our people across the continent, they had no fear of attacking at night.

Tensions continued as the Gunaikurnai people's game was chased away by settlers and food became scarce. Then in June 1843 Lachlan Macalister's nephew, Ronald Macalister, was speared near Port Albert – close to Yiruk (Wilsons Promontory: this place is called Yiruk in Gunnai, and Wammon in Bunarong). It was reported that his body was mutilated and his kidney fat cut out, which was a common practice associated with spiritual beliefs.[14]

It of course triggered a major reprisal from the growing number of settlers. The resultant attack on the Gunaikurnai, led by Angus McMillan, may have been the worst massacre of First Peoples in Australian history – the Warrigal Creek Massacre. While estimates of those killed range between thirty and 500, we will probably never know the real death toll, as there was a strict code of secrecy amongst settlers.[15] This secrecy had been heightened following the conviction and hanging of seven white men found guilty of the Myall Creek Massacre in New South Wales, just five years earlier in 1838.

Professor Lyndall Ryan, who is the lead researcher on a massive project to map all the documented massacres around Australia, described Victoria as a killing field. 'Victoria has far more massacres than I ever realised. I reckon at least half of the Aboriginal people that were actually killed in Victoria were killed in massacres.' Lyndall, who now lives in Newcastle, has been working on the project for over ten years and said that the project's definition of a massacre is where six or more people were killed. 'Some of my historian colleagues in Victoria just refused to believe it. They argue that the population was only 20,000. I think it was closer to 40,000 or 50,000, even 60,000. And that's a big story that needs to be told.'

Rob Hudson told us that one thing he wants people who visit the Krowathunkooloong Keeping Place to understand is the real story of history. He said that when many visitors read about the massacres they say, 'We never knew that. We were never taught that.'

But as Bruce Pascoe points out in his groundbreaking work *Dark Emu*, there is so much about First Nations history and society that is not well taught: 'Not only that the frontier war had been misrepresented in what we had been taught in school, but also that the economy and culture of Aboriginal and Torres Strait Islander people had been grossly undervalued.'[16]

What is known from sources close to the time is that it was largely the Bratauolung people who were surrounded at Warrigal Creek Waterhole, and slaughtered. One settler, Willy Hoddinott, using the pen name 'The Gippslander', wrote that the attackers mainly consisted of Scotsmen who called themselves the Highland Brigade, and who swore before God and their Queen to maintain complete secrecy of the affair.[17] Ironically, many of the Scotsmen had themselves lost their family lands, victims of the English policy of Highland clearances of the previous century, and were devout to their own clans and spoke their own language – but despite this they failed to find any empathy with the plight of the Gunaikurnai.[18]

Over a dozen more massacres followed, with a total death toll of between 300 and 1,000.[19] So many massacres that it chills you to read them from a list on the wall of the Krowathunkooloong Keeping Place. And the stories of settlers' children finding rows of skulls years later wakes you up in the night.

Some of the massacres were the consequence of a story of a mysterious white woman who was believed to have been kidnapped by one of the Gunaikurnai clans and was forcibly living with them. Just the thought of it sent hysteria through the good citizen settlers, who led several expeditions to find her. Some even included members of the vicious Native Police, a force resulting from the insidious practice of recruiting First Nations people from different and distant lands, with no connection to the people they were brought in to hunt down and 'pacify'. They were often recruited very young and indoctrinated into a brutal way of life that they could not escape.

According to the Commissioner of Crown Lands, Charles Tyers, at least fifty people were killed by the Native Police searching for this unknown and unsighted woman. This number may actually be a deliberate underestimate, as Tyers is believed to have taken part in one of these bloody expeditions himself.[20] Needless to say, no white woman was ever found beyond colonial imaginings. And suspiciously, the story had first been reported in the colonial press by that early squatter Angus McMillan, who, it could well be argued, had a vested interest in having the Gunaikurnai cleared out by overzealous avenging expeditions. In a newspaper article, he wrote that he had seen the woman being escorted away at spear point by 'these ruthless savages', leaving behind a dead white 'male child' and clothing 'all be-smeared with human blood'.[21]

Nineteenth-century fake news designed to stir up people's emotions? Maybe. However, recent research has uncovered Gunaikurnai songs, in the papers of A.W. Howitt, that seem to confirm the existence of this white woman, referring to a Lohan-tuka (white woman) from over the sea. But like many parts of this country's history, too much of the stories, or those who could tell the stories, has been lost, and we may never really know the actual truth of this matter.[22]

In the 1860s Gunaikurnai society was battered again, this time by Christian missionaries, who, albeit with good intent, took people off their land and onto missions. The first such mission, at Lake Tyers, was led by Church of England missionary John Bulmer, and was a fairly decent place, allowing people to hunt and practise their culture and language. But after Bulmer left in 1907, as Wayne Thorpe described it, 'It turned to shit.' He said the mission evolved into a place where people were treated poorly, subjected to tyrannical rules, and only allowed to practise their culture in secret.

Wayne Thorpe said, 'The government came with a bible in one hand and a gun in the other.'

If you want to understand just how heartbreaking and authoritarian missions and reserves were, go online and read some of the letters collected in the publication *Letters from Aboriginal Women of Victoria 1867–1926*.[23] So many are plaintive pleas from mothers to just be allowed to keep their children with them, or for their husband to be allowed to stay with the family. These letters also show how misnamed and heartless the Board for the Protection of Aborigines in Victoria was.

Living now mostly on missions, the Gunaikurnai used their experience with Marn Grook and their warrior prowess to turn out some talented footballers, who had to battle significant racial prejudices, as well as strict mission policies, to be allowed to play against white teams. In 1913 a highly skilled team from Bung Yarnda (Lake Tyers) were the first to play a Melbourne VFL club when they played Carlton at Lakes Entrance. It was reported at the time: 'In order to play, the latter [the team from Bung Yarnda] had to travel by foot from the station, nearly 10 miles distant, and return the same day – also per foot.'[24]

An even more ignoble game was played in 1900, when half the First Nations players were not given permission to leave their mission at Coranderrk to play – and so were replaced by whitefellas wearing blackface.

And yet the Gunaikurnai have survived. As the members of the Gunaikurnai Whole of Country Plan proudly state, 'We are Gunaikurnai, the first people of our Country. We have survived for tens of thousands of years, often against great adversity. We have looked after our Country and passed on stories and traditions through countless generations.'

They carry these traditions like their ancestor Booran carried that canoe, travelling from the past into the present and into the future.

Wayne Thorpe said that this is one of several things that white Australia needs to understand – how First Peoples are still practising their culture and looking after the land. 'We need to make our stance and invite people to come with us and look after our Country. All them foreign cultures need to learn that and look after family. As nature is family.'

Another key thing he said white Australia needs to know is that there was more variety in culture and languages across the continent than there was across Europe. And the meaning of words is important. Wayne argues against using the term 'Aboriginal', as he says it can be interpreted to mean 'away from the original'; and 'Indigenous' too often refers to plants.

But First Peoples?

'Yeah. We are the first people in the world.'

Gulaga (Mount Dromedary)
Yuin Country

Walawaani Njindiwaan.
Ngayaga bundj nguumbun muladha gumara muruul yuwinj wanggan njin dhugandha.

Welcome, everyone.
We recognise First Nations peoples as the first people and custodians of Country.

We saw the smoke of fire in several places; a Certain sign that the Country is inhabited.

Cook's journal, 22 April 1770

The land of the Yuin people stretches several hundred kilometres along the sandy beaches and rugged coastlines of the New South Wales south coast. It encompasses the land just north of the Victorian border, up past Nowra, and stretches over the mountains to the west towards Goulburn and Bowral.

Their land is full of mild beaches; large, protected estuaries; headlands, and gentle forests that run up to and over the mountain ranges. The Yuin tell that when their old people saw the *Endeavour* sailing northwards they tried to fit it into what they knew of the world, and saw it as a giant pelican. In their stories Gurung gabba the pelican was a greedy creature, and it appeared to have returned from the Dreaming – with unknown intent.

Wary of its presence, the Yuin lit fires on the headlands to warn people further north of its coming. Because such fires were only lit during certain ceremonies, the people to the north knew something strange was happening and would have been on alert, until they too saw the large pelican approaching.

While the ship's crew noted the smoke from the fires, they of course lacked the cultural knowledge to know it was because of their incursion into Yuin sea Country that the fires were lit.

Lawrence Joseph Perry, a Worimi man from near present-day Newcastle – whose ancestors would have been a part of the chain of signal fires along the coast – explained how First Peoples could communicate with each other over great distances without leaving their own Country, through smoke signals. He said that a fire would be lit on a specific headland or high place, and green branches thrown onto it to create a cloud of blackish-grey smoke. He also said that heavier branches could be used to alternatively cover the fire and release smoke puffs into the sky.[1]

The people wondered what Gurang gabba was after, and the old people feared – rightly so, it would eventually turn out – that the bird would come in closer to land and scoop up everything, and steal it.

As the giant bird came closer to their lands, some of the Yuin people went inland to hide, while the Elders sang up a westerly wind to send it away. And that wind carried Cook further northwards, until he was alongside a long low mountain with a hump in it. Fitting it into his own view of the world, he saw it as a two-humped camel and named it Mount Dromedary.

To the Yuin people this was Gulaga, their sacred mother mountain. And where Cook saw a camel sitting down, the Yuin people see a pregnant woman lying on her side, her head to the south, her feet to the north, facing the sea. Gulaga has always been there, from the time the sun and moon and everything was created, for Gulaga gave birth to all the Yuin people, and the people look to the sacred mountain for guidance and strength. It is also a place of ceremony, primarily for women.

Sharon Mason is a proud and energetic Yuin woman, and the creative director of the Djaadjawan Dancers, an all-women dance troupe. She lives in the small coastal town of Dalmeny, just to the northeast of Gulaga. She tells that the story most commonly told about the mountains is the fate of a mother and her two sons, Baranguba and Najanuka.

The older son, Baranguba, wanted to go out to sea and explore the world, so he ventured out into the ocean, and remains there today as the island named by Europeans as Montague Island. The younger child, Najanuka, wanted to go too but his mother would not let him go, and kept him close to her. He is the smaller mount, Najanuka (Little Dromedary), resting at the foot of his mother.

The island Baranguba dominates the ocean view from the coast around Narooma. People regularly visited the island in their canoes, but stories tell that on one journey a storm suddenly came down, tipping over canoes, and many lives were lost. It is a tranquil passage to the islands on some days, but don't be deceived, as it has moods of dangerous tempest.

Sharon said a less-told story of Gulaga is of the first waratah. 'Toonkoo and Ngaardi came down from the stars – like Adam and Eve, they were the first people. But Toonkoo disrespected the spirits and he got taken back up to his grandmother, the moon. And Ngaardi wept, climbing the mountain, Gulaga, looking for Toonkoo. She died from a broken heart and from starvation. That's the Creation story of the waratah – her heart.'

Gulaga saved the communities in front of the mountains during the Black Summer bushfires of 2019–20. 'Our ancestor saved us', said Sharon. But she added that massive fires and floods are a clear sign that we aren't looking after our mother the earth, the way that she looks after us. 'The sleeping giants are waking up. The rainbow serpent is stirring.'

It is therefore vitally important to get the peoples' laws back and into practice. 'And the only way to get our laws back is through

Gulaga/Mount Dromedary

Elders and through Country. Local communities need to start strengthening their connections to Country through their Elders.'

Gulaga sees increasing numbers of tourists each year, as more people seek out First Nations experiences, and there are mixed feelings about letting men climb the mountain, which is mainly a women's site, though there are men's sites on it too. Sharon feels it should be closed off to the public. 'Too much of our sacred stuff is lost,' she said. Marcus Arvidson, the CEO of the Twofold Aboriginal Corporation in Eden, said he would never climb Gulaga. 'It is not my place to go up there,' he said. But he understands the desire of visitors to climb the sacred mountain. 'As long as the cultural integrity of the space is being maintained and people are okay with it,' he said.

However, Marcus acknowledged that allowing large numbers of people to access a sacred area also puts such areas at risk of desecration. Near his office is one of the largest middens in the world, but such sites would crumble if people knew about them and were climbing all over them.

Eden currently receives over forty cruise ships a year – which is almost one a week – and many people on the ships are looking for a genuine Australian experience. Hoping to provide a carefully curated experience, the Eden Local Aboriginal Land Council is in the process of cataloguing and putting on display for visitors the dozens of artifacts and artworks it holds, as a curated keeping place.

Wayne Shipp, the CEO of the Land Council, says that he'd like to see cultural guides employed to educate visitors while protecting heritage.

Uncle Warren Foster is a Djiringanj Yuin Elder, and lives at the former reserve site of Wallaga Lakes, north of Bermagui. Google maps doesn't seem too familiar with the streets there, but the people sitting out the front of their houses prove much more reliable in knowing Warren Foster's place.

He tells a story that his grandmother's grandfather was one of the survivors of a Gunaikurnai massacre on the Snowy River, and how, like many First Peoples, he has wide family links across many different peoples.

Warren Foster's kitchen window looks out onto the mountain Gulaga, and he says that from seven different angles you can see a pregnant woman in the different stages of pregnancy. But of Cook naming it Mount Dromedary, Warren said, 'How the fuck do you see a camel?'

He also said that when he was a young man he was very angry about Captain Cook. 'I hated the bloke really.' But as he grew older he started going up the mountain with Elders, and they told him that Cook's story was now a part of the mountain's story. 'I started doing tours and talking about how he named the mountain, and talking about it, and going up the mountain, healed me of the hatred I had. It is a very healing place.'

The three major mountains of Yuin lore are Gulaga, Biamanga (Mumbulla Mountain) and Balgan (Pigeon House Mountain). Biamanga, located southwest of Bermagui, has both men's and women's lore sites, and is linked to Umbarra the black duck, which is the totem of the Yuin people.

Uncle Warren Foster tells the story of Umbarra. In the old days, a boy named Merriman had the totem of Umbarra the black duck, and wherever Merriman went Umbarra warned him of any danger by fluttering his feathers and diving down into the water, splashing loudly. When Merriman saw that bird doing that, he knew there was danger coming.

One day, all the tribe was out getting a feed of fish, bimbullas (shellfish) and djungas (octopus), and Merriman spotted Umbarra acting quite strangely. He was diving in the water, splashing about, ruffling his feathers up, which Merriman knew was a sign that there were people coming.

So Merriman told the tribe to get all the women and children together. He put them in the canoes and he sent them out to the island, Merriman's Island, which lay in the middle of Wallaga Lake. All the women and children, and the Elders, went to the island.

All the warriors, however, waited around the lakeside for these other fellas. They were coming here to steal the women. The night came and those fellas came. They were sneaking up and as they were getting nearer, the black duck he warned the people. When they came and tried to go to the island where all the people were, the warriors kept them off from invading that land and taking the women.

Uncle Warren Foster said that if you climb up Gulaga and look down on the island in the lake you will see that 'the island itself is a duck. It is a duck in flight. Taking off.'

He also explains that in addition to the black duck totem of all the Yuin people, each clan has their own totems, which represent special places or animals, and each person has a special totem too, which that person is responsible for looking after – and in return it will look after you. And while totems can be a plant or an animal, or a part of the landscape even, you have to protect your totem and cannot eat it. The totemic system creates a strong link between people and the land, which includes all the creatures that live on the land. It is a system that ensured proper balance and sustainability for our people for tens of thousands of years, supported by ceremonies.

The Yuin people hold a ceremony to bless the koontapool (whales) and their offspring on their migrations north and back south again. Whales are important to the Yuin people, and from May to November they migrate along the coast northwards. In the Yuin language, Dhurga, they would say, 'Walawaani Muriyira-Waraga.' Which means 'Greetings and safe journey whale-many.'

Whales would often be beached, which was seen as a way of the whales giving themselves back to the people, for whales were once Elders on the land, and there is a time for them to sacrifice their lives for the people and pass on their lore. When a whale was sighted on the beach an Elder would be summoned to ceremoniously spear it with a special hardwood spear. Then the whale would be turned over to regurgitate the lore. The spear would be pulled out in one piece, without breaking it, and a message would be sent to all tribes nearby to come for the feast.

Late Yuin Elder Uncle Max Dulumunmun Harrison told in his insightful book *Gurawul the Whale* that while the people were eating the flesh of the whale they would be learning more of the wisdom of the ocean and the land. He said, 'This was an important ritual to restore peace in the land. There were no wars or fighting. Gurawul gave up its life and its body so that people would unite.'[2]

There are just over a dozen tribes of the Yuin nation and they speak a common language called Dhurga, though clans can have their own languages too. The clans include the Walbunja, north of the Moruya River; the Murramurang, south of Lake Conjola; the Djiringanj, north of Bega; and the Brinja, from South Kianga to the Moruya River.

The Yuin lived a prosperous lifestyle between the sea and the mountains, due to the abundant resources of kangaroos, possums and echidnas, and seafood including oysters, abalone, pipis and mussels. Those whose land was by the coast were saltwater people, and those whose lands lay inland were freshwater people.

And coastal people had no great distinction between the land and sea, as both were considered a part of Country. This means that, like other peoples, the Yuin had a very different concept not just of land, but of the coast, compared to that of the settlers who came.

Yuin heritage was shaped heavily by the seasons, which indicated which foods could be accessed at what time. For instance, when the wattle was blooming it signalled the coming of bream and whiting. Then songs would be sung to Tootoowa (the wind creator) to bring fish into the stone fish traps, and songs would be sung to the rain to wash fish out of the creeks and rivers, which were then caught.

Many of our mob who grew up along the south coast would have memories of the Elders taking them down to the rivers to spear bream and eels at the full moon, when they'd come up the rivers. People would stand there perfectly still so as to not scare the fish, holding a homemade spear maybe made out of gum saplings or bamboo and the barbs from fence wire, determined to catch a fish for dinner.

As for all First Peoples along the east coast, such resources could only be taken in accordance with the lore that governed when they could be eaten and in what way, to ensure proper respect and also to ensure they would not be over-consumed.

The Yuin had nine different seasons, and each season was marked by different foods and could be indicated by different colours – such as the red bark at a certain time of year, or yellow blossoms at another. When the people went out to collect food from trees, they could shake the tree three times and after that must move on to another place, as that tree was not going to provide them with anything else that day. Lore told them repeatedly not to be greedy, like Gurung gabba the pelican, and to leave food for other mobs who might come along.[3] The people moved across their territory following the food seasons, moving onto new places and allowing the land to replenish itself. But the collection of food, whether by hunting or gathering, was also about connecting with ancestors and passing knowledge and skills on to a younger generation. So it was also about connecting with your Country, and managing Country and connecting with your Elders who had taught you the lore for gathering and hunting.[4]

During the summer months the Yuin people would follow traditional pathways onto the lands of nearby peoples in the mountains to collect bogong moths. This would also be a time of trade, ceremony and even arranging marriages.

One such pathway that ranged from Bega up into the Snowy Mountains is known as the Bundian Way, and is now a well-known tourist trail. It was traditionally a shared pathway, allowing for safe passage for the Yuin, Ngarigo, Jaitmathang and Bidwell peoples to travel between Turemulerrer (Twofold Bay) and up to near Tarangal (Mount Kosciusko). People would travel up into the high country in summer for the bogong moth feast and festival, and people would travel down to the coast in spring for ceremonies associated with whaling.

Walawaani njinidwaan is a greeting in the Dhurga language – 'welcome, everyone' – which is spoken across the lands of the Yuin people. It is an easy word to call out in either a loud voice or a soft one. Sharon Mason's mother, Aunty Vivian Mason – Yirrimar to her close family – teaches visitors how to say it properly, and she also teaches how traditional crafts are made. She sits on a blanket by the Wagonga inlet at Narooma and takes item after item out of her basket and passes it around to eager hands who examine it carefully. She explains that Narooma means 'clean water' in Dhurga, and Wagonga refers to a special quartz with magical abilities found in the waters.

Aunty Vivian, who belongs to the Walbanja clan, shows how strands of stringybark are used to make string, that is in turn used in many decorations. Shells are tied around the ankles for dancing, making a pleasant jingling sound. 'Shells like this were traded up the coast,' she says. Women gathered the shells by the shore while the men dived into the waters to hunt for sea foods. The ocean provided all their food, and everything was shared.

It was the role of the Elders to teach the younger ones about weather patterns, animal movements and the seasons, and about special places in the landscape. 'Some places are women's places,' she says. 'Some are men's. Some are places no one goes to. Like that creek where some of the mob from down south had been killed by Yuin. Those men had come north looking for wives. They found them, but did not seek permission. They were taking them back home when they were caught. They were speared as the law dictated.'

In the early 2000s a few determined Yuin people began to reclaim their language, working to have it taught in primary schools, and then ultimately at TAFE level. Words and phrases were collected from within communities, from early tape recordings of Elders, and from the written records of early explorers and settlers. Starting with about thirty words, they ended up with about 730. Not the complete language, but a significant amount. This work also led to the development of a Dhurga dictionary and learner's grammar, published by the Australian Institute of Aboriginal and Torres Strait Islander Studies. It has enabled both young and old to reclaim their language, which is an important part of knowing their culture.

Aunty Vivian tells that young kids are now being taken into the bush once more to learn the skills of collecting grasses and weaving, or learning about cultural burning. 'They learn to watch the birds and the wind to know when rain is coming. Black cockatoos can tell when rain is coming. Willy-wagtail brings bad news. If you have a bird totem – magpie, crow or kookaburra – they know what you are doing all the time.

'Your totem is given to you by an Elder and you need to look after your Country and look after your totem. You can't eat your totem animal.

'Birds come to tell you things. If you ask for permission to perform a dance, birds will give you permission by flying over.

'Look for signs to know when the rainbow serpent might be angry. If you take note of the earth, the birds, the trees, they can tell you something is going on. The trees dance when they are happy. Old girls live in the oak trees. You can talk to them.

'Talk to them.

'Walawaani njindiwaan.'

As Cook sailed further north, he named the land after random Englishmen or just equated what he saw with a name. Bateman's Bay was named after Nathaniel Bateman, a man he had previously sailed with. Point Upright was named on account of its perpendicular cliffs, and Pigeon House Mountain was so named because Cook saw a 'remarkable peak'd hill laying inland, the Top of which looked like a Pigeon house'. That would seem an odd decision for a sailor so long at sea, because there is plenty of material out there that states

Balgan/Pigeon House Mountain

the mountain was seen by the Yuin people as being shaped like a woman's breast. Today, most tourist information gives the mountain's name as Didthul.

But Uncle Noel Butler says that name is incorrect. 'Bullshit!' was the actual adjective used. He says the real name is Balgan.

Uncle Noel Butler is a Budawang Elder of the Yuin people, he is an extremely fit 74-year-old and has been a cultural educator for most of his life, teaching people about his culture and Country, both in Australia and overseas.

He says, 'The story I know on Didthul, where it comes from, if you go back and read the old histories recorded by Alexander Berry, Hamilton Hume, and the other surveyors with them who rode their horses up there, in one of those writings, they referred to it as "Millie's Tit". Now where that came from and who they were denigrating, I don't know. So it became Tit Hill.

'If you asked an old fella with a tooth missing out, "What do you call that one out there?" he'd say, "That one is Tithill."

'But how does a whitefella want to spell it or pronounce it? Were they linguists who wrote it? No, they weren't. They were everyday people. It's how you hear it and how you write it.' So that in turn became Didthul.

He says that much of the naming along the south coast, and even interpretive signs put up by the National Parks, are also incorrect. 'Ulladulla is said to mean "safe harbour", but when did blackfellas sit on a cliff and say, "That's a safe harbour. Let's put all our ships in there."' The proper name, he says, was Ngullada.

He says of the whitefellas who misnamed much of the landscape, 'They couldn't talk like us.' And he laughs.

Taking people out on Country near Murramurang Point, Uncle Noel indicates the metal signs erected by the NSW National Parks and says, 'It's not right. These are the things that we need to pull out and take over ourselves, and put the right information. We need to put the truth out. And we've tried for many years. I was an advisor

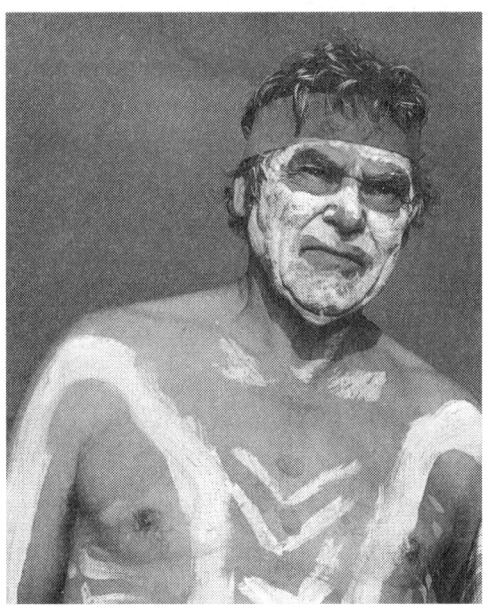

Uncle Noel Butler

on the New South Wales advisory board for National Parks. But in the years that we were there, they took no notice of everything we said.'

He says that the land underfoot was the largest midden in New South Wales, before it was dug up. 'I remember this and the old earth ovens where we cooked food and stuff, and it was just all sandhills and little tracks. Because I remember coming here as a kid and sitting on the headlands up here.'

Like too many of us, he also has memories of having siblings taken away, and of hiding in the bush from the government men. And while we're talking, a sea eagle glides down close on the wind. To our mobs, that is the ancestors or totems checking us out. Connecting with us.

Turning his mind back to the land about him, he says, 'But this was one of the biggest what they call digs for anthropologists and archaeologists, so they've turned it upside down and inside out, taking everything out of it. And where is it all? And we've been asking forever, "Can you get a keeping place where we can bring all that stuff back? You've done all your stuff and you're telling us about us, which we already know, and right under our nose, you know, and we're not allowed to touch anything, or even break a stick down for a spear or we get arrested, and now we're trying to get all that stuff back.'"

Uncle Noel says it is very important for his people's history to be taught alongside white history of Australia, and despite the disappointing result of the 2023 Indigenous Voice to Parliament referendum, work needs to continue on telling a shared history. 'All us mobs we will work together. We gotta work a bit harder, and work with the people who do want to learn their history and share their history and the knowledge, and just do it ourselves.

'Because then we can encourage our kids and stuff to come and learn from us and then we've got more teachers, to share, and we can confidently take other people around the country and teach them all the real value of this place that we call home.

'If they live here too, then they should be wanting or willing to learn about the Country where they live. Put the two histories together and put different value on the land, instead of monetary

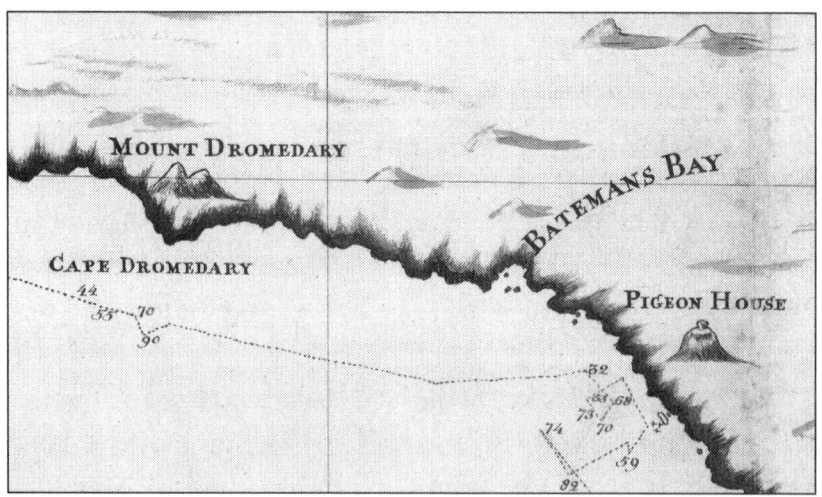

Cook's chart of Yuin Country

value with a piece of paper, and also have the willingness to then help protect and preserve what we've got left. So the future generations, those who follow us, they've got something to live with.'

A senior Yuin Elder, Percy Mumbler, had a story about Captain Cook landing at Batemans Bay that was told to him by his father. Cook had no way of knowing how his journey would enter into the stories of the people of this land, telling of his landings in places he visited as well as places he never visited, ranging from Batemans Bay right around to the Kimberley in Western Australia. But like understanding that Dreaming stories exist beyond the literal, you need to understand that many Cook stories also exist beyond the literal, and provide a deep understanding of what impact Cook had.

Percy Mumbler worked with the poet Roland Robinson, who collected many First Peoples' stories in the 1950s. He told Robinson the Captain Cook story, which goes in part: 'The big ship came and anchored out at Snapper Island. He put down a boat an' rowed up the river into Bateman's Bay. He landed on the shore of the river, the other side from where the church is now. When he landed he gave the Kurris clothes, an' those big sea-biscuits. Terrible hard biscuits they was. When they were pullin' away to go back to the ships, these wild Kurris were runnin' out of the scrub. They'd stripped right off again. They were throwin' the clothes an' biscuits back at Captain Cook as his men were pullin' away in the boat.'[5]

Joseph Banks and Cook were sometimes an odd couple, as can be seen not just from their differing backgrounds, but also from their journal entries. Cook was the son of a farm labourer who came to the navy late in life and was promoted due to his diligence and careful work. Banks was the rich son of a slave owner. Banks had paid handsomely to get his place on the ship, and had some expectation of being the boss of things because of it. But he slowly came to admire Cook and his skills.

Gunnai man Wayne Thorpe sums the men up like this: 'I see Cook as a public servant, paid to do his job. Banks was a spoiled fucken brat.'

The attitudes of Banks and Cook to the people they encountered are also evident in their journals. Banks' reads in part like he was on an extra-long gap year, sampling whatever culinary and sexual delights he was able to, while having Sydney Parkinson sketch the many hundred botanical specimens he had gathered – like posting Instagram pictures of the day.

Sharon Mason says of Cook, 'Cook wasn't the man who had all the soldiers in the harbour. He had a job to do, I suppose.' Then she tells that when she was in Sydney with her dance troupe recently, she went to the National Maritime Museum to see an exhibition of traditional shell fishhooks she had contributed to, and while there she went on board the *Endeavour* replica. The kids had asked if they could go on board the pirate ship there, but when she asked about it, one of the museum staff told her it was not a pirate ship, it was Cook's *Endeavour*!

'I went around that ship and looked at the places where Cook and that would have slept, and then went up the front of the ship where the artifacts were kept.' She gives a shiver. After seeing the artifacts there she had to get off the ship right away.

Sharing the past and sharing culture is something Sharon does regularly, and she is involved in tourism but thinks it could put a lot of pressure on a community, trying to meet the growing need for cultural engagements. Despite having worked as a tour guide herself, at The Rocks in Sydney, she says she has decided that her dance troupe, the Djaadjawan Dancers, are only going to perform for ceremonial occasions in the near future, and not for general tourism.

'Our culture is getting too loose. We need to strengthen it.'

The final landmarks on Yuin Country that Cook renamed were Cape St George (sighted on Saint George's Day, 23 April) and Long Nose (Cook finally succumbing to an anatomical reference), which make up the land either side of Jervis Bay. But he was not able to enter the bay and make his first landfall on the east coast there, writing: 'we had the wind it was not in my power to look into it and the appearance was not favourable enough to induce me to loose time in beating up to it'.

So he sailed on northwards, looking for a more favourable site to land, and entered Dharawal territory.

Contact

Eighteen years after Cook passed by, the eleven ships of the First Fleet sailed past Yuin land on their way to Botany Bay, and fulfilled that fear of the greedy pelican Gurung gabba taking more than it should. The coming of the fleet was the point at which the people's lives began to change, though not for the better and not straight away.

The first Europeans did not travel through Yuin Country until 1797, when a small party of survivors from the *Sydney Cove* shipwreck passed through their land. The ship had been wrecked on Preservation Island off lutruwita (Tasmania), with a large cargo of rum. Several members of the crew crossed over to the mainland by boat, which was also wrecked on the voyage, forcing them to walk all the way to Sydney to seek help. One of the men to survive the journey, William Clark, wrote of the Yuin they encountered: 'met 14 natives who ... kindly treated us with mussels, for which unexpected civility, we made them some presents These people seem better acquainted with the laws of hospitality than any of their countrymen ... For to their benevolent treat was added an invitation to remain with them for the night ...'[6]

That is a part of our culture, to be hospitable to those in need.

Clark's account also described how the people escorted the shipwreck survivors to the edge of their Country and handed them over to new people to escort them on their way. But helping strangers in need to move through your Country is clearly not the same as allowing strangers to come and settle on your Country.

As more convicts and settlers arrived at the colony in Port Jackson, settlers and explorers began moving up and down the coast, searching for fertile lands and timber and other resources. In 1806 a group of Yuin people at Nalluccer (Twofold Bay) attempted to forcibly remove a gang of eleven sealers who had camped on their land. The Yuin attacked with spears and the sealers responded with musket fire, killing nine.

Two years later, in 1808, bad weather forced a colonial vessel, the *Fly*, into Batemans Bay, and while some accounts say the crew were attacked 'without provocation'[7], it is more likely they had broken some lore or had caused offence. The result was that three crew and an unknown number of Yuin were killed.

What the settlers did not understand – or perhaps had no real interest in understanding – was that for the Yuin people land was a heritable possession for the whole tribe, and could not be traded or given away. Its use was governed by strict laws and ceremonies.

European invaders had an entirely different concept of land, and its individual ownership. To them land was owned if it was fenced and improved in some way, so a claim on the land was visible. And these two different views of the land inevitably led to clashes, and ultimately dispossession for the Yuin. They were not only moved off their land but were forbidden from speaking their language and practising their culture. Some women who ended up having children with white settlers, including those women kidnapped by sealers, became disengaged from the traditional customs and alienated from their own people.

A story that was told by a woman known as Coomee Nulunga, who died in Ulladulla in 1914, was that her grandmother had told her about the coming of the British ships as 'the first time the white birds came by'.

She also said, 'Where my people?' – a pause – 'Dead all dead. Coomee soon die too – then all gone … Why my people die?'

She attributed the death of her people to a change from healthy 'native food' to 'eat white man tucker – drink white feller grog … grog kill 'em ver' quick'.[8]

But the Yuin proved to be resilient and their language and culture is being reclaimed. There are schools along the south coast teaching the Dhurga language and the work of finding and reclaiming more lost words continues.

Warren Foster said, 'There is a big resurgence of language and dance and culture. It gives our children identity and they know where they come from.'

He said that when he was younger and the Elders had singled him out to teach culture and law, he was angry and told them that their culture was dead. 'But one Elder told me, "As long as that fucken blood runs through your veins, culture is never dead."

'It made me realise,' Warren said, 'that as long as we are alive, our culture is alive.'

Kembla (Red Point)
Dharawal Country

Bereewagal, naa niya.
Yura ngura dyi ngurang
   gurugal.
	People who come from afar,
	   I see all of you.
	Aboriginal people camped here,
	   at this place, long ago.

Ngoon dyalgala niya, ngoon bamaraadbanga ni.	We embrace all of you; we open the door to all of you.
Ngoon – mari ngurang – niya mudang yura ngurra.	We lend this place to all of you to live while we sleep.
Dyi nga ni nura.[1]	Here I see my Country.

A little way inland to the North-West of this point is a round hill, the top of which look'd like the Crown of a Hatt.
Cook's journal, 26 April 1770

Cook entered Dharawal Country on 26 April, passing modern-day Kiama and naming the large point he observed Red Point. To the Dharawal people it was a headland of the bay they called Kembla, which was a part of the landscape they called Woolyungah – and both are used today in the names of Port Kembla and Wollongong.

    The name Woolyungah is said to mean 'five islands', which is a central Creation story of the area and involves both the sacred Mount Keira and the five islands that lie offshore of Wollongong.

    As told by Aunty Lorraine Brown and her sister, Narelle Thomas, the west wind Oola Boola Woo lived on Mount Keira with his six daughters. But they were troublesome, and one by one he

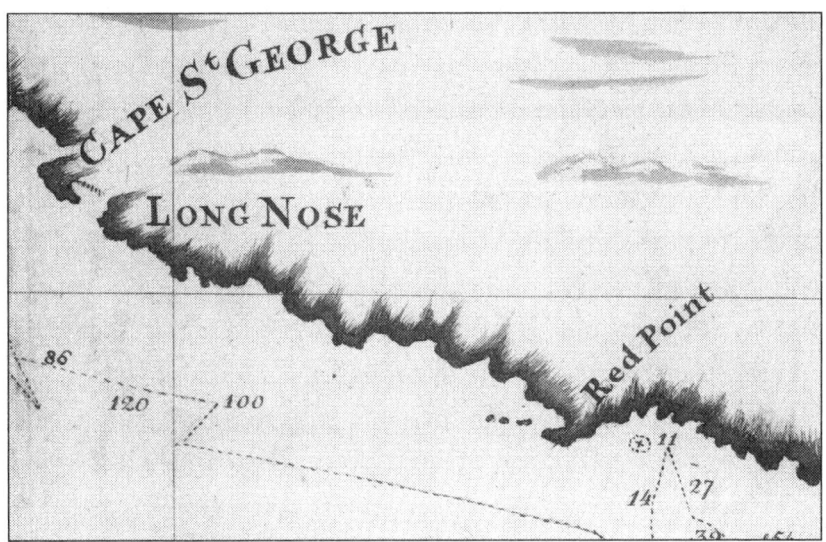

Cook's chart of Dharawal Country

blew five of them out to sea with the chunk of land they were on. They became the five islands. The one daughter who was left, Geera, fretted for her sisters and sat in one spot on the mountain until she was covered by the leaves and the moss. She became the top of the mountain, which is now known as Mount Keira.

And the five sisters, even though they also fretted, ended up turning into mermaids and they swim around the islands.

Stories of how the Dharawal people came to the land they now inhabit tell that they moved from the east as the seas rose and the hunting grounds became sparce. One story tells that they came across the ocean in a whale canoe – which is why whales have always been significant to the Dharawal people.

This was a time when the animals lived in a land beyond the sea, named Nurran. They were able to shapeshift between human and animal form at that time, and had resolved to leave that Country in a canoe and come to the hunting grounds where they now live.

As the whale man, Burri Burri, was much larger than any of the other people, he therefore had a canoe that was also very large. But he would not lend it to anybody else and their small canoes were unfit for use far from land. The people watched carefully in the hope that Burri Burri might leave his canoe so they could get it for their journey to the new land. But Burri Burri always kept a strict guard over it.

Now Burri Burri's best friend was Gunaagaan the starfish man, but he conspired with the people to distract Burri Burri to give the people a chance to use his boat to reach new hunting grounds. So one day Gunaagaan said to Burri Burri, 'You have a great many lice on your head, let me catch them and kill them for you.'

Burri Burri had been very pestered with these lice and quickly agreed to his friend's offer. He tied his canoe to a rock, on which he sat down. Gunaagaan gave the signal and the people quietly got into the canoe and rowed away.

After a while Burri Burri wanted to check on his canoe and looked back, and was surprised to see it was gone. He became angry and he and Gunaagaan began to fight. Gunaagaan grabbed a stick to defend himself and pierced a hole in Burri Burri. In his anger, Burri Burri split Gunaagaan's body into the shape of a star. Gunaagaan slipped down from the rock into the water and fell onto the sand at the bottom of the rockpools – where he still is today. His shape and rough appearance is the same today, and he lies alone at the bottom of the pools as a lesson not to trick your friends.

Burri Burri then jumped into the water and swam after his canoe, spurting water into the air through a wound in his head that came from the fight with Gunaagaan – something he has done ever since.

The chase lasted many days and nights, until finally new land was sighted. As they drew close to the land, two of the ancestors, Guradhawak (brolga) and Garilwa (koala), began to dance in the canoe until two holes were put in the bottom of it. In panic, Guradhawak flew onto the land and hid, and Garilwa turned the canoe over and pushed it out into the sea, before retreating to hide in the top of a tree, where he remains today.

As the saltwater, wind and sand blew across the canoe, Burri Burri was unable to recognise it, and Burri Burri's ancestors continue to come up and down the coast today, still looking for the canoe. And that canoe lies at the entrance to Lake Illawarra, as Windang Island, a reminder of how the rise of the sea level brought the Dharawal people to the Illawarra. And the people take their name from the Dharawal Palm that they carried with them on their journey.[2]

As the whale was an important totemic animal to the people of the land known as Woolyungah – the Dharawal and Wodi Wodi peoples – they would watch for them from rock lookouts along their land. And they would use the flowering of the gymea lily to tell them when the time was right to see the whales on their migration northwards, up to birthing areas in warmer waters.

Living along the coast, the people from the Dharawal nation identify as saltwater, freshwater, or bitter-water people – who live by swamplands. Wodi Wodi people identify as saltwater and mountain people.

The people moved around the lands in accordance with the seasons, remaining on the coastal plains during the warm seasons, where there were abundant marine resources. Lake Illawarra provided plentiful food throughout the year, and tribes would come from the south and north, being able to stay for three days gathering mussels, oysters and fish. About 250 plants supplied 80 per cent of the people's diet.[3] Following the seasons closely, the people would look for the blossoming of coastal wattle in the summer months to know that mullet were running. Other plants signalled the birthing of eastern grey kangaroos.[4]

The people had a Creation hero – or Creator – common to much of southeastern Australia and he was known by several names. Baiame is one widely known name across many peoples, but he was known as Mirriwal to the Dharawal and Wodi Wodi peoples. He – or she, in some tellings – created the features of the land and gave people their lore and initiation rites. Mirriwal sang the mountains into being and his son Duramulun was the law-giver, who taught the people laws and customs related to kinship and totems.[5]

Learning and understanding Country was the key to survival, and this was shared through stories, song, dance, art, and walking Country.

Richard Campbell is one of the founders of Gumaraa Cultural Tours and Education Group, and today he is waiting for a group of teachers to join him and his team of six, on the grassy slopes of the Killalea reserve at Shellharbour. It is a b-e-a-utiful day and down the slope is the secluded Killalea beach. Just to the north are the Bass Point wetlands. Bass Point itself, directly to the east, is a low sloping headland – the most prominent peninsula in the Illawarra.

Further away north you can see the city of Wollongong, but if you stand just so, all you see is the bush, the headland and the beach.

Richard has set up on a picnic table, now covered in traditional wooden tools and weapons, and one of his team has lit a small fire beside it. As the teachers arrive, wandering over from the car park in small groups, they are told the smoke is there to prevent anyone taking a spirit of the land away with them when they leave.

Richard begins by sharing his story. It is not an unfamiliar one for First Nations people, and includes him going off the rails a bit in his youth, but ends with how he came to set up Gumaraa – which means 'wise old man' – so that now he is able to teach people about his culture and Country.

'It is the best job I have ever had,' he says.

There are about thirty of us assembled on the grass, and each of the women are invited to place three ochre dots on the side of their face, which Richard says represent mind, body and spirit or soul. The men put two strips on their faces, across their noses and down

Richard Campbell

their cheeks, for the two rivers that bound the land – the Georges River and the Shoalhaven River.

Richard then proceeds with a Welcome to Country. It is so heartfelt and carries a genuine depth of feeling that many Acknowledgements of Country at official functions often lack. This clearly has a strong meaning to him.

He indicates the land all around us and tells us this is the land of the Wodi Wodi tribe, and tells us some of its stories. 'Bass Point is the second-oldest site on eastern Australia,' he says, 'having human presence dating back 32,000 years.' He indicates the wetlands between us and the point, and tells us it is a significant swamp, where the women were sat down and taught their knowledge.

'If strangers came to the land here they would twirl a bullroarer to let people know of their presence. Then they would wait for someone to come and ask their business. And only then might they be allowed onto the land, or to pass through it.' This is something that is consistent all across the continent, the need to respect other people's land and not enter it without permission.

Richard then tells us that Bass Point is where his people's bodies have traditionally been buried, including one returned from a museum. 'It was wrapped in bark, facing out to sea. Always facing out to sea,' he tells us. 'And when a tsunami is coming, the spirits of the dead buried there will tell the birds and the birds will let us know it is coming.'

The last tsunami here was about 6,000 years ago, he says. 'The people went up to the escarpment to escape it.'

Part of our learning today – the teachers as students – is a bush walk and explanation of the different uses that different plants were put to. We learn how a flowering banksia could be used to comb unruly hair, and a dead banksia could be lit to make a torch at night-time, or as a fire to carry around. Richard shows us the dianella bush, also known as the blueberry lily for its purple berries. And it's also known as the snake plant, because when you take the shoots of the plant and blow through them they make a high-pitched sound that Richard says attracts snakes, as they think it is a bird in distress. And when the snakes come, you catch them and kill them. Or as Richard describes it, 'Send them on their journey.'

The she-oak wood was used for making coolamons and shields, and the leaves of wattles could be rubbed all over your body to mask your scent when hunting game. Richard thanks the Elders for passing on all this knowledge and then addresses the Cook question. He says, 'Back in 1770 Jimmy Cook said he found Australia. He never *found* Australia.

'The Wodi Wodi people knew he was coming before he did,' Richard says. 'The mob sent smoke from Gulaga.'

When Cook tried to land a little further up the coast, he wrote in his journal: 'Being now not above 2 Miles from the Shore Mr. Banks, Dr. Solander, Tupia, and myself put off in the Yawl, and pull'd in for the land to a place where we saw 4 or 5 of the Natives, who took to the Woods as we approached the Shore; which disappointed us in the expectation we had of getting a near View of them, if not to speak to them. But our disappointment was heightened when we found that we no where could effect a landing by reason of the great Surf which beat everywhere upon the shore.'

If it had been a calmer day, then the Illawarra – probably Bulli or Thirroul – would have been the first place that Cook landed in Australia. And Richard tells us Cook was lucky he didn't land there. 'They [the local people] saw the ghost people on board,' he says. 'They were waiting on the beach with waddies [clubs].'

After a lunch that features emu and crocodile, the teachers are stood in a large circle. Richard takes a big ball of wool and hands it to one person and tells them to throw it across the circle, while holding onto the other end of the wool. It takes a while to work out how much wool to unwind to make a successful throw, but everyone soon gets the hang of it and is throwing the wool back and forth, until everyone is joined up by a crisscross of long strands of wool.

Richard tells us that First Nations societies were connected to each other before European invaders came. Then he produces a pair of scissors and walks in and around the circle, seemingly at random cutting threads. As he does he says, 'You were put in jail.' *Snip.* 'You lost the link to your mother.' *Snip.* 'You were taken away.' *Snip.* 'You lost your language.' *Snip.*

When he finally stops cutting, only about 20 per cent of the woollen connections are left. Some people are standing with nothing but the dangling ends of wool in their hands. Then Richard says, 'This is what has happened to my people.'

There were many well-known and well-maintained walking paths across the country that people would use to get from place to place, usually about a metre wide. One well-used path ran for 150 kilometres, from Jervis Bay through Kangaroo Valley to Robertson and Appin. The journey would have taken about five days, but some Elders covered the distance in amazingly short periods.[6]

And these paths were a songline or storyline, a path that had been travelled by a Creation spirit while bringing the Country into existence. Songlines join the continent like threads – some are short and some stretch for thousands of kilometres, crossing many different Countries and language groups. They were used for trade and they were used for connecting to Country.

Trading paths had existed across many generations, and involved travelling for hundreds of kilometres to meet and exchange gifts, often with familiar people in pleasant locations. It has been estimated that valuable items, like songs, stories and ceremonies, or quartz and ochre took about fifteen years to cross the entire continent.[7]

Dharawal people say everything lies on a songline, otherwise it was not created and does not exist.

The people knew the land intimately and knew what to expect at each new location, in terms of wood and water and foods. Their stories and laws were often based around protecting the Country, and their totems were a part of this system: never killing or eating a personal totem, but taking responsibility to care for that animal of plant, so that the whole clan would benefit.

To the Dharawal and other peoples and clans across the country, all life was connected – the Creation beings, the land, the sea, humans, fauna, flora, and all other natural phenomena. And all were respected and kept in balance – a way of life that had sustained the people and the land for tens of thousands of years. Ritual and ceremony were a way of entering a direct relationship with Creation spirits, to conserve the balance of everything in the world.[8]

Another significant site in the Illawarra is Dhgillawarah (Hill 60, which is one of the highest points along the coast, and overlooks the point that Cook named Red Point). It had been a traditional camping place for the Dharawal and Wodi Wodi people, but they were moved off in World War Two when it was taken over as an observation post and gun emplacement. Today the hill is

Three of the five islands seen from Dhgillawarah (Hill 60, Red Point)

one of the best places to see the five islands that are integral to the Dreaming story of the place.

You can ascend up to the viewing platform of the white observation building and get a more than 180-degree view along the coast. The five islands lie there before you in the ocean, a mix of green-covered and rocky platforms. The islands are Cobbyr (Flinders Islet, also known as Toothbrush Island), Munnungang, (Bass Islet), Martin Islet, Booirodoong (Big Island, also called Rabbit or Perkins Island) and Rocky Islet. Together they make up an area of about 26 hectares.

Now a heritage-listed Aboriginal site, the hill is frequented by rock fishermen (six killed so far in 2023, a sign warns), and paragliders who compete with the pelicans to ride the updraughts. A stunning and colourful mural built along a sea wall on the northern side of the headland tells that the shoreline was the area for coastal fishing with canoes and traditional woven nets, and it is still a special place, connecting the people's past and present to the future.

As a watching point for guiding fishermen, it would have been where the people saw the *Endeavour* make its slow journey north.

Dhgillawarah (Hill 60) mural depicting parts of the Five Islands story

Yuin woman Dr Jodi Edwards, who has kinship ties with the Dharawal and has been a leading advocate of Dharawal language reclamation, said of the key sacred sites of the region, 'We got our Grandmother mountain Mount Keira, Grandfather mountain Mount Kembla, the Five Islands out to sea, Hill 60. Then there's the escarpment, that's littered with several significant sites.'

If anything defines Dharawal Country to a visitor it is the imposing escarpment that rises above the mountain range to the west, continually drawing your eyes to it.

Dr Jodi Edwards said that her people have been fighting to have their lands returned for a long time and on one occasion, in 1998, the land seemed to be fighting along with them. The story, as told by mob, is that developers wanted to build houses at Sandon Point. The mob were protesting, saying it was a significant site, but the Land and Environment Court said it was not, as it was already being mined.

The Country then spoke for itself.

A big storm came through on top of a king tide, with the waves breaking over the lagoon there, and they uncovered the remains of a man in the sandhills. He was identified as being a Kuradji – or 'clever man', and over 6,000 years old. For perspective, that is twice as old as the ancient Egyptian Pharaohs.

Unfortunately a lot of development continued in the area, leading to a strong campaign to protect the site, including both radical action and court cases. In 2017 it was finally declared an Aboriginal site by the New South Wales government and is now protected by the *National Parks and Wildlife Act.*

Contact

In many history books the first European settler to move into the Woolyungah area is given as Charles Throsby, with his convict servant, Joe Wyld, in 1815 – though Wyld later claimed to have visited the area on his own much earlier. There had actually been many earlier encounters, as escaped convicts made their way south through the thick scrub. We know this because when Matthew Flinders and George Bass visited Lake Illawarra in 1796, they were told that a number of escapees were living with the people.[9]

In the early days, coexistence seemed possible, with Charles Throsby reminiscing decades later in 1863: 'the Aborigines were never particularly hostile to the whites. The Wollongong tribe numbered about one hundred. They were very much finer looking … [I]n the early days they had abundance of fish, kangaroos, possums, ducks and other wild fowl …'[10]

It has been estimated that in 1820 there were some 3,000 First Peoples living in the Illawarra region, but by 1846 that had diminished to fewer than a hundred, due to the encroachment of settlers bringing disease and dispossession.[11]

According to researchers at the University of Wollongong, Michael Organ and Carol Speechley, who have extensively researched the early days of the Illawarra, the arrival of Europeans was to change forever the way of life of the Illawarra people as it had existed for over 20,000 years. It led to the almost total destruction of their ancient culture within a single generation.[12] People were pushed off their land for sheep and cattle grazing and then punished if they speared one of the animals that had supplanted their kangaroos and wallabies. Women were abused. Children were taken from their parents. Even the vast shell middens along the coast were destroyed, to make lime for building – giving the township of Shellharbour its name.

The news of the First Fleet's arrival in Sydney in 1788 was met with much foreboding, and stories quickly circulated to explain the event. One such story, quoted by Organ and Speechley, was from as far away as Victoria, and told: 'The solid vault of the sky rested on props placed at the extreme edge of the earth. News came that the eastern prop [near Sydney] was rotting and if gifts were not sent to the guardian the sky would fall, and the white-skinned ghosts or reincarnations of all the blackfellows who ever lived would break through from the spirit world to swarm over the land. The landscape and all of its Dreamtime associations would be transformed. Everybody would be killed.'[13]

This proved to be true for too many of us.

And despite being 'largely seen as peaceful' (or harmless in colonial speak), the people were still subjected to massacres.[14] In 1818 a group of Wodi Wodi were massacred by Europeans along the Minnamurra River, north of Kiama, led by settler Lieutenant William Frederick Weston, his overseer Cornelius O'Brien, and seven convict labourers.

And yet some settlers did understand the people's strong cultural links with their land. In 1825 a deputy-surveyor was quoted by two members of the London Missionary Society as saying the people had 'a notion of the rights of real property, the lands which particular families occupy being marked out and bequeathed from the father to his children'.[15]

Dr Jodi Edwards said, 'Not stereotyping all non-Aboriginal people, but I feel they need to have an understanding of the interconnected relationship that we have with Country. I feel that's their major barrier.

'They don't understand that when we talk about Country as being alive, it's because that's how it is. It *is* alive. For example, the trees speak to the grass, and you see this when you watch cultural burning – in some cases when a tree doesn't need burning it will speak to the grass and that grass won't stay alight.

'Connection of responsibility to Country is not just land Country, but sky Country and sea Country. Sky Country is alive, always moving and teaching us the patterns we see between the stars and sometimes in the stars, like the Emu in the Sky and the Seven Sisters Dreaming (Malamalang). Sea Country teaches us about the connection between Grandmother Moon and Grandfather Sun – the tides, and currents, how to use them and respect them. That's why some fishermen are washed into the waters at Dhgillawarah (Hill 60). They don't know the lore and the connections. The Old Man of the Sea, he is hard and he will take you.

'I feel some non-Aboriginal people – those in caring for Country groups and planting tree groups and that – they're ready to hear. People who go out and pick up litter and that, they get an understanding of it when you yarn about Country being alive, or when you can connect the stories to song, to dance, to the sea and the sky.'

Mirroring the age divide apparent in the 2023 referendum, she said, 'I certainly think more people of the younger generation, between, you know, twenty-five and thirty-five, are listening and are ready to hear.'

She says that is where the future lies – with the younger generation.

And for her own people, she says, 'I just feel it's important as a community we remember to share knowledges, especially with the young ones, because they're the next generation and are the creators for the future. They're the ones that need the stories, songs, the dances, the art, and to be taken out on Country and shown the connections. Show them Country is alive. This way they will have the knowledges, and they can continue to pass on and share our culture.'

Kamay (Botany Bay) Dharawal Country

Naggangbi gweagalgulli nguranhung nhay.

Welcome – this is Gweagal people's Country.

At our first entering the woods we saw 3 of the Natives, who made off as soon as they saw us ...

Cook's journal, 3 May 1770

From the ocean, Kamay (Gamay or Botany Bay), is a largely hidden expanse of water whose size only becomes apparent as you sail in between the 1.5 kilometre opening of cliffs on the northern and southern shores. Sadly Cook, in his precise and measured prose, failed to capture the majesty of sailing in through the heads and finding the great stretch of emerald-blue water there. He wrote: 'In the P.M. wind Southerly and Clear weather, with which we stood into the bay and Anchored under the South shore about 2 miles within the Entrance in 5 fathoms, the South point bearing South-East and the North point East.'

But crossing that gap from the ocean to the bay marked the crossing of a cultural line that Cook and his men were unable to understand. For them the bay was a shelter where they could anchor safely and send out their boats. Somewhere they could reprovision with fresh water and fresh foods. Somewhere the naturalists could come ashore and botanise to their hearts' content. It had, after all, been over a month since they had left New Zealand and their drinking water was getting a bit old and could have done with replenishing.

To the people who lived on the shores of this wide beautiful bay – the Gweagal (or fire clan of the white clay) of the Dharawal people on the southern side, and the Kameygal (or spear clan) of the Eora people on the northern side – this land was somewhere they had lived for more thousands of years than the Europeans could have guessed. Season upon season, year upon year, they had lived there in a state of careful balance with the land and its resources. It was a place where sea and land met. Where freshwater and saltwater met. And they knew every facet of the land and they looked after it to ensure it was always abundant in the six Dharawal seasons.

Gweagal Country ranged from the southern shore of Botany Bay at Kundul (Kurnell) and Kurunulla (Cronulla), extending to the Woronora River in the west, and to the Georges River to the

Cook's map of Botany Bay compared to an aerial shot

south. Like many people of the Country, their boundaries were defined by landscape.

It is the Gweagal who have the most claim to talk about the impact of Captain Cook, as they were the first people on the east coast to meet these strangers face to face. They have the most well-known story of the clash between the two peoples, and they also have the most monuments and memorials to Cook on their land, on the shores of Botany Bay. They therefore often have to carry the main First Nations response to Cook's arrival.

Was he an invader? A transgressor? Or something more complicated than a single word can capture?

The Gweagal also have to contend with all the different stories of Cook that compete with their own stories. Cook the heroic explorer or Cook the exploiter. Cook the humanitarian or Cook the coloniser. Cook has made such a strong impact on First Nations people that he even exists in stories told in the Northern Territory, which tell of him shooting his way all around the coast from Sydney Harbour and up into the Northern Territory, taking land that he liked the look of, and never asking permission to enter the land.[1] So there is even Cook as the metaphor for colonisation.

It was also the Gweagal people who had to first defend their land from Cook, when he came ashore in 1770, and they then watched the British closely as they blundered around, breaking lore and protocols – until they seemed to have finally gotten the hint and sailed away.

But it has been Cook's own version of these events that has dominated history for most of the 250 years since he sailed into Kamay, as if it was the only version possible. Reading the ships' journals closely, though, you can't help but wonder how differently things might have turned out had a few different decisions been made. For instance, Banks wrote that when the ship's boat preceded the ship into the bay, checking the depth of the water and making sure the passage was safe for the ship, the sailors saw many people along the north shore. He wrote that they came down to the beach and 'invited our people to land by many signs and words', which he says the sailors could not understand at all. However, since the people on the shore were all armed with 'long pikes and a wooden weapon made something like a short scimitar', the crew declined to land there and instead looked to the southern side of the bay.

Nobody on board the boat or the ship could have known that the people on the northern shore were a different people to those on the southern shore. And when the ship followed the boat into the bay, Banks wrote that more men on the northern shore came down to the rocks 'brandishing their crooked weapons at us as in token of defiance'.

So the first 'what-if' proposition for the landing at Kamay is: What if Cook had landed on the northern side of the bay? Might he have encountered much larger opposition by a larger band of people, and might it have led to the deaths of any of his crew?

When the *Endeavour* turned away from the northern shore and sailed to the southern arm of the bay, Banks wrote that they saw four small canoes with a man in each fishing with a spear. 'The ship passd within a quarter of a mile of them and yet they scarce lifted their eyes from their employment.' Likewise as they came abreast of a collection of huts, the men on the ship saw an old woman with several children come out of the bush, and although she looked at the ship she 'expressd neither surprize nor concern'. The men fishing then came ashore and began cooking their catch, 'to all appearance totaly unmovd at us, tho we were within a little more than ½ a mile of them'.

For the Europeans, it was as if the people on the southern shore could not comprehend what they were seeing. As if the idea of a ship of the size of the *Endeavour* had not yet been created in their minds.

The Gweagal have a different interpretation of events, of course. Firstly, we know that they knew the ship was coming, from the signals and stories being sent along the coast. But like most of the clans across Australia, they had a very strict protocol for strangers to enter their lands, and even for acknowledging strangers coming onto their land. This involved politely ignoring the strangers until a reasonable time had passed, and then an Elder would wander over and ask them what they wanted, before choosing to invite them onto the land – or not. Added to that was the assumption that these white men were ghosts of the dead, or perhaps evil spirits, in which case they might go away if left alone.[2]

Dharawal man Dr Shayne Williams is an Elder of the First People's community at La Perouse in Sydney. He has a long background in education, telling his people's stories, and has said that seeing the world through a spiritual lens was logical for his people, and that is how they would have viewed the events of that day. 'Our spirit ancestors created Dharawal Country and its various life forms. This shaped our kinship, social structures and lore. Our Dreaming stories provide us with a spiritual reasoning for existence.'[3]

One such story tells how animals, once in human form, came to the Country in a big vessel, slowly transforming into animals on the voyage – the koala, the crane and the whale. Another tells how the spirits of the dead return to Dharawal Country in low-lying clouds.

Shayne Williams says that when the people saw the *Endeavour* coming up the coast, they first thought it might be garru (a cloud), and that the spirits of the dead were returning, but as the ship got closer it changed shape, so they thought it might be a floating baranggas (island). Then, as the vessel turned into the bay, the people saw sailors going up and down the masts, which they thought might be possums.

Finally, when they could make out the figures on board as humans, they saw they were white and assumed they were the spirits of the dead.[4] So each side was viewing the other through their own cultural lens.

Contact

The story of the British coming ashore is fairly well known. Having seen huts and some people on the southern shore of Botany Bay, Cook took two boats ashore, with forty or so men in them, hoping to speak to the people they had observed. But things did not go well. As the British approached the shore, two men came down to oppose them, each armed with a spear that was about 3 metres long. From the boats, Cook and the Tahitian navigator Tupia tried to talk to the men but they could not understand each other's words. This was a disappointment to Cook, as Tupia had proved an invaluable translator in New Zealand, where his language was close enough to the Māori language (te reo Māori) to be understood.

Sydney Parkinson, the ship's young artist, said they shouted, 'Warra warra wai,' which for years was believed to mean 'Go away!' It is now known more accurately to mean 'You're all dead' – a warning to others that they had encountered spirits of the dead.

Cook then threw beads and nails ashore from the boat, which the two men examined. They then made signals to Cook which he interpreted as beckoning them to come ashore. But this was a big mistake. As soon as they landed, the two men threatened them with their spears again, first throwing stones. In response, Cook had the marines fire at them, first into the air, and then at the men with small shot. The elder of the two men was wounded in the leg, but his response was just to go back to the huts to fetch a shield and more spears and stones.

Following that, a volley of stones and spears were thrown at the Europeans, one spear landing between Sydney Parkinson's feet, and two more muskets of small shot were fired at the Gweagal men, until they retired slowly back to the bush.

Parkinson wrote that during the fray the women and children nearby in the bush set up 'a most horrid howl'.

Several musket shots and spears and some thrown rocks did not make a good start to relations. Again, we need to understand it from the Gweagal point of view. In an essay on Cook's arrival written for the British Library from an Indigenous perspective, Dr Shayne Williams wrote, 'If you look at this same encounter from our perspective you would understand that two Gweagal men were assiduously carrying out their spiritual duty to Country by protecting Country from the presence of persons not authorised to be there.

'In our cultures it is not permissible to enter another culture's Country without due consent. Consent was always negotiated. Negotiation was not necessarily a matter of immediate dialogue, it often involved spiritual communication through ceremony.'[5]

The fact that it was two men, one young and one old, with bodies painted, who came forward to oppose the strangers indicates they were following proper protocols. This is reinforced by the fact that the two men first displayed their weapons and shook them above their heads, without using them.[6]

Theresa Ardler is a descendant of the elder warrior who stood to oppose the British landing on his people's Country that day. She said, 'He was my fourth great-grandfather, Chief Cooman. He was the Gweagal warrior with the Gweagal shield that was shot in the leg and died afterwards.'

In addition to having deep knowledge of her people's stories, Theresa has a degree in constitutional law. While walking across the land at Kurnell she is stopped by some teachers on an excursion, and after a short chat is asked if she would tell their students how her people encountered Cook.

She says, 'So when they actually came into Botany Bay, it was in the afternoon, I was told by my nan and that. And so when they came in the women and children were in their nuwis [canoes], so they got called in.

'And our people, the Gweagal people, Cook and that didn't see them at first because we had the full body shields, and only the eyes [showed], and they were just blended in like the trees.

'And as they came in they thought at first it was a big white bird. Then when they got closer they thought they were goonjas [dead].

'That's when my grandfather and his brother were going, "Warra Warra. Warra Wai," which means "Go away, we don't want dead people here."

'And because they could smell them when they come ashore, because they'd been on that ship, you know, so they sort of smelled like death.'

Having driven the two warriors away, the men of the *Endeavour* then went and examined the huts near the beach, where children were hiding in fear. They left the people nails and other gifts, and took away forty or fifty of their spears and at least one shield. They were scientists, and felt it their right to collect artifacts wherever they went.

Parkinson wrote that the shield he examined had two holes in it, which were there to see through. We will come back to the shield in a moment, but Banks seemed very keen to explain in his journal that, given the distance the elder warrior had been from the landing crew when he was hit by musket shot, 'no material harm' could have been done to him.

As we have seen, Gweagal people told the story a bit differently, in that the shots led to the death of the leader Cooman.

There is a detailed engraving of the warriors on the beach that is often attributed to the ship's artist, Sydney Parkinson, and treated as if it is an accurate depiction of the men, their weapons and body decorations. It shows the two warriors with white patterns on their bodies, with a streak round their thighs, two below their knees, one like a sash over their shoulders running diagonally downwards, and another across their foreheads.

That too is a European construct. Sydney Parkinson only made the briefest of sketches of the people of Kamay, and the engraving, which was based on his sketch, was done by the artist Thomas Chambers, who never visited Australia.

Wayne Shipp, CEO of the Eden Land Council, who has a military-history background, points out that the two men in the picture are actually depicted in classical Greek poses. 'It's a Hoplite shield,' he said. The engraving shows one warrior holding a round shield at his front and a sword at his back, and the other warrior holding a spear over his head – not even using a spear thrower, as is present in Parkinson's original sketch. 'And you won't find a wooden sword like that in the Sydney basin,' Wayne said.

That the British considered they had the right to enter people's dwellings uninvited and steal their personal belongings is clear from Banks' journal. He wrote, 'We however thought it no improper measure to take away with us all the lances which we could find about the houses, amounting in number to forty or fifty.'

Only four of the spears that James Cook and Joseph Banks took from Kamay are known to still exist today. For over 220 years they were in the collection of the Museum of Archaeology and Anthropology at the University of Cambridge – a symbol of everything taken from the Gweagal people. In 2023 an agreement was finally made to return them to Country.

The shield Cook and his crew took is known as the Gweagal shield. It is undecorated and made of red mangrove, with one pierced hole near the centre, and it has been the subject of significant conjecture. Firstly, was it really from Kamay? As it is made from red mangrove wood, which comes from trees further north, it has been questioned whether it was actually stolen by Cook later in the journey. Or could the shield have simply made its way south by a trade route? And the hole in the centre of the shield – was it a musket ball that caused it, or was it one of the holes made by First Peoples to look through?

The second issue is perhaps easier to address. A ballistic study concluded the hole was not made by a bullet or musket shot, and it is well known that shields did have holes cut into them for viewing through.[7] This is supported by the *Endeavour* journals. Cook wrote, 'a man who attempted to oppose our Landing came down to the Beach with a shield made of the bark of a tree; this he left behind when he ran away and we found upon taking it up that it plainly had been pierced through with a single pointed lance near the centre'.

Theresa Ardler says she is still waiting for the return of the Gweagal shield, which she says her ancestor Chief Cooman held to defend his people. It is still held by the British Museum.

One of the earliest known written Gweagal accounts of Cook's landing was recorded in 1863, in a letter sent from a Catholic priest and political activist, Father J. McEncroe, to a member of the New South Wales Legislative Council, Dr H.G. Douglas. In the letter, McEncroe recounted a conversation he'd had thirty years earlier with a local man whose father was witness to the *Endeavour*'s arrival. It is uncertain how accurately McEncroe recalled the conversation after three decades, but he wrote that the man had told that 'they thought at first that it was a big bird that came into the bay, and they saw something like opossums running up and down about the legs and wings of the bird; but on viewing them closer they thought them to be people something like themselves. They kept away, however, for a few days, wi[t]hout coming near the people who came from the ship to the land, although these people made several signs to the natives, who were lurking about the bushes, to come near them. At last it was agreed that two of the tribe would go down and meet the new comers; but they were directed by the women particularly, when going down to the water, not to eat or drink anything that the strangers may give them for fear of being poisoned.'[8]

The botanists on board the *Endeavour* – Joseph Banks and the more experienced Daniel Solander, and their assistants – found Kamay a treasure trove of new plants. They collected 132 species, of which only a few were known to European science, and of course Banks had one genus renamed after himself – the *Banksia* (guriidja to the Dharawal). They classified the specimens according to the European scientific framework, and described them by comparing them to European plants.

They had no idea of the people's knowledge, use and perspective of plants, as a part of the total cultural landscape. For the Dharawal people, different parts of nature related to others, so when different flowers were out they knew what dhanj (fish) were running. A special plant to the Dharawal people is the cabbage tree palm (dharawal), after which they are named. These are ceremonial trees, and in the Dreaming are connected with life and death ceremonies. The dead leaves can be woven into baskets, and fibres from the tree are used to make ropes and nets. The tree grows over 20 metres tall, and the tip is edible – though plucking it can kill the tree, so this was done sparingly.

As an important part of Dharawal lore was not to over-hunt any resource, so that there would always be more for future generations, they watched in shock as the British pulled up net after net of fish from Botany Bay, including taking a vast number of sacred stingrays. The stingrays were so prevalent that Cook first renamed the bay Stingray Bay, before crossing that out and writing Botanists Bay, later changing that to Botany Bay.

He conjectured that stingrays were not eaten by the people as they never saw the remains of one near their huts or fire places. In fact the people around modern-day Sydney had a taboo against eating both sharks and stingrays, which was later noted by Matthew Flinders.[9]

The Europeans had no such qualms. Cook wrote on 5 May 1770: 'In the evening the yawl return'd from fishing having caught two

Sting rays weighing near 600 pounds.' Dining on the catch, Banks proclaimed it excellent.

Cook also conjectured as to what the Gweagal people did eat, writing on the same day: 'shellfish is their Chief support, yet they catch other sorts of fish'. But what Cook failed to observe was that the people also hunted many land animals, which included gurawara (possums) and buru (kangaroo).

Over the eight days they were at Kamay the men of the *Endeavour* often saw large groups of local people ashore, but as they approached them they disappeared into the bush. The crew left beads and ribbons in their huts, but these were not valued and never taken by the people.

Much of the wildlife proved as elusive. The British got a quick glimpse of a kangaroo or wallaby, and the dung and footprints of animals they were unable to identify.

Despite several more attempts by the British to make contact with them, the Gweagal disappeared into the trees when approached.

One day, though, one of the midshipmen was walking in the bush by himself and came upon an old man and woman and some children sitting under a tree. They were surprised to see each other, and the crewman, trying to show he was friendly, offered them some parrots he had shot. The people refused the food, seemingly in fear of the sailor. He stayed with them a short time before seeing more of their people fishing nearby in canoes, and worrying they might come ashore to confront him, he left them. It was the closest thing to a conversation to date between our people and the newcomers – but it was held in silence.

Cook summarised the state of relations well when he wrote, 'all they seemed to want was for us to be gone'.

The southern point of Kamay has long been a significant ceremonial area, and people would travel hundreds of kilometres to gather the clay or white ochre that was found there. And because it was so abundant in food it could accommodate large numbers of people for such ceremonies.

It is still a place of ceremony, hosting community picnics, speeches, flag raising, ceremonial plantings, royal visits, re-enactments, and the laying of wreaths of mourning and remembering.

Each year, on or close to 26 April, descendants of the Dharawal and Eora, and others from across the land, gather there to remember that day in 1770 when the floating cloud came into the bay. It has become a day when both the black and white histories of the place are acknowledged. But it is near impossible to imagine how the land might have looked at that time, due to the large oil refineries and long pier that fill much of the bay's vista.

Theresa Ardler says, 'If my ancestors came back they wouldn't recognise it as their home.'

There are several more modern monuments, contrasting with the stone plinths and plaques, notably a huge mother whale and her calf looking out towards the mouth of the bay, and some metal canoes sitting on the rocks, depicting how the people's nuwis would have sat when Cook was there. Theresa Ardler, whose artwork the sculptures are based on, said that the whale is an important totem for her people.

The foreshore has been cleared and a long line of Norfolk Island pines planted. Theresa said, 'They actually planted them on my ancestor's skeletal remains, so we can never dig the trees up. They were all laid down with their feet facing out, so a splendid view while they were living and a splendid view in the afterlife and the Dreaming.

'And an archaeologist who has been working closely with me and the La Perouse community said that they can never be dug up because it'll rip the skeletal remains, because those trees, the roots go right down.'

For Shayne Williams, the impact of Cook is two-edged. He

said that Cook's landing is symbolic because it portended the end of his people's cultural dominion over the land, so any discussion of Cook sparks a sadness amongst his people. 'A sadness that laments Cook's voyage precipitating, some eighteen years later, the landing of the First Fleet. With the First Fleet came the legal fiction terra nullius, a fiction that was applied to justify colonial subjugation of us.'

Filling the holds of the ship with food and water and wood, the men of the *Endeavour* turned their minds to their onward journey north. But they left several things behind. Firstly, they left the body of one of their own. Forby Sutherland, a sailor, had died of consumption – or tuberculosis – and 'his body Was buried ashore at the watering place, which occasioned my calling the south point of this bay after his name'. Today there is a small memorial plinth to him on the shoreline of Kurnell, where Cook landed, and Sutherland Shire bears his name.

Also buried nearby, but not often remarked upon, is Cundlemong, who has been described as the 'last full-blood' chief of the tribe whose headquarters were at Kurnell. He died in 1846, seventy-six years after Sutherland.

Cook also left behind the first of many memorials, or committed an act of vandalism, depending on your perspective, stating, 'During our stay in this Harbour I caused the English Colours to be display'd ashore every day, and an inscription to be cut out upon one of the Trees near the Watering place, setting forth the Ship's Name, Date, etc.'

After seven days at Kamay, Cook decided he had seen all he needed to see, but was unable to leave the bay due to contrary winds. Finally, on 6 May, he was able to write: 'Having seen everything this place afforded, we, at daylight in the morning, weigh'd with a light breeze at North-West, and put to Sea.'

Watching the ship and the strange inhabitants finally sailing away, the people of Kamay may have been relieved but could not have imagined that their land would one day become a part of one of the largest cities of the world by area, displacing thousands of people and animals and irreversibly changing their land and waterways – putting enormous pressure on the people's relationship with the land.

Their understanding of the world, shaped by thousands of years of following the ways of their ancestors, was coming to an end. The *Endeavour* was gone – but more ships would be coming. In less than eighteen full seasons eleven British ships were in the bay, followed soon after by the French ships of La Perouse, who also anchored in Botany Bay. Both would sail away, but not before the French had built a stockade ashore and fired a few more musket shots at the Eora people, and the British ships did not go far, anchoring a few miles northwards, inside the next large harbour along the coast.

It was the start of the slow dispossession and degradation of the land at Kundul (Kurnell), ravaged by cattle, rabbits, industrialisation, and the Cookification of street names (Captain Cook Drive, Sir Joseph Banks Drive, Solander Street, Cook Street).

When the First Fleet arrived at Kamay, the Gweagal had clearly not forgotten Cook's time there, as according to Lieutenant Watkin Tench: 'We found the natives tolerably numerous as we advanced up the river, and even at the harbour's mouth we had reason to conclude the country more populous than Mr. Cook thought it. For on the Supply's arrival in the Bay on the 18th of the month, they were assembled on the beach of the south shore, to the number of not less than forty persons, shouting and making many uncouth signs and gestures.'[10]

Warrane (Sydney Harbour)
Dharug/Eora Country

Warami N'Allowah Mittigar.	Welcome. Come in, sit down friend.
Yangoo Borga-Mandoo-Ginee Yaddung Gee.	For coming here today we say thank you.

At Noon we were ... abreast of a Bay or Harbour wherein there appeared to be safe anchorage which I called Port Jackson. It lies 3 leagues to the northward of Botany Bay.

Cook's journal, 7 May 1770

If the wind had been a little bit more accommodating, and Cook had not just replenished his supplies of wood and water and fresh food at Kamay, he may have been more tempted to enter the harbour he renamed Port Jackson, and find, like Governor Phillip did eighteen years later, that it was 'with out exception the finest Harbour in the World'.[1]

He would have also found a flourishing culture of peoples living all around the harbourside, fishing and travelling in small but very stable canoes. He might even have observed women singing and nursing their infants while they fished. He might not have realised that the people were living in small family groups, but were united by a common language, with strong ties of kinship and a rich saltwater economy.[2]

Or he might have seen the people react as they had at Kamay, challenging him not to come ashore without invitation.

Of course Cook could not have known that there were about 1,500 people from twenty-nine different clan groups covering what became the modern Sydney metropolitan area. These people have come to be collectively referred to as the Eora (pronounced 'Yura') nation, although Eora was never the name they used to identify themselves. Rather it appears to be their word for 'people from here', or even just 'people', that they gave in response to colonisers when asked for their collective name.[3]

Understandably with such rapid colonisation and dispossession of the area, a lot of knowledge was lost, and today there is also some argument to support the word 'Dharug' for the people of the whole greater Sydney area. Though that is not agreed to by everyone either.

There is a bit more agreement about clans, though. Sydney's CBD stands on the land of the Gadigal clan, and their name comes from the gadi, or grass tree (*Xanthorrhoea*), also known as gulgady. The suffix '-gal' refers to the people, so they are the Gadi-gal – the

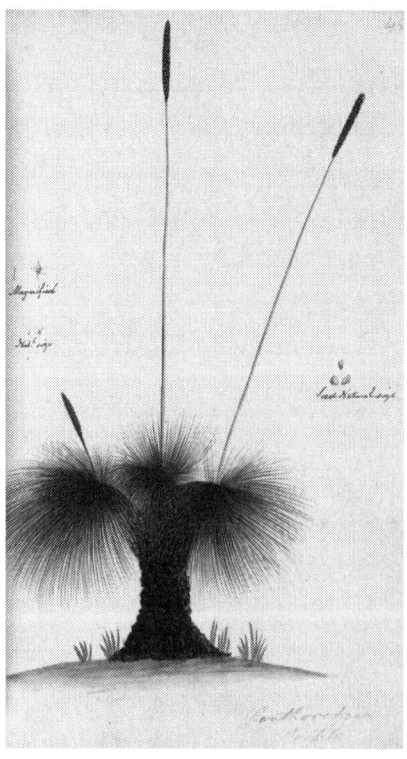

A gadi plant showing stems

people of the grass tree. Almost all the clans around the harbour have this suffix to their names, such as Wangal, Boromedegal, Gamaragal, Borogegal, Birrabirragal and Gayamaygal.[4]

The Gadigal had over twenty different uses for the plant they took their name from, varying from making spear shafts from the large stem to making glue from the resin and using the leaves for weaving.[5] The spears made from the gadi are not as heavy to hold or throw as those made from the wood from trees, and they are easily obtained and require little working to make a good spear – just hardening the tip in a fire and perhaps inserting oyster shell at the tip to make it sharp. Men had three different spears. One with three prongs for catching fish, one for hunting and one for battle.

And there's a high likelihood that the warriors of the clan had their spears in hand as they watched the *Endeavour* sail past the mouth of the harbour. They would have been aware that the strange beings or people had visited their neighbours to the south, with

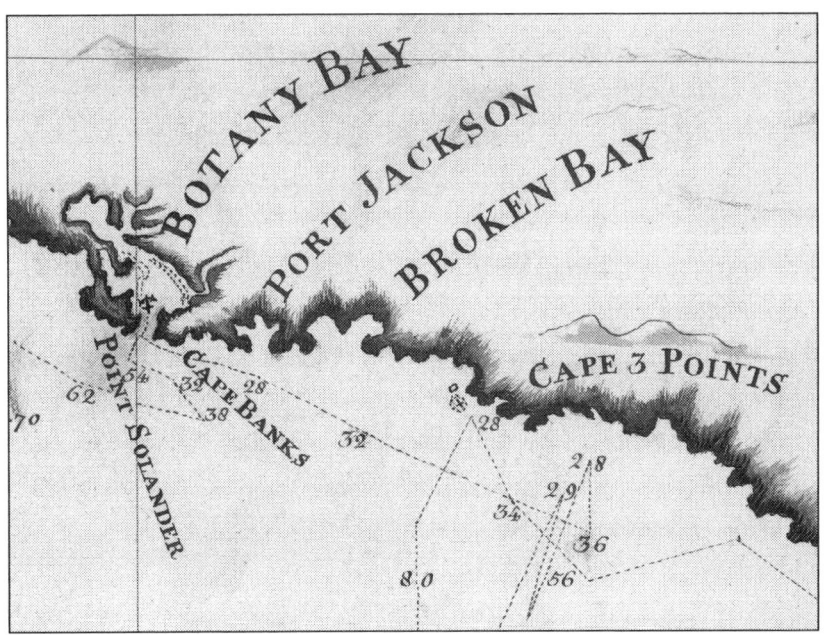

Cook's chart of the coast around Kamay (Botany Bay) and Warrane (Sydney Harbour)

stories travelling overland quickly. This may have been a significant event for them, wondering if the strangers were going to set foot on their land as well – but it was nowhere near as significant as the event eighteen years later, when Governor Phillip and the First Fleet sailed into their harbour.

Some of the people that Phillip met or wrote about – often forcibly abducting them to act as cultural interpreters – would have had a memory of Cook's ship passing by. Arabanoo, the first man abducted, would have been about eleven in 1770, as he was estimated to have been about twenty-nine when taken. Tragically he died of smallpox within a year.

Bennelong, the man Governor Phillip believed he had a close relationship with, and who travelled to England and back, would have been about six years old when Cook sailed past. Bennelong was a Wangal man, whose lands stretched along the southern shores of the Parramatta River. And the great resistance warrior Pemulwuy, a Bidjigal man, would have been in his thirties already.

Many other important people had not even been born when Cook sailed by, such as Bungaree, from the area Cook renamed Broken Bay, north of Sydney. Bungaree accompanied Matthew Flinders on his voyage around Australia between 1802 and 1803. He was not born until about 1775. Or Patyegarang, the young 'Port Jackson' woman who helped the ever-inquiring Lieutenant William Dawes learn some of her language. She was not born until about ten years after Cook sailed past. Patyegarang was the first teacher of an Australian language. Interestingly, Dawes's notebooks were lost in the archives for many years and only identified in 1972, and they reveal the complexity of some words, such as 'putuwa', which he stated meant 'to warm one's hand by the fire and then to gently squeeze the fingers of another person'. Or 'Tariadyaou', which means 'I made a mistake in speaking.'[6]

Tribal Warrior, the Redfern-based Indigenous community organisation, runs harbour cruise experiences on the oldest operating ferry in Sydney, now named the *Mari Nawi* (Big Canoe). Terry Olsen has been working with Tribal Warrior for many years, and says he has come out of retirement to help them out with a cruise today. He is not from the Sydney region, but has lived here for many years and learned the stories of the area.

The *Mari Nawi* leaves Circular Quay right beside the lines of people queuing up to ride jetboats. Each group of people looks at the other, believing they have gotten the better deal for the day.

With about thirty people on board, the *Mari Nawi* cruises out into Warrane – the waters of the harbour, and alongside the Opera House. Terry Olsen tells that the land it is on, Dubbagullee, was originally an island only accessible at low tide over a path of shells. He also tells that as a part of their initiation, young men learnt all the knowledge of how to hunt around the harbour, where they could go and not go, what to eat and not to eat, and they had to be able to explain that knowledge back to the Elders who taught them.

To the east side of the Opera House is the small bay where the First Fleet landed, on the foreshore of the Botanic Gardens, Wuganmagulya, or Farm Cove. Further to the east is Yurong, the site of what became known as Mrs Macquarie's Chair.

Terry Olsen says, 'Mrs Macquarie was so good for us. She noticed our people were getting sick and she tried to nurse our people back to health.' He also tells that it was the place that the European invaders first saw a traditional ceremony and dancing, when Mrs Macquarie, accompanied by Lieutenant Collins, was invited to watch one performance. Collins wrote: 'The place selected for this extraordinary exhibition was at the head of Farm Cove, where a space had been for some days prepared by clearing it of grass, stumps, &c.; it was of an oval figure, the dimensions of it 27 feet by 18, and was named Yoo-lahng. When we arrived at the spot, we found the party from the north shore armed, and standing

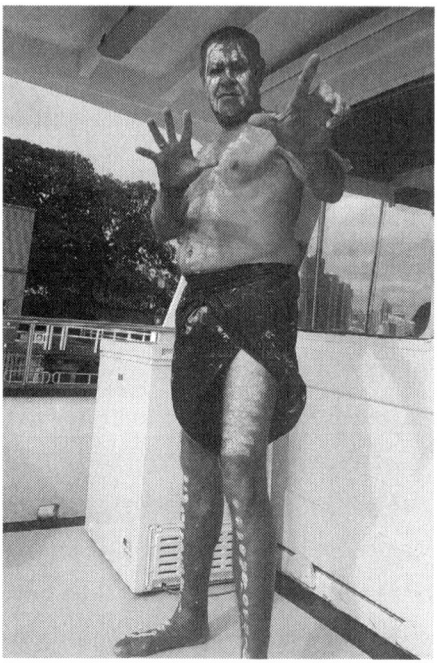

Terry Olsen on board the Mari Nawi

at one end of it; at the other we saw a party consisting of the boys who were to be given up for the purpose of losing each a tooth, and their several friends who accompanied them.'[7]

Terry Olsen indicates, as the *Mari Nawi* passes Mattewanye, or Fort Denison, 'All the islands in the harbour were places of ceremony, but Aboriginal people don't go *there* anymore, because convicts were tortured there and made it a bad place. There is bad energy and bad spirits coming up through your feet there.'

Cruising along the harbour's waters, it is hard not to agree with Governor Phillip that it is indeed 'with out exception the finest Harbour in the World', though it does take a leap of the imagination to visualise how it might have looked when Cook sailed past, without the tall apartments coming down to the shoreline. But there is just enough bushland where it is possible to shade your eyes and look only at dark green trees, speckled with yellow and white, framed underneath by the pale pastel orange and yellow of sandstone, which in turn sits atop the many greys of rock oysters that indicate the high tide mark.

The *Mari Nawi* ties up at Me-Mel Island – until recently known as Goat Island. The name Me-Mel is a reference to the eye of an eel, as the island is shaped like the head of an eel. The island was a shared space for the surrounding clans, and each were custodians of this sacred place that had many roles. It was a refuge, a place to practise culture and ceremony, a place of education, a place to rest and get your spirit back.

Terry Olsen and his partner David daub their bodies in white ochre and then put on a performance, with the gathered tourists looking on in rapt fascination, much as Mrs Macquarie and Lieutenant Collins would have done. David plays the didgeridoo, and they perform the welcome dance and then various animal dances.

The audience are told that 'didgeridoo' is not the instrument's actual name. It should be known as a yidaki, which is the name for it in the language of the Yolngu people of eastern Arnhem land in the Northern Territory, where it originated. The name didgeridoo was given to it by white settlers, trying to come up with a name that mimicked the sound it made. Or there are other stories that it may also have roots in the Irish words *dúdaire* (pronounced 'doodjerra'), meaning trumpeter, and *dubh* (pronounced 'doo' in the northwest of Ireland) and meaning black.[8] Many First Nations words in common use today have complex stories behind them.

The story that is associated with the island is that of the Eel Dreaming – Boora Birra. The story tells that once, there was no evil in the land, and the sea lay much further to the east than it is today, and a deep valley ran along the land that was home to the Parra Doowee – the Eel Dreaming spirit.

The valley was a special place for women to perform ceremony and teach the children important things that they needed to know when they came of age, like how to provide protection from evil spirits that could make you do evil things. The valley was flat and easy walking, with plenty of food. And as time passed the people there grew fat and lazy and forgetful. The men no longer honoured the spirits of the animals they hunted, even eating only parts they liked and leaving the rest to rot. And the women no longer paid their respects to the earth mother and did not give thanks for the food they obtained so easily, and they no longer taught the children the way of their people.

So the children grew to manhood and womanhood without learning the laws, and without knowing why they must obey those laws. The men and women formed into bands and roamed the flatlands, destroying gunyas (huts) of old people, stealing fishing spears and hunting spears and fighting each other.

One day a band of such people came upon an old warrior named Kamarai, who guarded the Great Eel. He welcomed the visitors, but the lawless ones surrounded him and laughed as he tried to avoid their jabbing spears. Bleeding from many wounds, Kamarai fell to the ground.

But deep in the river the Great Eel heard the commotion and the cries for help from his old friend Kamarai, and he swam to the surface to investigate. The lawless ones turned their spears on him in fear as he emerged from the water, moving his great body to protect his old friend. One of the spears managed to strike his tail.

But when the Great Eel saw that Kamarai was now dead, he cried out in grief and struck the ground with his great tail, causing the earth to shake violently. A chasm opened up and swallowed the lawless ones as they tried to flee.

Like most Dreaming stories, this one has an important moral lesson. The Great Eel said, 'Let this be a warning that the laws of this land must be obeyed, and the ceremonies must be honoured.'

The Great Eel watched the waters fill the valley and said that it would now be a place where the sea creatures could teach their children the law of the sea. 'This place will remain safe to hunt and fish and live, but you must teach the laws,' the Great Eel said, and slipped back beneath the waters.

Telling us a more contemporary story, but still with a moral, Terry Olsen says there was a whale that came into the harbour a few years ago that no one could get rid of. He said the authorities finally called a traditional man, and he came and put his hand in the water and he sang and the whale left.

'They asked him how he did it, and he said, "It's called connection."'

According to David Watts, at the Aboriginal Heritage Office in North Sydney, knowing the exact locations of different clans has become difficult, but the Australian Museum has put together a list based on what is known, acknowledging that there are multiple spellings for names that originally only existed orally. As mentioned previously, each clan name ends in 'gal', the word for people, and the first part of the name describes a place. So it is correct to call the land around the Sydney CBD Gadigal land – as in the Midnight Oil song – but it is not technically correct to call other areas, such as Sydney Olympic Park or the north shore, Gadigal land.

Here is a list of a few of the known peoples, according to the Australian Museum – though again, it is not agreed upon by everyone:

CLAN NAME	NAME OR DESCRIPTION OF COUNTRY
Borogegal	Borogegy, now known as Bradleys Head
Darramurragal	Associated with the suburb Turramurra, at the headwaters of the Lane Cove River
Gamaragal	Located on the north side of Port Jackson
Gameygal	Around Kamay (Botany Bay), possibly to the northwest of Gwea (home of the Gweagal)
Gayamaygal	Manly Cove

Gweagal	The southern shore of Kamay (Botany Bay)
Wallumedegal	On the north shore, opposite Warrane (Sydney Cove)
Wangal	Extending along the south side of the harbour from Tumbalong (Darling Harbour) to Parramatta

In addition to the many First Nations place names that can still be found around Sydney, such as Toongabbie, Parramatta, Wooloomoolo, Maroubra, Kirribilli, there are thousands of sites that contain rock art or other cultural artifacts, linking the present to the past.

The rock art on the north shore within national parks can be easy to find. The people who lived here created hundreds of galleries, engraved in the sandstone, containing totemic figures of sky heroes, men and women, clubs, shields, whales, sharks, fish, kangaroos, and other animals. According to the State Library of New South Wales's Eora Stories, these carvings were an eloquent witness to culture, art and spiritual beliefs, marking a time before the arrival of the Bèerewalgal – the 'people from the clouds'.[9]

At the Bulgandry Site near Gosford, on Darkinjung lands, a short walk down a bush track leads you to a wide expanse of rock with a boardwalk built around to protect it. There are several clear figures carved into the rock, including one known as Bulgandry – a large man thought to be an ancestral hero. He has an elaborate headdress, and one hand holds a small boomerang and the other has a circular object. A long, decorated club is horizontal across his waist.

Nearby engravings are of wallabies, fish and an eel. One figure, about 3 metres long, is a dolphin or a very large fish. Another shows a woman chasing a large kangaroo. Another is a fish with a spear sticking out of it. These engravings or carvings, technically called petroglyphs, are actually made by pecking holes along an outline, and over time weathering has made a single line. Getting the right time of day to best view the past can be tricky, as you need early morning or late afternoon sun that casts a shadow along the grooves of the carvings – but not too early or late when the shadows of the bush block a clear view.

Unfortunately there are too often reports in the news of vandals desecrating the carvings, by scratching them or even riding a motorbike over the figures. Heartbreaking to know that something so old, that should be considered a treasure, can be treated so poorly.

Contact

An often overlooked part of Australia's early settlement that needs to be much better known is the smallpox epidemic of 1789, which killed, among hundreds of others, the aforementioned Arabanoo, the first Eora man to be kidnapped by the British. Lieutenant Watkin Tench, quite a humanitarian, wrote pitifully of one boy: 'eruptions covered the poor boy from head to foot'. And he wrote of an old man: 'He bore the pangs of dissolution with patient composure; and though he was sensible to the last moment, expired almost without a groan.'

The epidemic began amongst the clans of the people of the harbour, but soon spread further outwards as the people fled the disease they called galgalla – or devil-devil.[10] When the more than 1,000 convicts and marines came ashore onto Gadigal land in 1788, Governor Phillip estimated the number of people already living around the harbour at about 1,500. Over half of those would be dead, or have fled, from the smallpox epidemic within eighteen months.

David Collins, the Colony's judge-advocate, wrote in April 1789: 'At that time a native was living with us; and on taking him down to the harbour to look for his former companions ... he looked anxiously around him in the different coves we visited; not a vestige on the sand was to be found ... It seemed as if, flying from the contagion, they had left the dead to bury the dead. He lifted up his hands and eyes in silent agony for some time; at last he exclaimed, "All dead! all dead!" and then hung his head in mournful silence.'

There have been many theories as to the cause of the smallpox outbreak: the French who landed at Botany Bay as the English fleet was moving to Sydney Harbour, or the Makassar fishermen from Indonesia, or even suggestions that it was actually chickenpox. But another thing we know from the journal of Lieutenant Watkin Tench is that the colony's surgeon, John White, had vials of 'variolous matter' – which would have been scabs or the pus from smallpox that was used for vaccinating people against it.

Watkin Tench, however, posed several questions as to the origin of the smallpox epidemic in a journal footnote, which included: 'Was it introduced by Mr. Cook? Did we give it birth here? No person among us had been afflicted with the disorder since we had quitted the Cape of Good Hope, seventeen months before. It is true, that our surgeons had brought out variolous matter in bottles; but to infer that it was produced from this cause were a supposition so wild as to be unworthy of consideration.'[11]

A lot of our mob think it well worth considering. According to Professor John Maynard, a Worimi man working with the University of Newcastle, 'It was unquestionably germ warfare.' He suggests it was a deliberate act, and identifies the most likely culprit as Major Robert Ross, who was in charge of the 160 marines of the First Fleet. John Maynard says that Major Ross had no time for the consolatory approaches of Governor Phillip, nor for humanitarian men like Watkin Tench.

According to researcher Chris Warren, we need to consider that much of the marines' ammunition had been accidentally left behind in England, and they also lacked the proper tools for mending damaged muskets.[12] Did the use of smallpox as a tactical weapon become something Major Ross considered when the numbers of marines and serviceable muskets started to drop, and resistance from the local people increased?

John Maynard said it is also known that Major Ross had served in North America, where smallpox had been released against the Pontiac people following a rebellion in 1763. It is documented that infected blankets and handkerchiefs had been given to the Pontiac people.

There is also the fact that the smallpox epidemic began on the northern shore of the harbour – not on the site of the colony – which suggests an intentional release. 'It was an instrument of destruction for us,' John Maynard said. 'The death rate in Australia was between 60 to 90 per cent [of those infected] and it led to enormous loss of cultural knowledge, of dances, of songs.'

The disease travelled along the trade routes, killing people. John said, 'An old fella said the sickness came through the grass and through the water. People from Sydney fled down the coast and to the north. It was a tsunami of sickness. It would have changed the dynamics so quickly.'

When explorers travelled further into the country they found that smallpox had long preceded them. 'Skeletons and graves were found along the Murray River,' John said, and stories from First Nations people in the South Australian Riverland describe a disease with smallpox-like symptoms that ravaged communities ahead of settlers arriving, an indication of how quickly the disease spread.[13] David Watts, of the Aboriginal Heritage Office in North Sydney, said the impact of smallpox, as well as other diseases and killings, was such that 'as far as we know there are no descendants of people from around northern Sydney'.

As with many aspects of First Nations history, not everyone agrees with this, and when so much cultural knowledge has been lost it is hard to weave back together the strands of the past. 'There is so much we really don't know,' David said.

But what is known is that for the clans around Warrane – that 'finest harbour in the world' – the impacts of settlement were the earliest and the most severe. Yet as many First Nations people stress, both those born in Sydney and those who have come to call Sydney home, they have survived and continue to practise their culture there today.

Whibayganba (Nobbys Head)

Awabakal & Worimi Countries

Nyura wubaliyn?	Welcome. What are you doing?
Nyura yiigu marala barraygu.	You have come here.
(Yii barraba barray.)	(This is my Country.)
Yii Gathangguba barray.	This is Gathang Country.
Gathay nyiirun.	Let us go together.

> *... a little way inland, is a remarkable hill, that is shaped like the Crown of a Hatt, which we past about 9 o'Clock in the forenoon.*
>
> Cook's journal, 11 May 1770

We now need to travel down some intricate pathways around naming and language.

Sailing northwards, the *Endeavour* passed the wide mouth of Broken Bay where the Hawkesbury River reaches the sea. Cook wrote in his journal on 8 May: 'at sunset the Northermost land in sight bore North 26 degrees East; and some broken land that appear'd to form a bay bore North 40 degrees West, distant 4 Leagues. This Bay I named Broken bay.'

The northern shore was Darkinjung Country, which took a full day to reach, as counter winds kept the ship very much where it was. Seeing three 'bluff points' to the north, Cook renamed it Cape Three Points. There is a Captain Cook lookout there now, with that name etched into the concrete base, and many people mistakenly believe it is a marker indicating that Cook landed there. Elder Uncle Gavi Duncan jokes that it has that name because when the Darkinjung people saw the ship coming they said, 'Look out, here comes Captain Cook!'

The ship's progress up the coast was fairly slow and Cook did not see the entrance to the Hunter River until three days later, when he noted a 'small round rock or island, laying close under the land'. This was later renamed Nobbys Head – but not by Cook, as it was one of the few times he seemed stuck for a suitably esteemed or random Englishman to name a landmark after. He also failed to name the 'remarkable hill, that is shaped like the Crown of a Hatt'. To the Awabakal people who inhabited the southern side of the Hunter River, the rocky island was known as Whibayganba. And the hill shaped like the crown of a 'hatt' (Mount Sugarloaf) was known to the Awabakal as Warrawelong and also Keemba Keemba.

There were two peoples around the Hunter River: the Awabakal,

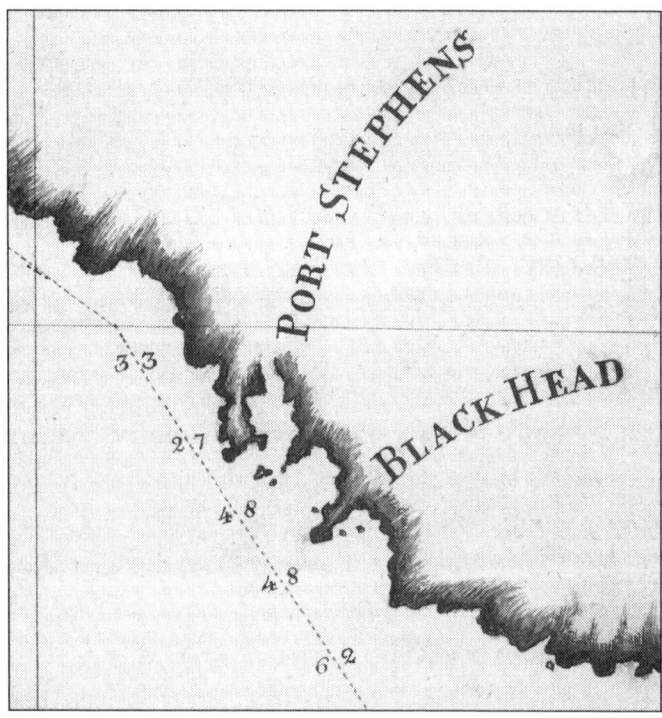

Cook's chart of Awabakal and Worimi Countries

south of the Hunter River; and the Worimi, to the north. However, the people around Newcastle who identify as the Awabakal people today generally know that their ancestors never actually used the name Awabakal. The name was conferred on them by a European anthropologist, John Fraser.

So here's another thing about names that we need to consider: while many First Nations people, including the Awabakal, are finding that they are able to reclaim their language and their traditional names for things, largely as a result of work done by anthropologists, anthropologists also got an awful lot of things wrong. And when it comes to getting things wrong, John Fraser is a good case study.

Fraser was a Scottish-born amateur ethnologist who migrated to New South Wales as a young man, settling in Maitland in 1861 where he became a schoolteacher. He took an early interest in First Nations languages, but his enthusiasm perhaps outweighed his diligence. He even took the work of another pioneering anthropologist in the Newcastle region and condensed and edited it, re-releasing it with the rather lengthy title: *An Australian language as spoken by the Awabakal, the people of Awaba or Lake Macquarie (near Newcastle, New South Wales) being an account of their language, traditions and customs, by L.E. Threlkeld; re-arranged, condensed and edited with an appendix by John Fraser.*

We will get to the Reverend L.E. Threlkeld in a moment, but Norman Tindale, another early anthropologist – of greater standing – described Fraser's work as: 'most unsatisfactory and unquestionably the most inaccurate and garbled account ever published about the aborigines'.[1] He also wrote, 'Examination of his map shows that his "tribes" bore little relationship to those now recognized', and that the names of several tribes were 'coined by himself to supply what he considered to be a lack'.[2]

The name Awabakal comes from an amalgam of words coined by Fraser: 'Awaba' is a plain or flat surface and was used to describe

Lake Macquarie. 'Ba' denotes 'place of', and the suffix 'kal' denotes the masculine, or man. Awabakaleen would have been the feminine form.[3]

Another of his 'garbled accounts' was in stating that there was a greater tribe named the 'Kuriggai' that stretched from Newcastle all the way south to the northern shores of Sydney. Hence the name Mount Kuring-gai for the northern Sydney suburb. But this name has been challenged by some First Nations people for being inaccurate, particularly the Guringay people whose lands lie between the Hunter and Manning rivers – hundreds of kilometres from the north shore of Sydney. Recent research suggests the name was a localised language around the Broken Bay district, and was the Karikal or Garigal.[4]

It has become hard to say what is definitely right and definitely wrong, as so many people were dispossessed of their land and had to use scant oral records and anthropologists' writing to rediscover their cultural history. But what do you do when the oral histories and anthropological reports clash, both with each other and with other oral histories and anthropological reports? Yuin man Richard Campbell captured the prevailing attitude of mob by saying, 'Anthropologists didn't always get it right.'

One anthropologist whose story is worth telling, though, was a missionary with the unlikely name of the Reverend Lancelot Threlkeld. He lived with the Awabakal people for many years, learning their language, stories and ways. And it is through his writings that much of their language is being reclaimed. For instance, he collected the Creation story of Whibayganba, which tells: 'At the entrance of Newcastle there is a small high island, called by the English Nobby's Island. The blacks have a tradition that it is the abode of an immensely large Kangaroo which resides within the centre of the high rock, that occasionally he shakes himself which causes the Island to tremble and large pieces to fall down, as any one can perceive has been, and still continues to be the case, on the eastern side of the Island.'[5]

However, there were important parts of the story that he was unable to obtain, which were later recounted by Percy Haslam: 'So there was this giant kangaroo, selfish and lustful, who, putting desire before code of behaviour, attacked a female wallaby. Such an act conflicted with the laws governing kinship pattern of survival based on the purity of blood lines. It destroyed the totemic structure, so strongly emphasised in the Bora teaching.

'After the deed became known, flocks of wallabies gave chase to the perpetrator, who fled over the hills and through the bush, heading for Newcastle. Though he kept ahead by superior leaping he knew that capture and death were inevitable because the sea offered no escape. But as he neared the sea a mist intervened and he was lost to the sight of his pursuers. He took advantage of this respite by swimming to Nobbys Island, which he entered and shut himself away from sight.

'The wallabies gave up the chase believing the sea had claimed the kangaroo. But, according to tradition, the kangaroo was never certain of his safety. Now and then he would jump up and down [in] his island and cause the cliff to tremble and break away as a warning to any wallabies and other animals not to come too close to his island refuge.'[6]

If you stand at Whibayganba/Nobbys Head on a sunny winter's day, the waves of the ocean batter the breakwaters as if they are attempting to get into the river mouth. And it is striking how Cook, Banks and Parkinson never commented on the light along the east coast here – that eucalyptus-tinged softness of the land, the contrasts of the deep blue of the ocean and the stark white of breaking waves.

North of the Hunter River and the land that Cook renamed Point Stephens and Port Stephens, after a random Secretary of the Admiralty, is the land of the Worimi people. They are a part of the three Gathang-speaking nations, which also include the Birpai and Guringay peoples.

Whibayganba/Nobbys Head

According to Worimi man Joe Perry, there were at least four Worimi clan groups, the Garuagal, Maiangal, Gamipingal and Buraigal, and each occupied specific tracts of land.[7]

Joe also said that the lifestyle of the Worimi was like most other First Peoples', in that they lived a semi-nomadic life, moving around their Country but not travelling great distances day to day. 'They never travelled out of their Nurra (territories) unless invited and required to attend specific ceremonies,' he said.

And the Worimi had no need to travel very far, as their land provided them with all the food and materials that they might need, and the environment was rich in resources, particularly seafood. Like all First Nations people, they knew 'every spiritual and physical aspect of their Country that was necessary for their survival and to fulfill their Dreaming obligations', Joe said.

The Worimi lived on a very varied diet consisting of makurr (fish) – including biiwa (mullet), darawang (flathead), ninang (oysters), dijaraa (crabs) and wira (lobsters) – as well as the meat of wambuyn (kangaroo), barrin (wallaby), bilu (possum), wurran (goanna), and plants such as faramalay (the apple berry), bangwaal (swamp fern) and bumiray (grass tree).[8]

Similar to other peoples along the coast, the Worimi women were required through Dreaming lore to undertake a ceremony that eternally connected them to the sea and the fish they desired. This involved tying a string around the first joint of the little finger so tightly that it died and fell off. According to Joe Perry, 'Depending on the clan the small piece of amputated finger was taken out into the ocean, harbour or river and thrown in. The belief was that fish would eat that small finger and forever be attracted to the hand from whence it came. This ensured that all Worimi women, after depositing their sacrificial personal lure in the waters, would always be successful fishing in the future and provide food for their families.'

There were close relationships between the Worimi and other Gathang-speaking peoples, with intermarriages used to cement alliances. The Worimi and Awabakal also had close relationships in trade and marriage and shared the same sex totems – with men being the bat totem and women the treecreeper bird totem.

Both Awabakal and Worimi were also believers in the sky spirit Baiame, as the creator who came from the heavens to create the world. He had two wives, named Biragnulu and Gunambali, and also a son called Daramalan. Mount Yengo, about 100 kilometres due west of Whibayganba/Nobbys Head, is a site of great spiritual significance to the tribes of the area associated with Baiame. It is the place where he descended to earth to create the world and everything within it, and also the place he ascended back to the heavens and flattened the top of the mountain in the process.[9]

But how do we adequately name and describe such spirits in English, without their full context? Many First Nations conceptual ideas are hard to pin down to a few written paragraphs, and even translating words risks losing some of the nuance of meaning.

Joe Perry has said that as traditional culture was learned orally, without the right words it is hard to convey communal religious concepts and belief systems that have existed for tens of thousands of years. 'When languages are no longer spoken and become extinct, we lose another world view that is unique to a living breathing culture,' he said.

He also said that the First Nations sense of belonging is at times indescribable. 'It's not something within your sight, or a thing that can be clenched in your hands or heard, but rather something that you feel and sense. The uniqueness of most Indigenous peoples is maintained through their religious beliefs and being able to interpret and comprehend the intangible world.'

How do you adequately put that into words in a book?

Worimi man Professor John Maynard has spent about thirty years working to restore First Nations stories into Australian history, to inspire young and old with the understanding that they have heroes and heroines embedded in their past. And ironically, his office at the University of Newcastle sits beside a park with an ornate Captain Cook fountain in it.

He said, 'Cook was a great discoverer – I'm not taking that away.' But, he said, 'we do know that when he sailed up the coast he didn't open up discussion with the people he encountered, and did not seek their consent to claim lands, as per his instructions from the Admiralty. Clearly it was an illegal act. Our sovereignty has never been ceded.'

But he does admit that large parts of his mob's history have been taken from them and lost. He describes First Nations history as a giant jigsaw puzzle, with the majority of pieces missing. 'And I have been driven to find and put those missing pieces back into the puzzle. I came through a school system of the 1950s and 1960s when we were conveniently missing, overlooked, forgotten, or dare I say erased from this nation's history except as a people that were described as belonging to the Stone Age and were a "dying race". But in my own family there were incredible histories of political struggle and triumph.

'Despite the school texts and history books of the 1950s and 1960s telling me nothing of Aboriginal history and culture, I drew upon my own family for memory, records and inspiration.

'What White Australia needs is to embrace Aboriginal history and welcome us back onto the page,' he said.

If Cook had been able to see the people of this area he would have undoubtedly agreed with early settler accounts that described them as very tall and healthy. According to one English observer in 1827, the natives of the Coal River (yet another early name for Newcastle) were 'taller than the Europeans. You seldom see a black under five feet eight or nine inches. I have seen them about six feet four in height.'[10]

The Awabakal and Worimi had an abundance of food from both the sea and the land, but as Cook sailed along the coast he and the naturalists onboard saw a continuation of land with not very much promise. No signs of towns or villages. No indication of precious metals or spices. But there were so many riches they didn't see. The great saltwater lakes of the central coast, like Lake Macquarie, just south of Mulubinbah, are such a deep blue that they exude a feeling of peace and tranquillity. They are protected from the elements and there is easy fishing in all but the worst weather, and abundant bird life for hunting. They are a part of the Dreaming track of the rainbow serpent (Yuulangaa to the Worimi people).

According to John Maynard, 'The greatest treasure we have is 65,000 years of Aboriginal connection to the Country.'

Some of the lifestyle enjoyed by the Awabakal people was captured by convict artist and forger, Joseph Lycett. He was sent to the penal colony of Coal River in 1815, for re-offending as a forger, and took the opportunity to study the local people closely, drawing and painting many scenes of daily life. John Maynard has written that Lycett was able to accurately capture a range of activities, such as ceremonies, burials, punishment, corroborees, hunting and fishing, 'as well as the idyllic nature of their existence'.[11]

And while Lycett's artwork has proven very valuable in recording how the people lived at the time of settlement – reflecting in great detail their pre-settlement ceremonies, night fishing, sporting and body decorating, among other things – he did take some licence in clothing people in loincloths or dresses, in order not to offend British sensibilities.

John Maynard said that there is a unique thing about the people of Mulubinbah, and that was their use of coal. They cooked with it and they feared it and even had Dreaming stories of coal. The main story tells that there was a great hole that fire erupted out of, and it covered the land in a great darkness. Everyone was very afraid. The Elders advised the people that they had to cover up the darkness that was spreading from the hole. So they buried it under the land.

'And the darkness of course is the coal,' John Maynard said.

He has also said that the Newcastle area was a manufacturing base long before the coming of Europeans, with the people making axes, saws, chisels, knives and hammers that were traded with other tribes who lacked suitable stone for making such tools and weapons.

Contact

One of the first known encounters between the Worimi and Europeans was in 1790, when a group of escaped Second Fleet convicts were taken in by the people. They spent almost five years there, until they were recaptured in 1795 when a ship took shelter at Port Stephens and found the escapees. It is reported that the men were soon given their freedom, as their knowledge had become a valuable resource to the colonial administrators.

There were other escapees who ended up living with the people in the area, and in 1796 some convict fishermen were shipwrecked around Port Stephens and the people escorted them most of the way back to the Hawkesbury River. Along the way the convicts observed seams of coal, and when they reported this the potential of the area was made known to the administrators.

First a penal settlement was established, which did not majorly encroach on the people's land, and they often sided with the officials in preventing convicts crossing their land to escape. They had no love of the convicts, who too often abused their women. In 1816 Commandant Wallis reported: 'Two runaways during Capn. Thompson's command namely Jack Sullivan and Thos. Kienan returned on the 23rd both badly speared the former not expected to live. Three men who deserted from here on the 20th have just returned all spear'd namely John Leas and Isaac Walker. Thos. McCarthy who ran also at the same time they report to have been killed by the natives. I consider all this fortunate for the Settlement.'[12]

Of note, and a strong exception, one convict, John Kirby, was hanged in 1820 for murdering a local leader, Burrigan. Although he was not the only white man charged with such a murder, he was the only man convicted in the first fifty years of settlement.[13]

Setting the pattern that was to occur all along the coast, the penal settlement was followed by free settlers being given tracts of the people's land as grants. According to Greg Blyton from the University of Newcastle, things began with the penal settlement at the mouth of the Hunter River in 1804, and colonisation crept its way up the waterway to around Maitland. The whole Hunter Valley was opened up for civilian occupation in the 1820s, when the penal colony was transferred further north to Port Macquarie.[14]

Competition for land and resources followed, with the Awabakal and Worimi having to actively defend their lands from the invaders. Settlers had Governor Darling send in military assistance, so determined was the Awabakal and Worimi people's resistance to the taking of their lands and the abuse of their women. The people's numbers dwindled as the violence and disease continued, or they moved away. At the time of white settlement there was thought to have been a population of about 400–600 Worimi living around the estuary of Port Stephens – though it may have been much higher. By 1873, however, it was stated that only fifty remained, and by 1900 there were very few tribal Worimi left.[15]

And that brings us back to the Reverend Lancelot Threlkeld. He arrived in the area in May 1825 and established a mission on the shores of Lake Macquarie for the London Missionary Society. Over the next twenty-five years he worked tirelessly recording the Awabakal language and translating the New Testament, finally abandoning it when he felt there were no longer enough speakers to make the effort worthwhile.

Yet his work has not been wasted, for while missions were generally a part of a system that suppressed traditional beliefs, languages and lore, Threlkeld's extensive work is today being used to reclaim culture. Though it needs to be said that much of the work was done by his Awabakal teacher, Biraban (called John McGill by Threlkeld). Biraban spoke English fluently, having worked for an officer in Sydney, and his name translates as 'eaglehawk' – a revered totem of his people. He was said to be a gifted guide, tracker, dancer and singer, and over time the two men developed a deep mutual respect and affection for each other. Biraban taught Threlkeld not just the language, but lore and Dreaming, and allowed him to witness some of the people's rituals.

Of note, Threlkeld wrote that the people we now call the Awabakal more often spoke of themselves as 'people belonging to Mu-lu-bin-ba' – their name for the area of Newcastle, which means the place of a particular fern (mulubin) that grows in the area.[16]

Daryn McKenny, the founder and manager of the Miromaa Aboriginal Language and Technology Centre, situated near Lake Macquarie, said that after white settlers insisted people give a name for themselves, many peoples across the country gave names that translated as 'no, no' or 'no name this place have', as wider tribal names often did not exist.

He also said that Awabakal was possibly the first language to have stopped being spoken in Australia, and while it is now being recreated from Threlkeld's meticulous work, Daryn did add that he thought Threlkeld was 'an arrogant prick'. Yet perhaps it has been the arrogant pricks of the past, who most refused to follow the dominant ways of thinking and behaving, whose actions have proved instrumental in preserving parts of the past.

Daryn McKenny also said we need to rethink the way that languages are being re-introduced, and that we need to achieve much more than just the positive emotional impact of being able to speak a few words. He is critical of linguistic approaches to saving or revitalising languages and says, 'We've not had one language that has been saved. All we've got are books on our shelves. Our language efforts, while great and vast, haven't given us the foundation we need. Saved is when it has a strong, safe and secure future.'

He believes that the pathways for learning local languages need to lead into careers, moving from environmental education to employment. 'Can they take their learning of language into a career pathway other than being a singer or an artist? Language has to take us somewhere, otherwise it is just for singing "Heads, Shoulders, Knees and Toes" – and we've wasted our time.'

Daryn said that language doesn't necessarily come from people, rather it comes from the Country and needs to be taken back out to Country, as landscape defines language. 'We need to let Country be our teacher.'

Both the Country and the history of our Country are defined by words, but we need to better understand the connection between words and the land, and words and the past. According to Ray Kelly, a First Nations cultural and language expert at the University of Newcastle, 'If we're truly going to understand the historical landscape, you can't do it unless you truly understand language, and that requires a deep knowledge.'

But as Daryn McKenny has said, all too often all that is available 'are these word lists that whitefellas have left us, and the knowledge has been filtered out'.

That is the bigger challenge for language revitalisation – linking language to cultural knowledge, which needs to be a part of language learning in First Nations communities. And for whitefellas, it should be about not just learning the words for a greeting in a local language and feeling good about it, but understanding something of the context of the greeting, and the deep meaning of the words used.

Dooragan, Booragan & Mooragan (The Three Brothers)

Birpai, Gumbaynggirr & Dunghutti Countries

Guudji Yiigu.	Greetings.
Nyaaga barragay Yii barray marrunggang balgarrabirang gurrwagu Yii Birrbay Barray.	See with me this Country is beautiful from the mountains to the sea, this Birrbay Country.
Nyiirun ngarragal bimaygabirang bangaygabirang marrung-ngarrayn.	We pay respect to the Elders, past and present.
Nyiirun yanyiyn dangaygalgubaga yabangga, wuunagi yabang nyiirunbagu burraydjarrgu.	We walk in the footsteps of the ancestors and leave footsteps for our children to walk in.
Nyiirun maray ngarragi ngarragi ngarragi Barrayga.	Let us all come learn, know and remember on the land.
Nyiirun marrung-ngarraliy gathagi wakulda.	Let us all respect each other and go as one.
Buwadi.	Let this be.

As the hills bore some resemblance to each other we call'd them the Three Brothers ...

Cook's journal, 12 May 1770

When Lieutenant Cook saw three inland mountains stretching across 35 kilometres from modern-day Taree to Port Macquarie and decided to name them the Three Brothers, he had no way of knowing that this was the same name given to them by the Birpai people. To them they are Dooragan, Mooragan and Booragan. The Birpai actually have a story saying that the land might have whispered to Cook, telling him the names.

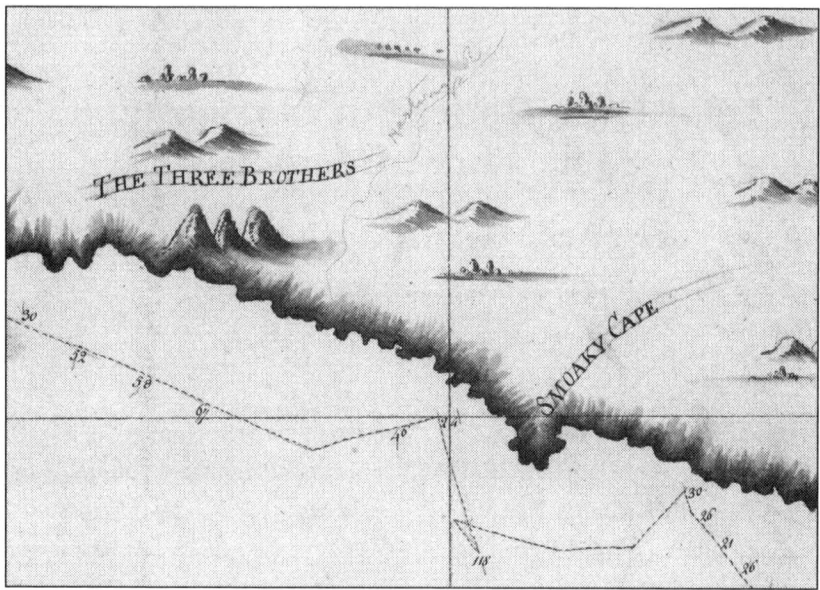

Cook's chart of the Birpai, Gumbaynggirr and Dunghutti Countries

There are many variations on the Three Brothers story, told by different clans. One version is told by Nardja Carter, a Birpai woman who works as a cultural guide with the New South Wales Parks and Wildlife Service. The story was passed on to her by her Elders. She tells that when the land was flat there was a large lake whose spirit was the mother of three brothers. Dooragan, the eldest, Mooragan the middle son, and Booragan was the youngest son, who had more favour in his mother's eyes than his siblings. As part of their initiation the brothers had been fostered out to the other clans among the Birpai nation. Dooragan was fostered out to the stingray people in the north, at Point Plomer. Mooragan to the crab people, also in the north, at Lake Cathie. And Booragan to the shark people of the south, at Harrington.

On their way north, Dooragan tried to persuade Mooragan to help him kill their youngest brother so that he might find more favour in his mother's eyes. Mooragan refused but this didn't stop Dooragan fleeing to the south to kill Booragan.

The willy-wagtail saw what had happened, and upon telling the brothers' mother she got very angry and killed the two brothers for murdering Booragan.

When the Great Spirit Eagle heard what had happened he also became very angry. As punishment for the mother, he turned the three brothers into mountains: Booragan into the mountain to the south, Mooragan into the middle mountain, and Dooragan into the north mountain, dividing his mother's lake domain into two, which are now known as Watson Taylor Lake and Queens Lake. Also as punishment for the mother's actions, he turned her into the Comboyne mountain so that she would forever look over her sons, the three brothers, and know her wrongdoings.

So the learning from the story – and all Dreaming stories have a learning – is that favouritism leads to jealousy, which can have terrible consequences. And one other consequence of the mother's actions is that women are not allowed to go up onto Dooragan (North Brother Mountain – also known as Big Brother Mountain, though it is the smallest of the three mountains).

Regardless of differences in the stories, the Three Brothers Mountains are a spiritual place for the Birpai people, who feel a connection to their Country and their ancestors when they go there.

Nardja Carter said that there are reasons that stories are different: it's not uncommon to be told different stories about a landscape by different clans and peoples, because rivers and mountains can be shared by different peoples. As she is from the northern Birpai clan, her focus is on North Brother, while around Taree their hero is South Brother. She also said that whitefellas need to know that the stories they get told might not be the same story that is shared by Elders. In the same way, she says, that the story she might tell a five-year-old would be different from the story she might tell a 55-year-old. 'It's not the story that's important, it's the lesson that's important,' she said.

Nardja Carter

She also said it is quite spooky when you go out onto the headlands and look back at what Cook might have seen – those Three Brothers. 'And to think that he saw them the same way makes your hair stand on end.'

Nardja said it was not widely known that behind the Three Brothers are three mountains associated with women, known as the Three Nellies. 'Nelly refers to a woman's breast,' she said. 'But also a woman at the time was known as a nelly.'

The drive up to the top of Dooragan, North Brother, is an easy one, but the drive that is really worth the effort is Mooragan – Middle Brother Mountain. If the track is dry. The bumpy, rocky track takes you high up the mountain, over 500 metres above sea level, where the tallest surviving blackbutt trees in New South Wales can be found. They stretch almost 80 metres into the air, with a trunk circumference of 15 metres. These massive trees were saplings when James Cook sailed past and renamed the mountain.

For the Birpai, all the land was created during that time when the ancestral beings wandered the world, and all the rivers, mountains, plants and animals have a Creation story about them.

Major totems of the Birpai include the shark, stingray and crab, and when John Oxley explored the region in 1818 he noted that the people ate abundant sea food but refused to eat any shark that had been caught.

Nardja Carter said that one animal that was taboo to all Birpai was the koala, and if you ate it, it would bring on a drought. She also said stingray was most closely associated with the northernmost Birpai clan, around Point Plomer, while the crab was one of the major saltwater totems of the Birpai clans of the Bonny Hills, south of Port Macquarie. Those people could eat lobsters but not crabs.

Other totems include the porpoise, which was associated mostly with the Birpai clans around present-day Port Macquarie (Guruk), and women would sing the porpoises close into shore as a method of bringing schools of fish with them.

The Birpai tell that all totemic animals had played a part in the shaping of the land, which was done by the Creation figure Goonbarbi, who made the rivers and landscape. The boundaries of the Birpai people's land were marked by those rivers and mountains. Goonbarbi then created Goomarrunga, who was his trusted keeper of the land, and it was Goomarrunga who created the first man and woman, Yeeindi and Werin. He passed onto them all the knowledge that Goonbarbi had passed onto him, with Yeeindi being taught men's business and Werin being taught women's business.[1]

The Birpai lived in close accord with the land, following the lore that was provided to them, ensuring that they understood the land and abided by the lore that kept it abundant for them. For the Birpai there were two main seasons, summer and winter, that regulated their annual land-use patterns. In summer they lived near the sea, taking advantage of seasonally abundant fish and shellfish, and fruit such as figs, and in the winter they moved into the mountains and hunted game and gathered wild vegetables.

They farmed the country with fire, which was easily controlled by the many rivers, creeks, lakes and swamps, and the entire coastal land and eastern slopes were burnt in small patches over time. They also had to adapt to climatic changes. About 30,000 to 12,000 years ago, the land was struck by long droughts, and then, about 10,000 years ago, the sea levels changed. The oceans rose so high that coastal areas where they had once gathered shellfish slowly became very far out to sea.[2] This is why many coastal middens date back only about 7,000 years.

The Birpai made tools for hunting and fishing, including tidal fish traps made of stones located along the coast. Some of their implements were traded over long distances, such as the water carriers that women made from the leaves of Bangalow palm trees. They were laced together with such a tight weave that no water escaped from them.

Unlike many First Peoples, the Birpai were known to live in villages alongside rivers and around lakes for much of the year, and the explorer and son of Governor Philip Gidley King, Phillip Parker King, commented on their houses in 1819. He wrote, 'The native

Birpai fish traps

huts were more substantially built and contained 8 or 10 persons. They were arched over to form a dome with the opening on the land side, enabling them to be screened from the cold sea winds, which were generally accompanied by rain.'³

An examination of the traditional role of Birpai women by Narelle Mathews, *Her Story*, acknowledges that the early records give us some useful material, but that they were all written by Europeans, and thus the documents that historians often refer to as primary sources are actually second-hand reports. Nevertheless, such reports do give us some valuable information to be confirmed by oral histories and family stories.

Mary Bundock, an early settler and pioneer in cultural anthropology, collected a wealth of information on women and the different practices of different tribes. For instance, she reported that while the Birpai women cooked small marsupials by wrapping them in leaves or ti-tree bark and then steaming them inside a hollowed-out ants nest, the women of the Dunghutti to the north cooked in a ground pit. More complex food preparation included pounding nuts, such as those of the bunya pine, into a cake, then roasting them. And the seeds of the Moreton Bay chestnut were first soaked, to removed their toxicity, before cooking. ⁴

In a type of home-schooling, children followed their mothers to learn bush skills and were taught to observe and mimic, but as boys got older they would spend more time with their fathers. Women had a valued role in society, and were valued not just as producers of food but as reproducers of children.⁵

Narelle Mathews also wrote that the place of women's work was closely related to the sites where their children had been born, and that as part of the religious belief system the site of a baby's birth was related to a plant or animal. This was called its Dreaming or totemic identity.

Aunty Rhonda Radley is a Birpai-Dunghutti woman, language activist and proud grandmother, and is very keen to tell the real stories of her people's culture and history. She says because the early anthropologists were all men, they didn't see what the women were doing. 'And they didn't have that cultural lens, you know, for all the subtleness around the camps and the movements of the people. They're just seeing the men out there doing their thing, but we had very strong men's business and also strong women's business and community business. And so I believe, in some ways, by not acknowledging the woman and the power of the woman, they disempower the woman.

'And some of our men had taken that on as well. But the first part and the last part of the men's law was women. So the boy stayed with a woman to a certain age, and the woman sort of gave them over to go do men's business, such as initiations and hunting. And there was a point that they accept them back as men.

'So being with the women was a big part of their learnings, the women were their first teachers, they developed this really strong bond with the women. Women were very protected and honoured in traditional life – but that didn't come through with the recorded documentation.

'And there's a lot of information about men, but women had their own initiations and responsibilities, and a lot of this was never recorded. We're filling in the puzzle now, women have still got knowledge, pieces of the puzzle. These pieces are coming together, for us as women to reclaim and do our own business. Women are knowledge holders and are the nurturers.'

Nardja Carter said that her grandmother was the source of all her knowledge, and her great-grandfather was a language speaker. She tells that her grandmother and her sisters were sent away to the Cootamundra Girls' Home when she was young – over 750 kilometres away. But she and her sisters all made their way back to reconnect with their land.

Aunty Rhonda Radley

Nardja also said that while there is some knowledge that has been lost, there is lots being retained and passed onto younger people. 'But a lot of knowledge hasn't been recorded, because that's not how it was shared.'

She said that it is important to know that cultural knowledge is a privilege and not a right, as you need to prove yourself worthy of that knowledge. 'I use my cultural knowledge in a different way. Advocacy.'

Nardja leads regular tours of the Sea Acres Rainforest, one of the few stretches of rainforest along this part of the coast that has not be cleared. She said that there once would have been a thin strip of rainforest all along Birpai lands, where her people sought out special plants or hunted for snakes. She also tells that the Hastings River, that flows through Port Macquarie, used to reach the sea at Melaleuca, 25 kilometres to the north. But a major flood about 300 years ago – pre-settlement but within close memory of her people – caused the river to change course and reach the sea at its current location.

She says the land of the Birpai here is unique, as it is the furthest north for many species and also the furthest south for others, so the area is very rich in plants. The small rainforest here is a living botanical museum.

Nardja leads people along a sealed path along the outer edge of the rainforest, stopping to show how different trees and plants were used to make tools or to get medicines. For instance, the lower end of a palm frond is soaked and then bent in half, and the two sides stitched up with twine to make a carry bag. With another piece of twine for a handle, it was hung on a person's back with the twine across the forehead, leaving the hands free.

She stops to point out a large tree that has been engulfed by the thick strands of a strangler fig, that surrounds it like an exoskeleton. The inner tree is dying but is held up by the strangler fig, and becomes a home for insects and small animals.

Nardja then demonstrates how the python tree, which has one of the hardest woods, could be used to make clubs or boomerangs. For instance, the hunting boomerang, which was shaped like a number 7, was carved from the curve between the tree base and uppermost part of the roots. It was used for many things, like a multi-tool. For instance, with both points sharpened it could be used to peel bark off a tree to make a canoe, it could be used as a club, it could be used to dig.

Another tree, the sandpaper fig, has a rough leaf that was used to make wooden implements smooth.

Nardja then pulls small berries from a native ginger tree. She tells how you need to swish them around in your mouth and suck out the juice then spit the many seeds out.

Further along, the path curves around past Shelly Beach where there is the outline of a large fish trap, made by building a rock wall that joined existing ocean rocks. It is easy to see how at low tide the

Hunting boomerang

fish would have been trapped there. It is less easy to see how the early settlers to the area did not recognise it as a fish trap.

Pulling strands of dried pandanus, Nardja shows how twine is made. Roll the fibres on your leg to get rid of the small strands, then fold it in half. 'Twist it three times away from yourself, then turn it over and twist the other strand three times away.' Slowly it forms into a long cord that is surprisingly strong.

She next picks a dried banksia cone from a tree and says that the cones would be set alight and then carried around in a pouch of wet leaves, so that it would be easy to start a fire at the next campsite when her people were on the move. 'The person responsible for the cone would blow on it to keep the fire going, or wet the leaves if needed.'

On the way back she stops to pat one large tree that is covered in a strangler fig, providing lots of hand and footholds for a young child to climb. She says, 'To think my grandmother would have played on this tree as a little girl – and possibly further back.'

Cook renamed two more places along the coast over the next few days of his trip, though neither seemed to warrant the name of a great man of the British empire. The first, Smoky Cape, was in the sea Country of the Dunghutti/Dhangatti people, and the second, Solitary Islands, was in the sea Country of the Gumbaynggirr people.

Cook wrote on Sunday 13 May: 'a point or head land, on which were fires that Caused a great Quantity of smoke, which occasioned my giving it the name of Smokey Cape.'

The Dunghutti names associated with Smoky Cape are Guuwa Miirlarl (meaning a special place of fog), and Jumbulba Guuwa (fog or mist). The tribes that occupied the coast around Smoky Cape used smoke to communicate with other tribes, as well as producing smoke when they undertook firestick farming – but was the smoke that Cook saw from firestick farming or was it a warning?[6]

The entire Smoky Cape area is of profound spiritual significance to the Dunghutti people and marks the place of the last recorded large ceremony along this part of the coast. There had also been numerous carved trees, located where the national park now is, which were removed and transported to the Australian Museum in Sydney.

The cape is a high headland that has yet another Captain Cook lookout. It also has a lighthouse situated at the top of a steep path, with neat picnic grounds, kept immaculately trimmed and fertilised by kangaroos. It is a spectacular view to the northeast, not what Cook would have seen, but what the Dunghutti people would have seen as he sailed away from their lands.

Cook never actually named the Solitary Islands in his journal, but he did write them in on his chart. On 15 May he wrote: 'Between 2 and 4 we had some small rocky Islands between us and the land; the Southermost lies in the Latitude of 30 degrees 10 minutes, the Northermost in 29 degrees 58 minutes, and about 2 Leagues or more from the land.'

Alison Williams, the creative director of the Wadjar Regional Indigenous Gallery at the Yarrawarra Aboriginal Cultural Centre, says there are many different Gumbaynggirr stories of the Solitary Islands, but they all explain how the two islands were formed. One such story tells how a hero ancestor, Bunyun, sailed his canoe into the island, splitting it in two.[7]

She agrees that it can be a problem that many First Nations stories have been written down and interpreted by white anthropologists, which perpetuates the dominance of anthropologists' accounts over oral histories – a problem that is also prevalent in native title claims.

Another of the stories about the Solitary Islands tells of Yuludarla, the all-powerful guiding spirit who created the Gumbaynggirr nation, and who lives between the Nambucca River and the Clarence River.[8] Up the road from the Yarrawarra Cultural Centre, north of Coffs Harbour, you can stand on the headland referred to in the story and look at South Solitary Island to the south. You can see the lighthouse built there and see how the island appears to have been cut in two: a larger grass-covered island and a smaller rocky island.

Further south, at Nambucca Heads, there is yet another Captain Cook lookout, sitting high on a beautiful headland. All the headlands along this coast seem to be trying to outdo the others in spectacular vistas. To the north of the lookout is a long, curved beach and to the south there's the mouth of the Nambucca River (Baga-baga Bindarray), that curves back and forward as it makes its way to the ocean. Straight out you can look to the far, far horizon, though it feels like you might be looking much further. Using the occasional boat as a reference point you can see how small the *Endeavour* would have looked out there.

There were an estimated 1,000 Gumbaynggirr people when Cook came past, and the Bagabaga (Nambucca) ancestors belonged to the sea and the rainforests. In each area along the coast the people were as distinct as the landscape itself, and each jagun (or clan homeland) was fiercely loyal to their own land, dialects and traditions. The clans were united by women, who were expected to marry outside their own clan but inside the Gumbaynggirr tribe.[9]

The museum at the Yarrawarra ('happy meeting place') Cultural Centre tells how people lived before invasion and after. One of the displays is of a sorry place. 'In the 1880s members of the local Aboriginal community at Red Rock were driven off the headland and shot by white police in a massacre. Today Gumbaynggirr descendants, especially women, avoid this place. It's become a place for reflection for both Aboriginal and non-Aboriginal people.'

A study of the archives by local historian Geoffrey Watts estimated that the Red Rock massacre was most likely conducted between July 1888 and July 1889, by a party of hot-headed young men returning from the races. He stated, 'It is hard to believe that Europeans then directly cleared the whole district of Aboriginal people. But it is easier to imagine that the Aboriginal people fled the local district as a result of the Red Rock massacre.'[10]

Alison Williams says that people moved away when there were killings, and as a result a lot of knowledge was lost. But today the Gumbaynggirr culture is being revitalised, largely through an initiative by Elders who got together in 1996 to start teaching language classes. This grew into the Muurrbay Aboriginal Language and Culture Co-operative, that produces a wide variety of courses and publications in language. Its work has spread across six other First Nations languages along the coast: Awabakal/Wonarua, Bundjalung, Darkinjung, Dunghutti, Gathang (spoken by Birpai, Worimi and Guringay peoples), and Yaygirr/Yaegl.

Contact

At the time of European settlement there may have been 6,000 people in the Birpai nation. Together with their Worimi neighbours to the south and the Guringay to the north, they were the

Gathang-speaking peoples. Each of these three tribes, or peoples, were divided into a number of nurras, or clans. And each nurra occupied a particular part of tribal territory.

All the tribes lived in close accord with the land and the seasons and they did not need writing to record their knowledge, which was passed on generation after generation. They had a rich cultural life and lore and education and technologies – very little of which was appreciated by the first Europeans to visit the area, and even less so by those who came to settle and saw the Birpai as a nuisance.

The first Europeans to arrive with an eye on some sort of permanence were convicts and their overseers, with Port Macquarie being chosen as the second penal settlement in New South Wales, after Coal River (Newcastle). The Birpai and the neighbouring peoples had already experienced considerable loss of life from smallpox that spread north from Sydney Harbour, and they had barely recovered from the epidemic when the British arrived to establish the penal settlement at Port Macquarie. This was in 1821, and by 1829 the registry for Births, Deaths and Marriages was already recording children being born to white men (most likely convicts) and local women.[11]

It is unknown how many of these unions were consensual, and certainly more interactions led to the taking of life than the creation of it. The settlement, named after Governor Macquarie, was established when an 1816 edict by the governor was still in force, stating: 'no Black Native, or Body of Black Natives, shall ever appear at or within one mile of any Town Village occupied by or belonging to any British Subject, armed with any Warlike or Offensive Weapons or Weapons of any description, such as Spears, Clubs or Waddies, on pain of being deemed in a state of Aggression and Hostility and treated accordingly'.[12] That was vague enough to endorse violence.

As the penal settlement grew, the Birpai were dispossessed of their land, and when Europeans discovered cedar, large numbers of loggers arrived chasing 'red gold'. By the 1840s the Birpai had decided to fight back, and with the help of the neighbouring Dunghutti Nation, undertook several reprisal attacks. It was brave, but the men stood little chance against firearms, and many were killed.

The settlers, in general, failed to recognise the people as knowledgeable custodians of the land. They saw them as a nuisance. One site, Blackmans Point, is said to be the location where around 300 Birpai were killed. But for many years this massacre was not recognised. It was again a case of oral history versus written history, and different interpretations of a story.

The background to the event was the killing of two loggers, who had gone to Blackmans Point to split shingles in 1826. A third man survived the attack and was able to make his way back to the settlement and report what had happened. A troop of soldiers were then sent out to administer colonial justice.

Henry Lewis Wilson, son of Lieutenant William Wilson who oversaw the convicts, wrote in his diary of the raid: 'and right well was the work carried out. The soldiers got round the blacks and shot a great many of them, captured a lot of women and used them for a immoral purpose and then shot them.'[13]

In a rare instance of rightful colonial justice, the story goes that the offending soldiers were actually sent to Sydney to be tried for their actions – but as was less rare, they escaped punishment.[14]

Based on official records and known limitations of how long it took to shoot and reload a gun at the time, some historians initially estimated that perhaps only thirty or so people had been killed at Blackmans Point. The Birpai people, however, knew that it was more like 300, and had to continue to press until recognition of the massacre was given – to add to the unfortunately large list of massacres across the land.

Aunty Rhonda Radley, who grew up in Guruk (Port Macquarie), said that she knows of multiple massacres but only three were ever officially recorded. She tells that over fifteen years ago, when they were trying to get the Blackmans Point massacre accepted, they had held a meeting of the First Nations residents to discuss it. But the invitation was also sent out to residents of the area. 'So when we turned up to our own meeting, all these residents there were yelling at us screaming, "Where's your proof? Where's your proof? Nothing happened down at Blackmans Point."'[15]

She says that Guruk can be 'a hard-arsed place. Grandfather used to say, all the whitefellas come here to die, because there's so many aged care facilities.' But she acknowledges things are changing. In the schools, in the community, with local government. 'Our ancestors are so proud that this is finally happening,' she said. 'The young ones, the young ones are really open. And they're more culturally aware and connected.'

By 1838 random killings across the colony had reached such a point that it was causing outrage in the press. A report in the *Sydney Gazette* on 6 February on the treatment of Aborigines at Port Macquarie stated: 'the disclosure of a series of cold-blooded atrocities perpetrated on the wretched aborigines who frequent the settlement, almost without a parallel among the barbarous massacres which disgrace the earlier years of our colonial progress'.[16]

Eighteen thirty-eight was also the year of the massacre of approximately thirty Wirrayaraay people at Myall Creek, that led to seven men being convicted and hanged – an act that divided the colony. There was outrage that white men could kill so wantonly, and outrage that white men could be hanged for such killings. Always more than one story.

And as happened in many areas, the only way the Birpai were able to stay on their own land, that they had fought so hard to defend, was to work for settlers, or under the instruction of the Aboriginal Protection Board, clearing land.

Aunty Rhonda Radley said, 'Colonisation happened on Country here, and our landscape changed because of that contact. Because our mob were pushed out, put on reserves – which is part of my family history – and we couldn't fulfil our obligations of looking after Country and custodianship. We were shut out of our own land, so that had a major impact on our mob, spiritually, physically and of course, you know mentally.'

But she wants truth-telling that is inclusive of all peoples.

'I think you know if we start telling the true story of the history of some of these towns, I think that brings people together in an understanding of why we are, or where we are, at this moment in time together. And I think that can support, you know, Aboriginal mob in healing because there still needs a lot to be done in regard to intergenerational trauma. I see it in the kids and I know it's not just coming from their experiences, it's coming from their parents and their grandparents.

'Trauma has been handed down through the generations and we just gotta stop this from happening. And I think white Australia can support us in healing our young ones, by allowing the truth to be spoken and for the history books to change.

'It's Aboriginal and non-Aboriginal history. It's the history of the land, and we all should know the history of the land where we walk.'

She said, 'Looking after Country is not just a blackfella thing, it should be all people's thing.'

Wollumbin (Mount Warning)
Bundjalung Country

Ngali na jugun.	We belong to this Country.
Ngali Garima mala jugun.	We look after this Country.
Wana janjma mala gunugala jugun.	Don't do wrong around here this Country.
Ngali wana janja mala jugun.	We don't harm this Country here.
Ngali na mala jugun.	We belong to this Country.

A Tolerable high point of land bore North-West by West, distant 3 Miles; this point I named Cape Byron. It may be known by a remarkable sharp peaked Mountain lying in land North-West by West from it.
                                    Cook's journal, 15 May 1770

Cook came close to losing the *Endeavour* when he was offshore of the place he had appropriately renamed Point Danger. He had earlier in the day renamed the headland Walgun, calling it Cape Byron after Vice-Admiral John 'Foul-Weather Jack' Byron, who was another British navigator, and grandfather of the 'mad, bad and dangerous to know' poet, Lord Byron. But as Cook continued on his way north, late in the day he had to suddenly change course to the east, having encountered a dangerous reef that ran out nearly 5 kilometres from land.

Had he arrived at the reef an hour or two later, after dark, it might have been the end of his voyage, striking that sudden reef. The reason it was so unexpected was that it was actually a lava flow from a large volcanic mountain that lay some distance inland, and had formed there about 20 million years before.

But Cook had not escaped the danger yet. When he awoke the next day it was to discover the ship had actually gone backwards

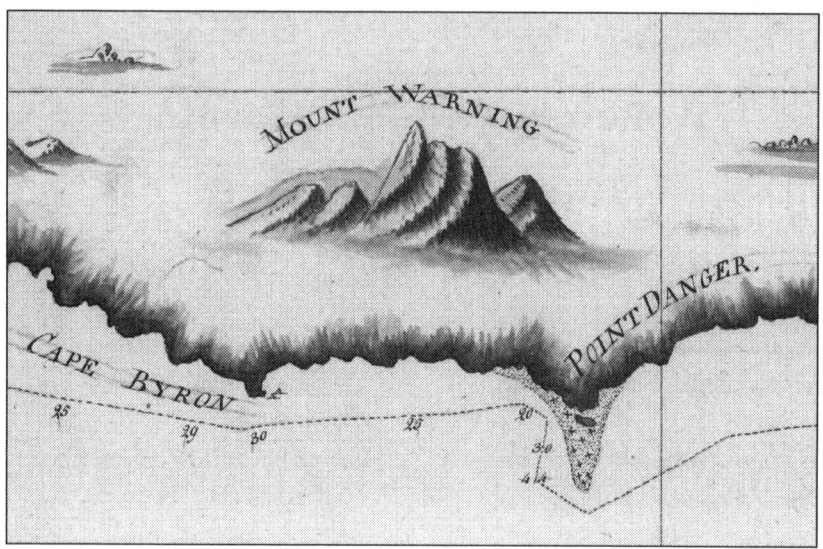

Cook's chart of Bundjalung Country

overnight, despite there being a strong southerly wind, as if the reef was calling him back to it. He therefore turned away from the reef again and renamed the area Point Danger. He also wrote a warning to other navigators – that it could be known by a particular peaked mountain some distance inland that he renamed Mount Warning. A story and names that he hoped would serve as a lesson for future navigators.

Of course, both landmarks already had stories and names. Point Danger was Booningbah, the place where Booning (the echidna) was chased into the ocean, and Mount Warning was Wollumbin, the cloud catcher, where the bush turkey settled after being speared in the head.

Although if you go to Point Danger today, you won't actually be at Point Danger. This was the fault of one William Johns, aboard the ship *Rainbow*, who in a chart published in 1831 marked it in a different place, further to the north, right on the New South Wales–Queensland border. So Cook's Point Danger is not the Point Danger you will find on many maps, rather it is the point named Fingal Head just a little to the south – clearly identified as Point Danger on Cook's charts because of the nearby island. This island was later named Cook Island, though not by Cook (and properly its name is Joong-urra-narrian). Becoming clear? Or just clearly confusing? To add to things, Point Danger – not Cook's Point Danger – is the site of the largest monument to Cook along the east coast, standing a massive 20 metres tall. (Or about ten Captain Cooks standing on each other's heads.)

Wollumbin to a geologist is the remnant vent of a mighty volcano, the central point of one of the largest calderas in the world. The reef that Cook nearly hit was made by a lava flow stretching from that mountain out to sea. But to the Bundjalung people of northern New South Wales, Wollumbin is something more, and highly significant to them. According to the Wollumbin Consultative Group it is a sacred ceremonial and cultural complex, linked to traditional lore and custom. The mountain is also interconnected within a broader cultural and spiritual landscape that includes Creation and Dreaming stories and men's initiation rites of deep antiquity.[1]

Wollumbin (Mount Warning)

Kyle Slabb, a descendant and Traditional Custodian of the Tweed Coast Coodjinburra people, maintains his family's cultural knowledge and beliefs and says that there are multiple stories of Wollumbin, as different clans see it differently. One of the stories sees the mountain as 'fighting chief of the mountains', and the thunder and lightning storms observed around the peak are the warrior spirits of fighting ancestors engaged in battle. And the landslips on the mountain's face are the resulting battle scars.[2]

According to Kyle Slabb, there is a story of a bush turkey that was speared in the head and settled where the mountain is, and the caldera is its nest. He says it is important to know that when a bush turkey hatches, its parents are not there and it has to know lore from within itself.

'That is why the bush turkey is important to our lore.'

Kyle also noted that the word his people use to describe Wollumbin is jagun, which means 'mother', and while the top of the mountain is a sacred men's site, there are sacred birthing places for women on the mountain too.

The Bundjalung people, like the Dharawal people south of Sydney, have one of the few migration Creation stories, which tells

Wogan (bush turkey)

that their first ancestors – three brothers – came to the land in a canoe from across the ocean in the Dreaming. They landed at Goanna Headland, just south of Evans Head, one of the most easterly points on mainland Australia, that from above looks like the head of a goanna. This headland is the place of origin of the Bundjalung people, who have lived on and visited Goanna Headland for at least 12,000 years. In their Creation story the goanna (Dirawong) and the rainbow serpent gave shape to the lands and islands along the coast, and the goanna protects the people from the rainbow serpent.

Although there are several variations on the three brothers story, including one in which they came from a land 'at the centre of the world' that had been destroyed by a massive catastrophe, the brothers are generally known as Mamoon, Birrung and Yar-Birrain. Together with their people, they spread out in different directions across the land. Mamoon and his people went to the west. Birrung and his people went to the south. And Yar-Birrain and his people went to the north. The brothers made a bora ring, which was where lore was made, and the Bundjalung people have followed that lore for thousands of years.[3]

While there are three major clans of the Bundjalung, as with many First Peoples in Australia there are clans within those; approximately fifteen are known, including the Yugembeh to the north, and the Arakwal around Cape Byron.

Bundjalung spokespeople have stated, 'A common feature of our Aboriginal identity is language, which is known in the Tweed and further south as Bundjalung; but in southeast Queensland people call it Yugambeh; and further west, in Kyogle Shire, people use Githabul as both a language and name for group identification.'[4]

The Arakwal were the people that Cook had spied on Seven Mile Beach the day before he renamed Point Danger. Banks noted that the forty or so people completely ignored them, writing they were, 'intirely unmovd by the neighbourhood of so remarkable an object as a ship'. While this has sometimes been used to conjecture that the *Endeavour* was not the first ship the people had seen, his description is very similar to how some of the Gweagal people reacted when the ship entered Kamay (Botany Bay). Some of the people there appeared to deliberately avoid looking at the ship, following their own protocol to strangers, until the crew had lowered boats and come closer.

The Arakwal have their own stories of Wollumbin, which can be seen from their lands. And while Cape Byron (Walgun) might be the most easterly point on the Australian mainland, Wollumbin is the first part of the mainland to be touched by the rising sun.

Other stories associated with that land tell of animals and how they became as they are today. The name Joongurra-narrian (Cook Island), for instance, literally means 'the place where the pelican played', and is closely associated with Joongurra-bah'ta (the small mountain known as the Razorback at Tweed Heads), which means 'the place of the pelican', and which has a Dreaming story associated with it explaining how birds got their different colours.[5]

According to Kyle Slabb, the birds had all gathered at the mountain to paint themselves, and the parrots could not decide what colour to paint themselves and so used all colours. The crow decided to paint itself black with ash. Joongurra the pelican, who glides so well through the air and swims so well on the water, was clumsy walking on the ground, and the crow laughed at the wobbly way it was walking. So Joongurra, who was painted white, threw white clay on the crow's eye. Now the crow has a white ring around its eyes to remind you not to disrespect people who are different.[6]

Another story tells not how an animal was formed, but how the animal changed the land. The story, recounted by Ian Fox and Kyle Slabb in the book *The Fragile Edge*, tells that in the Dreaming a young man went out hunting, and when he saw a kangaroo he threw his spear into it. But the spear only wounded the kangaroo, hitting its thigh, and as the man came closer the kangaroo hopped away. So the young man followed. And everywhere the kangaroo hopped it left blood. It travelled over much of the Country until at last it came to a mountain cave, and it went into the cave and died there. And when it died the blood from its wound turned into the red clay paint (goodjin), which the warriors wear. That paint in that cave, which is near the town of Kyogle, is much redder than any clay found elsewhere.7

Stories of the land and the animals and waterways formed a wide network of songlines and story places that had once connected and traversed the entire continent and, in some cases, beyond.8

A lot of Bundjalung stories and artifacts have been preserved by the Tweed Regional Museum in Murwillumbah, and also at the Minjungbal Aboriginal Cultural Centre and Museum at Tweed Heads. Minjungbal has a stunning bora ring, and a bush walk that enables you to learn about different trees and plants and what they might have been used for. The walk leads you past the mangroves of the Tweed River estuary, where you can stand and gaze at the mangrove shoots and thick trees across the water towards Ukerebagh Island, much as it would have been when Cook sailed past.

Ukerebagh Island Reserve is the birthplace of Senator Neville Bonner, the first Indigenous person elected to parliament in Australia. He was born under a birthing tree on the island, as was common practice.

As for the bora ring, it is spectacular. You walk along a small path into thick bushland and come upon it suddenly. Surrounded by tall gums, the ring is marked by a low fence but you can walk around the outside to appreciate the size of it – about 40 metres across. A slight mound marks the outside of the ring, that would have been cleared to make a flat surface for dancing and ceremony. Standing there you can feel the ancient ancestors of that land, and even feel like you could be seeing them doing corroboree. Right there in front of you.

Minjungbal museum

Tribes from all over the Northern Rivers regularly gathered on this sacred initiation ground. Month-long ceremonies leading up to the initiation of adolescent boys were held by firelight in this arena.

Bora rings like this one were made up of two separate rings. The first, larger ring, was used for dancing and performances, in which all the tribe and visiting clans took part, with each tribe or clan taking it in turns to present their own special dances. At the climax of the dancing, around dusk, the young boys awaiting initiation were snatched away by elder men and carried to the second, smaller ring. Early anthropologist R.H. Mathews recorded initiation ceremonies and described in great detail the trials and hardships the novices had to undergo at the hands of the Elders. This took place over several days, until the boys were considered initiated and had acquired the right level of wisdom.[9]

There are still remnants of the path that led to the smaller bora ring at Minjungbal. That ring it is now lost and could be under nearby houses, but we will never know.

And anyone who visits such bora rings today should know that regardless of their physical condition, the locations of all bora grounds still remain imbued with intense spiritual and cultural significance.[10]

That the larger bora ring at Minjungbal has been so well preserved is due to the efforts of Arakwal woman Margaret Kay. In 1961 she successful convinced the Tweed Shire Council to have the area preserved. There is a display specifically holding the items that were a part of Margaret Kay's original house museum, that allows great insight into Bundjalung life. But it needs to be stated that the artifacts and knowledge that have been preserved represent only a fraction of what would have once existed.

Such artifacts include woven dillybags that were used by men rather than women, and worn snugly under the armpit for carrying important tools like flintstone knives. These knives were indispensable for skinning animals, cutting women's hair, and for the ritual marking of initiates.

And while women traditionally had their hair cropped, men wore their hair long, often piling it up high on top of their heads, fastening it with twine and padding it out with bits of bark. Honey or clay was also used to give the hair more volume and stiffness, and finally, cockatoo's crests and other colourful feathers would be studded into the hair, with it all being held in place with a dingo-tail headband.

Although little clothing was ever worn, belts of possum-fur string were used to carry axes, boomerangs and throwing sticks, which left a person's hands free. Water could then be carried in a vessel made from the broad leaves of the Bangalow palm.

Because the Bundjalung lands were so rich in resources, there was less need to move around seasonally, which meant they were able to stay in one place much longer than many First Peoples of the wider land and were able to construct settlements or villages. European travellers to the area in 1823 reported on huts that were quite substantial, weather-proof and large enough to stand up in.[11] The longer periods of staying in one place also enabled more time for making sophisticated implements, like nets, fish traps and canoes.

And within the rainforests men would climb trees to hunt game by tying a vine around their waist and around the tree and using it as a back brace. The climber would move up the trunk in jerking motions until he reached a safe branch.

The Bundjalung people have a natural calendar comprising six seasons. Indicators in nature announce the seasons, such as when the wattle starts to bloom, then the mountain possums are fattest. The six seasons are:

Yirrimbu, the wet season. January–March, when the winds are predominantly from the north. Possums are fat during this time, shrubs and trees are loaded with berries and fruits, goannas are feeding and beginning to breed.

Guyumbu, the mullet season. March–May, when the winds are from the west and the last of the rains come. Many groups travel to the coast for the migration of the sea mullet, and Elders sing to the dolphins which help herd the mullet to shore, where they are caught with nets and spears.

Waringu, the cold season. June–July, when the winds come from both the west and the south. People go to the coast to collect bream, tailor and jewfish, and the whales begin to migrate north to their feeding grounds. The banksia flowers are in full bloom, indicating it is lorikeet and honeyeater season.

Yarrgehmbu, the windy season. July–August, when there are strong, changeable winds and it's the start of the echidna and turtle season. There is rain in the mountains, indicated by the sounds of the black cockatoo on the coast.

Gagabalingu, the goanna season. September–October, when the wind begins to turn to the north and the weather begins

TOP *Gulaga*, Cheryl Davison
MIDDLE *28.4.1770 – The Arrival of Captain Cook*, Kevin Butler
BOTTOM *Twelve Turtles*, Wanda Gibson

Terra Nullius, Gordon Bennett

TOP Therese Ardler in possum-skin cloak with the whale sculpture at Kamay (Botany Bay), designed and sculpted by her and Julie Squires RIGHT Therese Ardler and Julie Squires' canoe sculptures at Kamay

Mary Ann Cowan, a likely ancestor of Shauna Bostock, wearing a dingo-tail headband

The young Gudang woman taken to England by missionary William Kent, wearing her distinctive shell necklace

Sketch of fishermen at Kamay by Polynesian navigator and holy man Tupaia

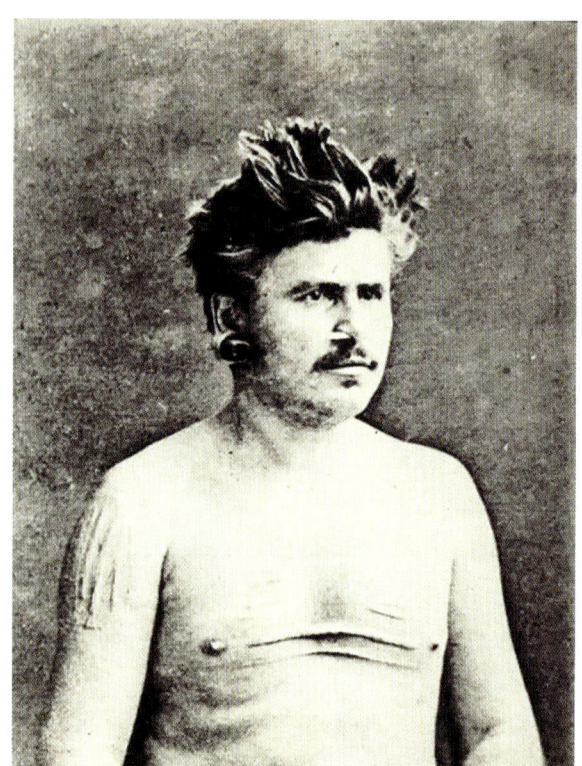

Frenchman Narcisse Pelletier, who spent 17 years living with the Uutaalnganu people of Cape York

Castaway James Morrill, after his return from living with the Juru and Bindal people of north Queensland

ABOVE *Endeavour* artist Sydney Parkinson's original sketch of the warriors of Kamay
LEFT The more well-known lithograph based on Parkinson's sketch, *Two of the Natives of New Holland, Advancing to Combat*, by Thomas Chambers, who never visited Australia and has shown the warriors in classical Greek style

Signs of Cook: at Seventeen Seventy (TOP & BOTTOM RIGHT), Kamay (RIGHT) and Townsville (BELOW)

TOP The Cook monument at Minjerribah, famously prised off on 'Australia Day' 2019 and used as a barbeque grill

LEFT The Cook monument at Thuined (Possession Island)

ABOVE The Cook monument at Seventeen Seventy

Queensland native police, Cloncurry, 1870

Archibald Meston's Wild Australia Show (circa 1893)

Auntie Dot,
Julie Dowling

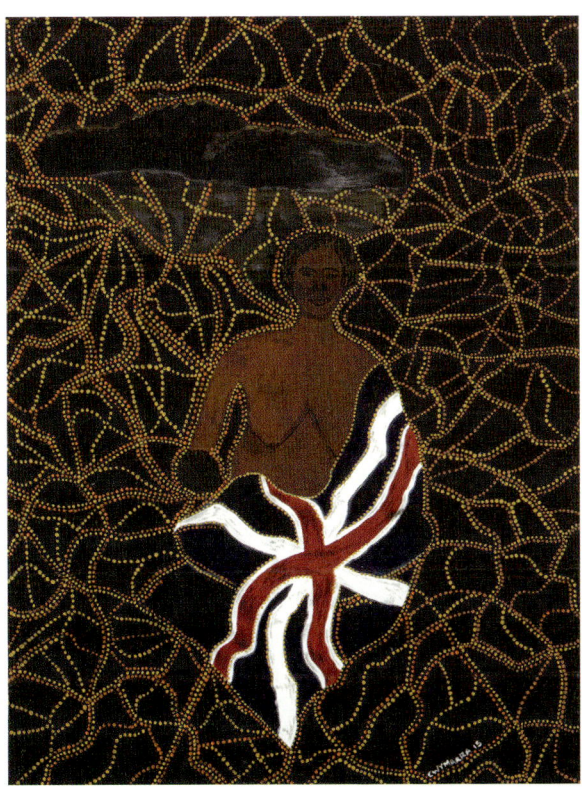

Eyes of Innocence,
Colina Wymarra

Bus stop at Bung Yarnda (Lake Tyers Aboriginal Trust)

Bus stop at Waiben (Thursday Island) reading 'Welcome to Country'

to warm up. Goannas, snakes and other reptiles wake up and begin to move around. Silky oak flowers start to bloom, indicating that the turtles are fat. Whales migrate back south with their young.

Moogerahmbu, the storm season. November–December, when the winds can come from the north, the northeast and the south. Many bird species begin to hatch now and many plants and fruits begin to emerge. Koalas begin to breed and bush turkeys are fat and abundant.

Like most of the people in the Northern Rivers and southern Queensland, every three years the Bundjalung would travel north to take part in the bunya feast in the Bunya Mountains, inland of the Sunshine Coast. People would travel up to 300 kilometres to collect the 30-centimetre-long cones filled with large seeds from the towering trees and eat them raw or roasted.

And while travel was permitted for certain ceremonies and gatherings, and there was regular trade between adjoining tribes and peoples, there were also complex and strict rules governing trespass. If there was no good excuse for being on another tribe's land there could be little mercy shown.

There were also times when tribal fights arose, triggered by either a woman being taken or an accusation of murder. These could escalate into full-blown tribal fights. However, these were very ritual in nature and there were rarely fatalities. Men of each tribe would line up facing each other with spears and boomerangs, and often a small wooden shield. Women were also known to join in, fighting with sharpened digging sticks.

There were rules to be followed, such as certain parts of the body being off limits, often everywhere but the back and thighs, and after an acceptable length of time a tribal champion could be nominated to take part in a one-on-one battle with another champion. The two men would face each other armed only with a flintstone knife or club and shield. The fight then became a contest of leaping and feinting and parrying as each tied to cut the other. Once blood had been drawn, things cooled off and a reconciliation was achieved.[13]

Until the next time.

Contact

In 1823, fifty-three years after Cook sailed past, John Oxley was on a journey to find a good location for a remote penal settlement, which he ultimately found on the Brisbane River. However, before that he came upon a river that he renamed the Tweed River, and wrote: 'The scenery here exceeded any thing I had previously seen in Australia – extending for miles along a deep rich valley, clothed with magnificent trees, the beautiful uniformity of which was only interrupted by the turns of the river which here and there appeared like small lakes, while in the background.'[14]

Five years later Henry John Rous found the entrance to the Richmond River, south of the Tweed, and explored 32 kilometres upstream. Word was getting out about the rich land, and the large red cedars that grew there, and by 1842 the first cutters had arrived looking for 'red gold'.

Bundjalung historian Shauna Bostock says in her book *Reaching Through Time*: 'Settler encroachment onto Bundjalung Country occurred with incredible speed: in the nine years from 1880 to 1889, there were 683 conditional purchases sold, and most of the accessible land to the east and north or Murwillumbah had already been taken up by settlers.'[15]

Conflict was inevitable. The first recorded incident was the so-called Pelican Creek Tragedy in 1846, when five European cedar cutters were killed, for reasons unknown. A reprisal led to around a hundred Bundjalung people being massacred at Evans Head – on the Goanna Headland that is so important to the Bundjalung people.

Historian Rory Medcalf describes the tactics employed by the settlers: 'Whites with firearms would form a cordon around a camp at night, and simply move in at dawn, guns blazing. This tactic was used on the Orara River and the Upper Clarence in 1841, at Evans Head in 1843, and at Ballina in 1853 or 1854.'[16]

As more settlers arrived, the native police were not far behind them and in 1853–4, at an area close to the present-day East Ballina golf course, the native police slaughtered at least thirty to forty Bundjalung Nyangbal men, women and children while they slept.[17]

The European settlers of East Ballina were said to have been disturbed by the unprovoked attack on the 'friendly natives', and reported the massacre to the New South Wales government. No action was taken.[18]

Oral tradition records a later mass poisoning at South Ballina, where the Arakwal people, who numbered about 200, were given poisoned flour. They took it to their camp on the Beach at South Ballina and made it into damper. The old people and children refused to eat the food and when they woke the next morning they found almost 150 adults dead.[19]

Added to this was the toll taken by European diseases, with smallpox, dysentery, diarrhoea, venereal diseases, measles, and the common cold killing more people than were killed by guns in the 1800s. The earliest diseases were carried by convicts escaping from Moreton Bay to the north. Researchers have been able to pinpoint individual convicts, such as one man named Baker, who had previously been exposed to smallpox and then escaped and lived for some time with the people of the lands he travelled through, infecting them in return for their kindness as he went.[20]

North of the Tweed River, the explorer William Landsborough recorded, 'I learn that small-pox killed off a large portion of these tribes both prior to the appearance of the Whites in this part of the continent and subsequently.'[21]

Tellingly, the census figures of 1871 to 1887, which were gathered for police magistrate Joshua Bray, show that within fifty years of European settlement, over 90 per cent of First Peoples may have perished in or fled from the Tweed area.[22]

Some Bundjalung people found an uneasy peace working as labourers for the European invaders, which allowed them to 'stay on their lands and continue their traditional economic, social, and ceremonial practices'.[23]

An early settler of the area, Mary Bundock of Wyangarie, on the upper Richmond River, wrote in her diary in the late 1880s: 'The young men too, they do not use the spear or the boomerang as their fathers did. They work spasmodically on the stations and like riding and work amongst the cattle, but drink and gambling are their curses. Our tribe is fading away though we do all we can to save them. I fear another generation will see few if any left.'[24]

But Shauna Bostock said that her people have survived. 'We are survivors of invasion, massacres, violence, land theft, segregation, stolen children and inequality. European colonists brought with them a foreign concept called government that robbed us of financial equity, our land (which was our independence and livelihood), and stripped us of our soul equity (the wealth of our cultural way of life, the use of our language, and even our children). We were kicked off our sacred Country and forced to become propertyless paupers in a nation overflowing with natural abundance. There was absolutely nothing civilised about the way European society, then Australian society, treated Aboriginal people.'[25]

Shauna Bostock's research has also looked at the impacts of harsh government policies on her people, and the collusion between organisations like the United Aborigines Mission (UAM) and the clearly misnamed Aborigines Protection Board (APB). She writes: 'What I found unsettling was that a religious group such as the UAM, who preached the tenets of Christianity, found nothing wrong with being active participants in the separation of very young Aboriginal babies and children from their mothers and families. Some of the children deemed neglected and who were not old enough for indenture were taken to the APB's institutions at Cootamundra Girls Training Home, or Kinchela Boys Training Home. If they were very young, or babies, these removed children were taken to the UAM's Children's Home at Bomaderry.'[26]

They are places that send a shiver through any of our mob who have had family taken to them, knowing the impacts of such institutionalisation. And we know it is a practice that continues this day, under the name of different welfare bodies.

Despite efforts by First Nations political groups like the Australian Aboriginal Progressive Association (AAPA) to stop these policies, they continued under the tyrannical administration of men such as Robert Donaldson – known by mob as the 'Kid Collector', and often cited as the most hated man in New South Wales in the first two decades of the 1900s. He had a seemingly paranoid fixation on taking children away from their families.

John Maynard, whose grandfather was a founder of the AAPA, is studying the impacts of the Aborigines Protection Board and told that he had been contacted by Donaldson's grandson, who said he could remember when his grandfather died, in 1936, at Bondi: 'them throwing drawers of papers over the cliff into the sea'.

John Maynard said, 'This is just getting rid of evidence, as far as just one man was concerned.'

The archives may be thin in places but the determination of First Nations people to have the truth told is strong, and the stories will be told.

Bundjalung people, like most of the mob we talked to along the coast, want people to know that they have not only survived, they are actively recovering their culture and language – after the number of speakers of Bundjalung proper dropped to only 113 in the 2016 census (with twenty-six speakers of other dialects), out of about 13,900 First Nations people living in the Bundjalung area.[27]

There were originally at least twenty dialects of Bundjalung, spread across the twenty or so different tribes.

Today the language is being taught in schools and in community, using recordings of Elders, DVDs and books to assist in learning, so people can know their culture through words and more easily be able to say with pride, 'Jinghi-wahla. Ngay waymalehla nganyahya nguyaya.' (Hello. I am speaking my own language.)

Beerwah & Tibrogargan (The Glass House Mountains)
Kabi Kabi & Jinibara Countries

Ngara Wunya Ngulum!   Hello and welcome!

These hills ... are remarkable for the singular form of their elevation, which very much resembles a glass house ...
                                         Cook's journal, 17 May 1770

This is a story of mountains and trees.

But first, Cook's continuing voyage northwards, where he sailed past the lands of the Yugambeh, Yugera, Quandamooka and Turbal, until he passed the headland he renamed Point Lookout. And to highlight the wide variety of spellings that exist, just looking at the Yugera and Turbal peoples, they have also been known as Yugerra, Yagara, Yaggara, Yugg-ari, Yackarabul; and Turubul, Turrabal, Turrubul, Turrabal, Terabul, Torbul, Turibul, Toorbal.[1] And of course, there are also many clan names that exist within these groups.

To the Quandamooka people, whose traditional lands include the renamed Point Lookout, that headland has always been Mooloomba, and unbeknown to Cook, it was a part of the island of Minjerribah (Stradbroke Island). That lookout is known locally as Cook's Look, and has a memorial to Cook on the grassy headland. It is a squat, square stone marker shaped like a rocky step-aerobics platform, with a plaque that commemorates the bicentenary of Cook's naming the headland.

On 'Australia Day' 2019 the plaque was levered off by Traditional Owner David Yowda Stevens, and used as a barbeque grill. Cooking on Cook. And the steaks even had the words of the plaque burnt into them. David stated he did it for his ancestors. In an act of great irony to the local mob, he was charged with wilful damage and theft.[2]

Sailing on, Cook saw some spectacularly shaped mountains inland. And when he renamed them the Glass House Mountains he was not actually thinking of glasshouses, as in where you might grow plants in the winter. He was thinking of glass furnaces, such as existed in his native Yorkshire, for making glass. Their conical brick towers looked similar to the shape of some of the mountains he saw. European eyes trying to find a comparison for what they were seeing.

The type of glass house (left) to which Cook compared the mountains he saw

The mountains lie on the traditional lands of the Jinibara and Kabi Kabi (Gubbi Gubbi) peoples, and individually they each have names and stories behind them. Of the fourteen accepted mountains (or lava plugs that remained after the landscape around them had been eroded), several have retained the original names:

Mount Tibrogargan: comes from the words chibur kakun, which mean 'flying squirrel biting'.
Mount Beerwah: comes from the words birra and wandum, meaning 'sky and climbing up'.

Mount Coonowrin: comes from kunna waruin, meaning 'crooked neck'.

Mount Miketeebumulgrai, whose name means a place where lightning has struck.

Mount Elimbah takes its name from Yilam, which means 'grey snake'.

Mount Tunbubudla East: comes from the words tunba-bulla bulla, meaning 'two mountains'.

Mount Beerburrum: comes from the word bir-barram, meaning 'the sound of a king parrot's wings'.³

Cook's chart of Kabi Kabi and Jinibara Countries

The key mountains in Kabi Kabi and Jinibara culture are Tibrogargan, the father, and Beerwah, the mother. Several of the stories associated with the mountains involve Tibrogargan and Beerwah and their children. One story, recorded from locals in the mid-1800s by Mrs Gwen Trundle, tells:

'Tibrogargan the father, and Beerwah the mother had many children. There was Coonowrin who was the eldest, Beerburrum, the Tunbubudla twins, Coochin, Ngungun, Tibberoowuccum, Elimbah, Micketeebumulgrai, the little plump Round Mountain and Wild Horse who was always wandering off to paddle in the sea. One day, Tibrogargan saw that the sea was rising. He called for his eldest son to go and help his mother while he himself gathered up his other children to take them to the safety of the mountains in the west. But Coonowrin disobeyed his father and ran off by himself to play.

'This made Tibrogargan so angry that he struck his son a great blow with his nulla nulla, dislocating his neck. After the sea had subsided and the family had come back to the plains, the other children teased Coonowrin because of his crooked neck. As a result, Coonowrin went to ask for his father's forgiveness, but Tibrogargan was so filled with shame at his son's behaviour, that he merely wept and his tears flowed out to the sea. Coonowrin then went to his mother, but she also wept as did the other children as he went to them in turn and there have been many streams flowing out to sea ever since.

'Then Tibrogargan called out to his son and asked him why he had not helped his mother when told to, and Coonowrin replied that as she was the biggest of them all, he thought she should have been able to look after herself. Tibrogargan was so filled with shame at this answer, and he turned his back on Coonowrin, vowing he would never look on his son again. Beerwah, whose great size was because she was pregnant once more wept even more for the disgrace of her son. Beerwah is still large and heavy with child as it takes a long time for a mountain to be born. There are still many streams flowing across the plains beneath the mountains as Tibrogargan gazes forever away from his son and out to sea.'[4]

Kabi Kabi and Waka Waka man Kerry Neill runs the cross-curricular Indigenous learning experience TribalLink up in the bushy hinterland of the Sunshine Coast. He enjoys teaching about

Mount Coonowrin (locally known as Crookneck)

his people's culture and history, and says, 'The stories about the mountains have been here longer than anybody else. And that's the connection that I think a lot of people don't realise. I think there is quite a lot that needs to be told, you know, it absolutely needs to be told that the Glass House Mountains weren't always called that. It's only been quite recently. And that's important for people to know.

'And even here on the Sunshine Coast there's many different stories about that place, and each one of us tell that story in a little different way, you know, to teach different perspectives. You can't talk the same ways you talk to children when you talk to adults, and there's deeper learning as you get older and older and older.'

Of the two peoples whose land the mountains sit on, Jinibara Country takes in the western part of the mountains, and Kabi Kabi Country takes in the eastern side down to the coast – so some different mountains sit within different people's territories. There are still many ceremonial sites within the mountains where gatherings

Kerry Neill

are held, and both the Kabi Kabi and Jinibara people have requested that visitors think carefully about their desire to climb the mountains, out of respect. Particularly Beerwah, the pregnant ancestral mother, and Tibrogargan the father. Being the tallest mountain at 556 metres, Beerwah is very popular, and so many people climb it (28,000 people in 2019) that they have worn a visible scar into the side of the mountain. And this is despite warnings that climbing the mountain can bring bad luck – which appears to be borne out by the statistics. Over a hundred people had to be rescued in the Glass House Mountains in 2018–19, which is ten times more than on any other mountain in Queensland, and there is a death from a fall there every few years.[5]

People really need to know there are many ways to connect to Country that do not involve conquering summits and pitting yourself physically against the landscape. Aunty Zeitha Jalamala Murphy is a Jinibara woman who is active in asking visitors not to climb Beerwah. She says, 'It is just my son and I who get out there and fight these battles to stop people climbing Beerwah. Climbers say they want to respect your culture, and they say they are standing in solidarity with us – but they really just want to climb it.

'They say that climbing the mountain is really good for their mental health. But what about our mental health? It is disrespecting our lore.'

Aunty Zeitha Jalamala Murphy knows a lot about being disrespected, as a survivor of the stolen generations. She says, 'I was taken away because I was fair skinned and pretty and they just wanted to assimilate me into the white world.' She was a couple of months old when she was taken, and she suffered racism, violence and sexual abuse and never got to see her birth mother again.

Aunty Zeitha Jalamala Murphy

Even when her mother was dying, she says, the authorities debated whether or not she could visit her. 'I was the only one that my mother asked for because she'd met all the others. She hadn't met me. But on the day that they organised for that to happen my mother died. So, I never got to see her. But I carry her spirit.'

Aunty Zeitha has spent most of her life recovering from the trauma that being stolen caused her, but she has found several paths to reconnect to her heritage and to her Country. She says, 'I went to America, and I spent three months with the Native American people, and that was sort of a catalyst for me – when I came back home – to find a way that I could create a better version of myself.'

She also decided to get a good education and she got a job as a research assistant for Professor Matt Sanders, founder of the Triple P – Positive Parenting Program. And that got her interested in studying human behaviour and psychology. She says, 'Doing the research was really good because I got to meet a lot of people, my mob, and that gave me an insight into how we are all challenged to find a pathway that allows us to lead to some sort of serenity in our mind. It helped me understand the stolen generation, and how the intergenerational trauma plays out. I have found how to walk on my own, and be proud of who I am as an Aboriginal woman.'

She also says that so much of her people's connection to Country and being a part of the land got broken up after Cook came.

She says she wants to help her kids find their way back into their Aboriginal heritage, and is interested in supporting men who are also victims of domestic violence, 'because there's not enough out there to support our men'.

'When Captain Cook came here, these guys took away the many roles from our men. For our men would go out hunting, and bring home food, and the women would be closer to the camp for safety, you know, they were the nurturers who provided and protected the children. But the men also protected the women and the children as well, you know, so the man's role got taken away.

'Our men are still trying to find a way back to their cultural connections. You can only find that within yourself. It's not something that anybody can give you. And you have to create that space for yourself.

'You'll find it if you go out and walk on Country.'

Kabi Kabi family Elder Uncle Tais K'Reala Randanpi, whose bloodline and connection is to the Muckan family, believes in teaching people – all people – how to better connect to Country. His great-grandmother was born along the banks of the Maroochy River, and he tells, 'That's our tribal and blood connection to this Country. The Undambi people within the Kabi Kabi nation.

'We all got our different names and versions of our cultural ways and stories, and spiritual connection, because until we get to understand and know that spiritual connection to mother earth or the father creator, then who are we? What are we? How can we share that story unless we get truly connected?'

He greets people onto his Country – on a large block nearby the old highway – where he guides people around and shares his wisdom. He starts by gentle conversation, challenging people to share their own stories and think in new ways. Then he leads you down to the back of the block where the scrub is thickest.

He points out trees and their uses. Which can be eaten. Which are medicinal. And he shows the differences in First Nations and settler approaches to treating plants and trees.

'The difference between a steel axe and a stone axe,' he says. 'We used to grind it all down and make a sharp stone axe, you know, and make it sharp enough. And then we'd go along and we'd take out that bark that we need for that time, alright.' And as an example he shows where bark has been removed from a tree to perhaps make a coolamon.

He says that a steel axe, however, does a lot more damage to a

Uncle Tais on Country

tree, cutting the bark, leaving it vulnerable to fire. 'We only bruise the bark with a rock axe, and when the fire goes through here, all that [scarring] gets burned out, but the bark is still protecting the tree. Our old people knew all that, they had generations to learn all that.'

He takes the group to another tree and says, 'See the red sap coming out of that one, bleeding – if you had a wound on your body, you'd break it down, and then you find a medicine tree. You'll find another herb or plant close by and mix them both together as a medicine to heal the wound. My cousin still uses this today, as he had a problem with the nerves in his back. He was standing up on hot bitumen one day, without knowing it he didn't even realise, but he was standing on it, and it burned a hole in the base of his foot. So what he did, he said he got some of this stuff, and he crushed it down, it's not like a dust, it's like salt crystals. But then he used some other herbal stuff here with it and he applied it on there like that. He went to doctors, they wanted to do skin graft and everything on that leg. But he wanted to use bush medicine – and before he knew it, the sore started to heal up and the skin started to grow back again.'

Uncle Tais tells that people who come on his tours are extremely receptive to learning about First Nations cultures. 'Oh mate they are hungry. I think the biggest group I ever had in one day was 120.' He says it with pride, knowing that he is contributing to more awareness of his culture.

'That's why I started my own business, you know, my own company to do that, because I'm sick and tired of working for the so-called man, working for somebody else, when you can make your own decisions and choices.'

He then takes the group deeper into the bush and tells everyone to look around carefully at the trees and things. Then he says, 'If I can take that image in your mind and turn that image upside down and take the dirt away, you'll see all the roots connected. All the brown ones, green ones and yellow ones, they all look different. And yet they all survive.'

Then he asks, 'So why can't we do that?'

Then he tells everyone that they are now going to experience for themselves the spiritual side of the tour. 'To look with your spiritual eye and tell me what you see.'

Everyone is encouraged to look deeper into the land, and try to learn how to read the land, and perhaps consider looking deeper into their own land when they return home, and consider the ancestors and what they are thinking about how Country is being treated.

Everyone stares around, looking into the trees and the leaves and the shrubs, until eventually someone looks over at Uncle Tais and visibly startles. There is the face of an old man in the tree there above his head. Staring out of the bark. Something you don't notice at first, but once you see it, you can't not see it.

Uncle Tais tells that many of the trees around him have faces appearing in them, and points out some more. 'That's just the spiritual side of our culture, you know, that's why you've got to allow the scales on your eyes to drop away.'

He tells of how the spirts of the old people are coming back in the trees, because they are not happy with how people are living – chasing a material culture and not working on their spiritual culture.

'That's why them old people are looking. Because if we don't acknowledge them, or we don't recognise them, then there's no connection.'

The Kabi Kabi people (who were granted native title over 365,345 hectares of land and water on the Sunshine Coast in 2024) deeply understood the lands they lived on as they did not need to move around very far, nor often, having such an abundance of foods. The ocean and rivers provided fresh and saltwater un'dia (fish), yuan'gan (dugongs), yu'lu (eel), mib'ir (turtles) and shellfish. The wetlands provided many species of dhip'pi (birds) and their bam (eggs). And the bushlands provided both plants and animals, such as dha'roan (kangaroos), possums, dhun'kal (bandicoots), kun'ang (lizards), yams, waterlilies, figs, native plums and nan'gu (bunya nuts).

Especially important was the bunya feast, though it was much more than a feast or a festival as Western words describe it. It was an important time for the many tribes and clans to come together and discuss important topics, plan marriages or settle disputes. People camped in discrete locations reserved for their particular group, and took the opportunity to catch up with relatives, totemic relations, or friends from other clans or tribes. Such meetings needed to be held on land that was bountiful, so coinciding this with the bumper crop was necessary. The feast had been conducted for tens of thousands of years – with particular bunya trees being the responsibility of a particular person, and that responsibility being passed down from father to son – until it was disrupted by settlers and many of the ancient trees were tragically cut down.

Contact

After Cook's brief sail-by, the next known European visitor to the area was Matthew Flinders in 1799. He was also the first European to climb one of the mountains, climbing Beerburrum and visiting the base of Tibrogargan. He reported favourably on the local people he met.

He was followed by former convicts and castaways. Three that we know of were Thomas Pamphlett, John Finnegan and Richard Parsons. They were blown way off course in 1823 while trying to get from Sydney to the Illawarra. They finally landed on Mulgumpin (Moreton Island) and spent some time with the Ngugi people before crossing over to Minjerribah, and then making their way to the mainland. They were well treated by all the people they stayed with, and at one gathering Finnegan said there were so many huts that he could hardly count them.[6] They saw the river later renamed the Brisbane River, and when rescued by explorer John Oxley in 1823 they told him of the river, which led to it being chosen as the site for another convict settlement, Moreton Bay, in 1824.

Poor old Thomas Pamphlett, though, after surviving this ordeal was arrested back in Sydney for stealing flour, and sent to Moreton Bay with a seven-year sentence.

The penal settlement at Moreton Bay had several relocations, and mixed relations with the Turrbal and Yuggera people, whose land it was on. It started at present-day Redcliffe, and then moved to Cleveland before settling up the river where the current Brisbane city lies.

The second commandant of Moreton Bay, Captain Bishop, established good relations and undertook frequent trade with the Turrbal and Yuggera. However, in 1826 he was replaced by the sadistic Captain Logan. Logan was hated by the convicts and his own men, and often clashed with the First Peoples – ultimately leading to his death when he was attacked by the local people while exploring on his own in October of 1830.[7]

In 1839 the Moreton Bay penal colony was closed and in 1842 the area was opened up to free settlers, with the former convict barracks being rented out as accommodation. As settlers moved inland searching for pasture lands, conflict of course ensued, with tribes coming together to resist the settlers.[8] It was heroic resistance, but ultimately futile, as it was widely across Australia.

Kerry Neill's mother, Dr Hope O'Chin – Aunty Hope to those who know her well – is an acclaimed artist and educator. She was born into the dormitory system on Cherbourg mission, and rose to become a senior executive within the Queensland education system.

She says, 'Listen, we've got nothing against where you fellas all come from – but you're here. Our mob have always welcomed everybody onto their land. They've provided chaperoneship for everyone. That's what acknowledgement and welcome means, because that was civilly practised in ceremony right across the whole of this continent.'

She says she is proud to see so many people acknowledging Country now, but adds, 'I want to be reminded of what happened when we were ignored. We were persecuted and we were slaughtered when this country was invaded. I want to be reminded of that.' Then she clarifies, 'But not in a way that it eats me up. So that I can personally reach out to others. To share in empathy, you know.

'We can't turn back the waves of newcomers coming to this shore. They'll always come because people will always need to have a place of refuge, right across the world.'

In many places across Australia there were those settlers who really wanted to learn about the First Peoples of the land and find a way to live with them. This seems a suitable place to point out that not all settlers were motivated more by greed than humanitarian concerns. There were settlers who sheltered First Nations people on their runs. There were some who worked hard to understand their culture and learned some of the language. There were some who sheltered deserting native police. There were some who wrote outraged letters to the press when they became aware of atrocities.

One such person was Tom Petrie. Born in Edinburgh, he came to Australia when he was only a year old, and moved with his family to Moreton Bay in 1837. As he grew, he was allowed to mix freely with the local children and learned to speak the language of the Turrbal people. At the age of fourteen he was taken to a bunya festival and was accepted by many people there as a friend.

His father, Andrew Petrie, understood the importance of the bunya nuts and the bunya festival to the local people and was able to successfully persuade the enlightened Governor Gipps down in Sydney to make a proclamation protecting bunya trees. It was proclaimed in 1842 and limited European settlement on the bunya lands and forbade the felling of any bunya trees.

It seemed a great and progressive outcome. But tragically, in February that same year, as many as sixty members of the Giggabara clan of the Kabi Kabi were killed by flour laced with either strychnine or arsenic at Kilcoy station, west of the Glass House Mountains.[9] The shepherds who gave the poisoned flour were employed by Evan MacKenzie, the lessee of the station, who had been expecting a contingent of Scottish workers.[10] It has been conjectured that, fearing these workers would be put off by the presence of so many First People, he decided something needed to be done.[11] The murderous act has been described in terms that should bring shame to any descendants of those involved, as 'a desperate attempt to disperse a threatening and immovable indigenous multitude ... to ensure that this apprehensive but valuable addition to the Scottish labour force would remain at Kilcoy'.[12]

So at the next Bunya festival in the summer of 1842–43, the tribes met to discuss what they should do about the settlers and their violence. A decision was taken to actively resist settlers and their abuses of traditional laws. And this in turn meant that the newly formed Bunya Bunya reserve became a bastion from which the people launched their attacks on settlers.

The Kabi Kabi joined up with their northern neighbours, the Butchulla, to defend their lands, and from 1847 to 1853 an estimated twenty-eight squatters and shepherds were killed by them.[13] Ray Kerkhove, who has done in-depth studies of First Nations resistance, points out that the heightened awareness of massacres in recent years has tended to depict the First Peoples as helpless victims, when in fact they had clever tactics and were able to adapt them quickly to changing situations and advances in European weapons.[14]

Boe Spearim, a Gamilaraay and Kooma man, and the creator and host of the podcast *Frontier War Stories*, says of researching the frontier wars: 'the most important fact, you know, is that it overturns that myth that blackfellas didn't defend themselves, or we didn't have an organised resistance, and that we actually defeated whitefellas on many fronts in different parts of the country. We delivered genuine fear in the colonies.

'A surprising thing is, you know, mob didn't just sort of wipe those fellas out as they came. They gave them a chance and they said, "Look, don't you harm or hurt our women and children, don't destroy this part of the country." They let them know the areas that they can't go to. But the whitefellas they punished and stole and hurt and destroyed our land and our children and our women, and as a response to that the conflicts started.'

The settlers were outraged, of course, and in addition to complaining bitterly about the attacks by the local people, they were eyeing off the bunya lands and the timber of those glorious bunya pines.

So when in 1859 Queensland became an independent colony from New South Wales, almost immediately the government repealed the bunya proclamation. It was replaced by the *Unoccupied Crown Lands Occupation Act*, which brought a flood of settlers onto

First Nations lands, felling timber and clearing the land for stock and farming.

So resistance, by necessity, took a different turn, with individual resistance fighters waging guerilla war. These attacks were often described by settlers as one-man rampages, rather than heroic resistance, but the heroes of this period include the warriors Dundalli from the Dala clan of the Jinibara, Mundrobin and Moppy of the Yuggera, Eulope from Minjerribah (Stradbroke Island), and Billy Barlow from the Kabi Kabi.

Dundalli alone should be better known. He was chosen to lead retribution under customary law, after ongoing attacks and the mass poisoning of his people at Kilcoy pastoral station in 1842.[15] He led payback attacks – a form of restorative justice – for a decade, until he was finally captured in 1855. He was charged with several counts of murder and robbery, and was hanged before a large crowd at the site of the Brisbane General Post Office. He was the last person publicly executed in Queensland.

Other resistance fighters and outlaws who don't make the history books include Billy Lillis, Captain Piper and Kit Guru.[16] It is also shameful that most Australians can certainly name more North American First Nations resistance fighters than they can name those from their own country.

Boe Spearim said, 'We're talking about two different forces, two different ways to conduct war. In the British way it's, "We're here to claim this land, so if you don't listen to us and abide by the King's rule, we're just gonna kill you off." And the blackfellas, we had our own way and roles and structures, and battlegrounds to conduct these things on, which were overseen by a council of Elders.

'It wasn't necessarily about who won. It was about feeling that they got their chance. It was in a controlled space and usually ceremonies happened after, and if it wasn't too bad between individuals, maybe there was a marriage that happened.

Jinibara resistance warrior Dundalli

'And then these whitefellas came and they had no concept of this and would indiscriminately kill us. But a lot of the times we defeated them because it was on our terms.

'So in Toowoomba they have the Battle of One Tree Hill, where Jagera (Yugerra) mob had soldiers chasing them up the hill, and then they threw boulders and spears everything else at these fellas to defeat them and to force them back off the land.

'And we had Dundalli here in southeast Queensland, fighting up to a twelve-year resistance. Same as Pemulwuy and Yagan and Jandamarra, like all of these battles that we fought with these whitefellas was on our terms and we picked the ground we needed.'

But we know that the armed responses by government and settlers were able to eventually overwhelm even the most skilled resistance fighters, especially as more advanced guns started arriving in the colony. Killings, poisoning and massacres and then forced removals continued, as the numbers of Kabi Kabi and Jinibara diminished.

A Jinibara heritage study published in 2017 stated: 'The Jinibara People had to cope with the outcomes of resistance. Our clan numbers had been decimated. Our surviving people were restricted in where they could live, often having to retreat into mountains fringing our traditional Country which were still seen by non-indigenous settlers as having less economic value. Alternatively, people chose to stay on properties owned by settlers who allowed such occupation, usually because our people were a source of labour.'[17]

Ironically, Kilcoy station – site of the 1842 mass poisoning – became one of these safe properties where people could trade their labour for safety.

Uncle Tais K'Reala Randanpi said, 'Just north of us up here, there was a massacre up there. But instead of placing a memorial marker it has buildings on it.'

By 1895 the number of Kabi Kabi living on their lands was so small that some were already considering them a vanished people. High on that list was a scurrilous, self-proclaimed expert on First Nations people, Archibald Meston. We will get to him in more detail in later chapters, but it's worth knowing for now that he was a self-educated, self-styled and self-important anthropologist and journalist who was eventually given the completely inappropriately titled role, Protector of Aborigines. Waxing lyrical on the Glass House Mountains, he wrote: 'The wild savages who roamed the pathless forests and sang their peace songs and war songs beneath the shadows of those grey trachyte rocks, cores of the old volcanoes, have vanished forever, bequeathing to us, as their last legacy, only those immortal rock sculptures from the studio of mighty Nature.'[18]

But they hadn't quite vanished forever. They had largely all been forcibly removed from their lands and relocated to Cherbourg and other missions.

Uncle Tais then turns to healing. He leads the small group he is teaching down to a stony creek. It is much cooler under the shade of tall trees. He tells that this is where his great-great-grandparents lived, sharing his deep connection to that land there. Then he asks everyone to find a bit of red ochre on the ground somewhere, which he says is a type of old ancestor's blood that is still in the land. He paints the men and women's faces with the red ochre, and shares how it represents a family totem, the wedge-tailed eagle.

Standing there by that creek you get a feeling of what a very, very ancient place it is. Then Uncle Tais has each person share a secret moment, standing at just a particular spot, and you feel welcomed by the ancestors there, and he tells that you'll always be a part of the land there after going through that ceremony.

It is such a confusing mix of emotions that everyone is quiet on the walk back up to the wooden benches where all the conversations started, and where the final questions are asked and answered. It feels like so much time has passed and everyone has come out of the bush with a little more understanding. More willing to look and listen. More willing to have a different perspective on what connection to Country means.

When asked about Cook, Uncle Tais tells, 'A lot of the Australian history is built on shifting sands. Botany Bay and what I see with that is the first seed they sowed when they put their big foot on the beaches, there was this – they sowed the seed of divide and conquer. And that tree has been growing ever since they hit that beach. And with the system, with their negativity and criticism, it actually waters that seed, whether it's black against black, black against white, white against black, white against white. That seed of divide and conquer has been growing ever since they put their foot on that beach and we need to come back and uproot those weeds.

'And the only way we can do that is with the strength of allowing us to sit at the table of decisions, to make decisions for the betterment of everyone in going forward. And that goes for everybody. That's the only way I see Australia going ahead.'

And Kerry Neill, when asked what he most wanted white Australians to know about his mob, says, 'What I would want people to know is that a lot of us, especially in my own particular family, have a connection to Country that goes back – it's indescribable – and connection to Country for us is not a straight line. It's not a geographical location. It doesn't have a start or a beginning. It's more like a sphere.

'It includes lots of different things. The sky and the water and trees and wind, and knowing that all things are alive. And, you know, the reality is humans need the Earth more than it needs us.

'And I think that knowing that is something that is super-important, and it's our responsibility to be reminded of that mortality and our connection, and our responsibilities to look after the Country.'

And Uncle Tais answers with, 'So come and visit us. Come and talk with us. Come and sit with us, and you will know that it's not just coming from a book. Mate, them days are over.

'It's no good just looking at one blackfella or black woman and say, "Oh, well, I know their story," and then have a generalised idea for the whole of the nation. No, it doesn't work that way.

'Come and sit down with us. Come and talk to us, and then you will know about our mob. Come and talk to each and every one of us to find out.'

K'gari (Fraser Island)
Butchulla Country

Galangoor djali! Galangoor.
Butchulla bilam, midiru K'gari galangoor nyin djaa.
Ngalmu galangoor Biral and Biralgan bula nyin djali!
Wanya nyin yangu, wanai djinang djaa.

Good day. Welcome!
Butchulla people, Traditional Custodians of K'gari, welcome you to Country.
May all our good spirits be around you throughout the day.
Wherever you go leave only footprints.[1]

From this last the land Trends a little more to the Westward, and is low and Sandy next the Sea, for what may be behind it I know not ...
                                    Cook's journal, 20 May 1770

Cook was now sailing past the largest sand island in the world, but could not distinguish it from the mainland and so drew it on his map as a cape. Sailing north from the Glass House Mountains, he had already renamed the peninsula of Double Island Point, just south of the island. He wrote it looked 'like two small islands lying under the land'. So a bit of country that was actually a point looked to him like islands, and the bit of country that was actually an island looked to him like a point. I think you get the point yourself by now, about Cook's distorted view of the land.

Anyway, he went for a plain and simple name for the wide bay that swung around from that point – Wide Bay.

He was also limited in his understanding of nature and landscape by the understandings of eighteenth-century natural science. Thus he described the island he was viewing as 'of moderate height, appears more barren than any we have seen on this coast, and the

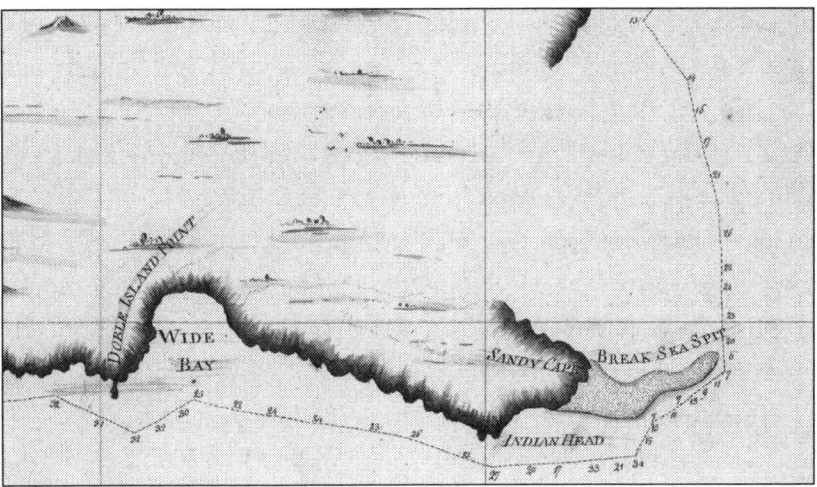

Cook's chart of Butchulla Country

soil more sandy, there being several large places where nothing else is to be seen'.

A more contemporary scientific view of the island has it that for hundreds of thousands of years sand had been carried up the coast from the Hawkesbury, Hunter and Clarence rivers, accumulating on the volcanic bedrock that provided a natural catchment. Such a view would also state that the island is currently about 125 kilometres long and 22 kilometres wide, but that between 20,000 and 10,000 years ago it may have been a part of the mainland, when the coast was about 25 kilometres further to the east.

To the Butchulla people the island is the physical form of the spirit princess K'gari. The Creation story tells that Beerall, the great God in the sky, made all the people, but after having done so he realised that the people had no lands. So Beerall sent a messenger, named Yindingie, to create lands for the people. Yindingie came down from the sky and set to work making the sea and the land, and when he reached the land that is now known as Hervey Bay, he had a helper – the beautiful white spirit Princess K'gari.

K'gari helped Yindingie make the seashores, the mountain ranges, as well as the lakes and the rivers. She enjoyed her work so much that she worked tirelessly to create all this natural beauty. One day, however, Yindingie became concerned and said to her, 'K'gari, you had better rest, otherwise you will be too tired to continue our work. There are some rocks over there in the sea. Why don't you go and lie down and have a sleep?'

So Princess K'gari lay down on the rocks and fell into a long and deep sleep. When she finally awoke she asked Yindingie, 'I think this is the most beautiful place we have ever created. Please, Yindingie, may I stay here forever?'

But Yindingie said, 'Oh no, I cannot allow that. You are a spirit, and you belong with me!' But K'gari pleaded with him, until he agreed. And K'gari still lies there looking at the beautiful land they created.[2]

When Cook sailed past the rocky cliffs that rise unexpectedly out of the K'gari sand beaches, he renamed them Indian Head, not knowing that they were one of the rock formations K'gari had laid her head upon – known as Takky Wooroo. He chose that name, he wrote, because at 10pm on 20 May, he could clearly see 'a number of the Natives were Assembled' on that high rocky headland.

Luke Barrowcliffe is a Butchulla Traditional Custodian, and is the manager of Studio K'gari, a sub-company of Butchulla Enterprises Limited. Luke is a deep thinker, and has spent a lot of time considering what Cook wrote about his ancestors, and what his ancestors were doing on the sacred headland watching him. He has even considered how much light there might have been, finding that on that date over 250 years ago there had been a waning crescent moon that would have provided about 30 per cent of the illumination of a full moon.

He said, 'On a moonlit night it's incredible how bright the light is on the Back Beach. I've been on the beach a few times during a full moon, and it's just like you're in the main street of Brisbane. Like it's just that lit up.'

He also said his people would have known of Cook's arrival from smoke signals being passed up the coast, and would have assembled to see who or what the ship was. The Butchulla actually wrote a song about the coming of the *Endeavour* that has been preserved. It goes:

Gabrin wuna'la yaneen, Areeram
Ngun'gu'ni wiinj gung'milung
Nyundal wun'yamba dhali dhak'kin'bah, Gebeer barine
Moomoo gumbir'l'im bundi burree, Yauwa dhan man'ngur
Yuang yangu moomoo gumbir, Billi'ngunda
Tin'gera dan'da gung'mungalum minya?

There are several translations of the song into English, and one was recorded by Edward Armitage, an Irish-born timber-getter and skipper, who recorded the original song and a translation in 1923:

These strangers, where are they going?
Where are they trying to steer;
They must be in that place, Breaksea spit, it is true.
See the smoke coming in from the sea.
These men must be burying themselves like the sand crabs.
They disappeared like the smoke.[3]

Other translations state that the ship was 'breathing smoke rhythmically from its rear', but the general meaning is similar – who on earth were these strangers and why were they heading to the dangerous shoals at the end of the island?[4]

Or as Luke Barrowcliffe put it simply, 'Before Cookie the only visitors we had were from the mainland, and when he turned up it was like, "What is this thing and how did it get out there?"'

According to Luke Barrowcliffe there were between 2,000 to 3,000 Butchulla people living on K'gari, and on nearby parts of the mainland, when Cook sailed past. Across the wider island, he said there were six tribes, though he acknowledges that others

Takky Wooroo/Indian Head

state there were only three tribes: the Dulingbara to the south, the Ngulungbara of the north, and the Butchulla of the central regions.

He takes cultural tours across the island, working with the Indigenous Rangers, travelling across the thick forest to the wilder west coast where four-wheel drivers have churned the sand into many channels of tyre tracks. He looks wistfully at the impacts of the vehicles and tells how life was lived on the island in the older times, and how important it is to comply with the three Butchulla laws, first documented by Wondunna Elder Olga Miller:

* Minyang galangoor gu djaa, kalim baya-m – What is good for the land comes first.
* Minyang waa nyinung, waa bunmalee dhama-n – Do not take or touch anything that does not belong to you.
* Wangou nyin gamindu biralunbar, nyin wumga-n – If you have plenty, you must share.

Luke said his deep knowledge of Butchulla traditional life and lore was given to him over several years by Olga Miller, who held pre-contact knowledge of Butchulla society, history and culture taught to her by her grandfather.

'We had an Elders' hierarchy or council who would meet and make the decisions on behalf of the whole group. Whatever they said went. There was no discussion about it.

'We were a fairly gender-segregated society and had men's and women's areas, and even within the clan group structure, you know, men and women would spend most of the time separate.

'Usually marriages were set up, not decided by the individuals themselves, also making sure they were keeping the bloodlines and the genes strong.

'So when you think about that level of understanding and knowledge of your societal makeup, your level of thinking is so much more strategic. You're thinking about seven generations ahead and we need to make sure this person marries this person, and then their kids marry this from this mob.'

Luke also said that each clan group of the Butchulla had a different responsibility to manage for the whole group.

Luke Barrowcliffe on K'gari

'We had a clever women's clan beside the women's area, where the birthing ground is. We had the clever men's clan, which was beside the men's area. There were hunter and fishermen clans. The clan land areas continued across the Great Sandy Strait onto the adjacent mainland as well, and the roles and responsibilities were across all of Country. So the fishermen's clan, they maintained all the fish traps, but they didn't actually have any fish traps on their clan lands. All the fish traps were essentially on other people's clan lands, but that was their responsibility.'

Luke said that, like the bunya gatherings in the Bunya Mountains, there would be a tailor fish gathering on the east coast of K'gari, that other tribes would come for. 'A message would be sent out. There were also environmental indicators – the wattle flower – so people knew when to start walking.'

For the Butchulla, when the cicada shed its skin it indicated it was time to go to the bunya gathering. 'It probably took a couple of weeks if you were going hard every day, but if you're meeting people and stopping to do ceremony it could take a month. And then the same here for the tailor, people would be over here for a couple of months. So there's this constant movement of people through the landscape, all across Australia.'

But, he added, things changed with Native Title, where there was an attitude of 'that's our boundary and don't you talk on behalf of our people and Country'. He said in the old times you might still know where the boundary was, and there would be a process about how you entered a neighbour's territory, but it was a bit more friendly. 'You were all living off the land together.'

K'gari is renowned for its over one hundred freshwater lakes and many streams. Luke said that fresh water was almost endless. 'The purest waters are in the creeks that come out all along the beaches. It's from the rain, and then the sand filters it.

'I often talk about our diet being mainly seafood, and then the fruits, nuts and berries from the rainforest. But we had to go to the mainland for that bigger game, the red meats, the kangaroo, the emu. So our diet was not your three veg and one meat a day. The cycle of your diet is a twelve-month thing, not a daily thing. Same for the mobs out west who would come here for their seafood.'

Evidence of the abundance of seafood can be found in the 200 or more shell middens found on the island, dating back more than 5,000 years.

With several different ecosystems on the island, ranging from ocean to rainforest, each provided different foodstuffs, and Luke said pipis were hugely abundant on the ocean side of the island and were very easy to gather. Many Butchulla lived on the island fulltime, and would have followed what was in season at any given time.

Takky Wooroo is still a sacred place, a pale rocky headland well covered with vegetation that rises out across the long flat sand beach. It is one of three headlands all within a short distance of each other, the other two being Champagne Pool and Waddy Point. Each is a rare rise of rock on the otherwise sand-covered island.

Before going up on the headland, Luke undertakes a ceremony – smoking and ochre painting, one wide stripe across the forehead – to ensure the old people will protect any visitors he is bringing from any harm. But women and children cannot go onto Takky Wooroo.

Whales in the ocean below Takky Wooroo

From the clifftop, where Luke's ancestors stood, there is a strong feeling of their presence. Of being looked after by them. And it is possible to look down and see turtles, whales and sharks swimming in the turquoise waters far below, as the ancestors would have seen them. And looking out to sea, it is easy to imagine how out of place the *Endeavour* would have been there, and that it demanded some explanation, some song.

It is a privilege to be allowed onto Takky Wooroo.

Coming down off the headland, we meet a family of five tourists on their way up. They are stopped by one of the Butchulla rangers, Dwayne 'Bob' Broome, who tells them politely that the headland is closed to random visitors. The eldest man in the family bridles at this and insists he has been coming up onto the headland for many years, and wants to know when it was closed off.

Bob tells him that he can go ahead up the headland if he really wants to, but it will cost him a thousand-dollar fine, and he points to the sign indicating it is a restricted area. The man bridles some more and his wife and children try and convince him to respect the request not to go onto a sacred area.

Luke says, 'For some people it's really doing their head in. They can't handle it. Like our mate saying he's been coming up here for thirty years, you can't stop me!'

The sense of entitlement of some tourists is frustrating – driving and camping where they like, taking over places once restricted to the Council of Elders.

Luke said, 'We're still grappling with this contemporary use of our traditional Country.' And then added that it shouldn't be that hard for people, as they've still got 150 kilometres of beach to play on.

The second European known to have visited K'gari was Matthew Flinders, who actually visited three times. But the history of K'gari is most closely linked to the visitor whose name the island bore for many decades, Eliza Fraser. However, trying to find the truth of her story is like trying to find a particular shell amongst a vast midden.

The story starts with another shipwreck. The *Stirling Castle* was on its way from Hobart to Singapore in 1836 when it struck a reef off present-day Rockhampton. The eighteen survivors, including Eliza Fraser and her sickly and incompetent husband, Captain James Fraser, took to the ship's longboats – along with his invaluable writing desk! They drifted for five weeks, before reaching the shores of K'gari.

No real spoilers in telling you that Eliza Fraser was eventually rescued. The trouble is that with each retelling, the story got more sensational, as did the titles of the accounts of it, such as the 1838 publication by John Curtis: *Shipwreck of the Stirling Castle: containing a faithful narrative of the dreadful sufferings of the crew and the cruel murder of Captain Fraser by the savages: also, the horrible barbarity of the cannibals inflicted upon the captain's widow whose unparalleled sufferings she stated by herself, and corroborated by the other survivors* ...[5]

In one account the survivors are captured by the Butchulla people and forced to work for them, with her husband being taken away and speared to death. Then there is the story of her being pregnant and having a baby onboard the ship's boat, who tragically drowned soon after birth. And in many accounts the Butchulla are cruel savages and cannibals, and regularly beat her, and even kicked her out of their shelters when she attempted to enter to escape rain.

Eliza Fraser stated of her treatment by the Butchulla: 'I was visited by a very great number of their squaws, accompanied by their children, who first commenced with a close examination of my person, then to beating and maiming me with clubs, and, at the same time encouraging their children to follow their example, to pinch me, to pull my hair and to throw dirt into my face and eyes ...'[6]

Fortunately for those trying to find the truth in her narratives, we not only have the stories of some of the other survivors, but the stories of the Butchulla people. Firstly, there is the account of one of the survivors, Robert Darge, who with five others chose to leave the shipwreck party and walk to Moreton Bay to seek help. He stated of the Butchulla: 'I cannot call them a cruel people.'[7] And survivor Harry Youlden wrote years later: 'The wife of the captain ... was a terrible liar, and the most profane, artful, wicked woman that ever lived.'[8]

And in 1874, Archibald Meston – that so-called Protector of Aborigines – seemed to have gotten it right for once, when after speaking to some Elders at K'gari, including some who had seen Eliza Fraser when they were younger, wrote an account of her time on the island. He reported that they told him that the shipwreck survivors were received in a friendly manner, and were passed on in canoes to the mainland, where they could make their way to the other white people at the convict settlement at Moreton Bay. Meston wrote of Eliza Fraser: 'she must have either had a serious quarrel with truth or else her head was badly affected by her experiences. Certainly she gave a wildly improbable tale in Brisbane, accusing the blacks of deeds quite foreign to their known character, and quite unheard of before or since in aboriginal annals.'[9]

And despite her hogging the headlines, there had actually been other European visitors to K'gari in the years before Eliza Fraser, mainly runaways from Moreton Bay. The first of these was probably James Davis, who escaped in 1820 and lived with the Butchulla for some time. He was known to the people as Thuribis, the reincarnated son of an Elder who had been killed in battle several years earlier.[10]

That escapees were considered returned spirits of the dead is important to understanding Eliza Fraser's story, for in Butchulla culture a dead person would have their outer skin cut away, exposing the white flesh underneath. Certain ceremonies were then conducted, and the body buried in the sand and the spirit allowed to travel up to the skies.[11]

So a more realistic telling of her story is that when the white people arrived on the beach like spirits from the ocean, the Butchulla people were hesitant about approaching them, but as the survivors walked down the beach of the island they engaged in barter with them, trading food for their clothing. When all their tradeable clothing was gone, the survivors were then taken into the tribe and separated, given into the care of different families so as to lessen the strain on resources. And they were expected to perform the normal tasks required of a member of the tribe, such as fetching wood and water, and, for Eliza, minding the children.

But being nervous of their possible status as spirits, the Butchulla would have kept them out of their shelters. Also, as Eliza proved increasingly unable to do her share of work, she would have been derided and teased, particularly by the children.

And Eliza, used to a different type of life and being well treated as a captain's wife, was unable to see this as anything other than cruel and barbaric treatment, fuelling her anger and disrespect of the Butchulla, which she seemed more than happy to cash in on when she was finally rescued.

Butchulla scholar Rose Barrowcliffe has said that Eliza Fraser was known to be a sensationalist, who made her story more and more salacious as time went on in efforts to garner more money from sympathetic supporters. This had a long-term effect of contributing to Indigenous peoples being vilified around the globe.[12]

And First Nations author Larissa Behrendt has said, 'It would be easy to dismiss Eliza as a racist but I think she is more complex than that. She was resilient, surviving a shipwreck that killed several others ... Yes, she believed in her own cultural and racial superiority, considered Aboriginal people to be barbaric and savage, was dismissive of their knowledge and technology, and was ungrateful for their help. But in a lot of these attitudes, Eliza was simply a product of her time and reflected the prevailing views of the day.'[13]

Another story where fact and fancy were too easily blurred is the so-called white girls of Fraser Island. In 1859 rumours of two shipwrecked white girls who were living with the Butchulla on K'gari began circulating. On the back of Eliza Fraser's wild stories of the callous ill-treatment she experienced at the Butchulla's hands, the good citizens of the colony were determined to protect those young girls from such hands. The colonial government in Sydney offered a £400 reward to have the girls returned.

The rescue expedition found two light-skinned girls, aged about twelve and eighteen, near Takky Wooroo, and paid money to their people in order to take them back to Sydney, promising they would only be gone for two months. However, it soon became evident they were both half-caste children and spoke no English. But rather than being returned, the girls were kept in the migration centre at Sydney.[14] 'Kitty' Mundi, the eldest of the two, was said to have suffered severe mental distress and died there soon after. The other girl, 'Maria' Quoheen, survived in Sydney for about twenty years. But she was never returned to K'gari.

To add colonial insult to injury, the money paid to the Butchulla for the girls turned out to be commemorative coins, not legal tender, leading to worsened relations with all white settlers.

Callous ill-treatment indeed.

Contact

Six years after the Eliza Fraser incident, in 1842, colonial authorities decided to close the convict settlement in Moreton Bay and open up Queensland for free settlement. Scottish engineer Andrew Petrie (father of Tom Petrie, mentioned in the chapter 'Beerwah & Tibrogargan') is credited with reporting on the vast timber reserves on K'gari in 1842, and later established a sawmill on the island. Meanwhile settlers travelled up the Mary River (Moonaboola) and soon established the town of Maryborough as a good port. Immediately there were clashes between the people and the settlers, which led to the first known massacre of Butchulla people.

Luke Barrowcliffe said there were stories of at least two massacres – that we know of – on the mainland, and as more and more settlers continued to arrive they pushed the Butchulla and other people off their lands, killing their game and clearing the land.

One old settler, James Fairlie, described how the whites, 'in taking their lands and felling the scrubs, made it difficult, almost impossible, for them to live in their native way. The scrubs, in which for ages they had hunted wallabies and dug yams, were destroyed and the trees, in many places felled into the river, prevented them from fishing with their nets along the riverbanks close to the mangroves on which the mullet found food.'[15]

In 1849 people started settling K'gari, and of course violence on both sides grew. Eventually the dreaded native police were called in. On Christmas Eve 1851, Commandant Frederick Walker and twenty-four native policemen travelled to the island with the intent of arresting some Butchulla. They spent eleven days on the island, engaged in what was euphemistically called 'dispersing'.

According to historian Jonathan Richards, one party tracked a group of Indigenous people across the island to the east coast, where they pursued them into the open ocean near Takky Wooroo, which was described in the subsequent report as being 'dispersed into the sea'.[16] But Luke Barrowcliffe said that there was recent research that suggested the massacre may have happened further to the south. He said his mother had a really odd experience one day on one of the sand dunes further south. 'She was just walking along the track, just walking, and the next thing she just heard a gunshot. And a man, one of our mob, fell out onto the sand in front of her, and she turned around to look where the bullet had come from, and she's seen a settler with a gun hiding back in the bushes.'

Butchulla artist and academic Dr Fiona Foley, who has explored many aspects of colonialism in her work, wrote, '[We] were not allowed to bury our dead after massacres had taken place. I believe this country carries deep wounds from the trauma of these frontier wars. We carry it inside our souls, whether we are conscious of them or not. The brutality, in turn, has also affected the perpetrators and their descendants. Many oral histories of genocide are carried, in the living memory, by Aboriginal people.'[17]

And Luke Barrowcliffe said, 'As you know, all those native police were brought in from outside areas. And our oral history is that we had all these black trackers. We had this sentimental thing that they were black trackers, but they were really just native police.' He said he had talked to historian Jonathan Richards, who has done extensive research into the native police – about why there was often little choice for people recruited into the native police, and also the attraction it had for young men. 'You can take off and go bush and forget everything you knew, and hide out, or you can become a native policeman. You get a horse, you get a uniform, you get a gun.'

One of the rangers who works with Luke Barrowcliffe, Dwayne 'Bob' Broome, said that he was related to a member of the native police, who was in fact one of the six troopers taken down to Victoria to track Ned Kelly in 1888 – with the promise of 50 pounds in payment.

Wannamutta was born on K'gari in 1855, and was taken from his family by Constable Thomas King at the age of fourteen and put to work as a trooper in the Queensland Native Mounted Police. He later changed his name to Jack Noble, and was first sent to Rockhampton where he took part in massacres. Young men like Wannamutta were treated harshly, and if they deserted, their fellow troopers would hunt them down and kill them. It has been estimated that in the sixty years they operated, the Queensland Native Mounted Police killed between 24,000 and 60,000 people.[18]

It is a difficult thing for First Nations people to know that their ancestors were members of the native police, and descendants have talked about trying to understand how they were victims of the colonial system themselves, often being young and impressionable when they were recruited, and then finding themselves in a system they could not get out of.

Jack Noble was one of the few who did get out of the force, though his direct descendant, Dr Galiina Ellwood, says it is difficult for his descendants when he continues to be used as a poster boy for the Queensland Native Mounted Police, while the other important parts of his life are ignored. In 1889, after twenty years in the force, Jack left and returned to K'gari, living on the Bogimbah

Jack Noble and wife Alberta at Yarrabah in 1902, when he was out of the force but still wearing his uniform

mission there. The mission – set up by the 'protector' Archibald Meston – proved a complete failure. As the number of people there steadily increased, being sent from across the regions, the mission was unable to properly support them. It was described as a hellhole of deprivation, lacking medical supplies, food and shelter, and when it was closed in 1904 the residents, including Jack, were sent to other missions.[19]

And Archibald Meston went on to another failure when he attempted to mimic Buffalo Bill's Wild West Show, with his Wild Australia Show, using First Nations people as living exhibits. The show toured Brisbane, Sydney and Melbourne, where Meston attempted to pass off the twenty-two participants as untouched by European influences. However, he ran out of money in Melbourne and deserted the troupe there.

By 1905 it was estimated that there were fewer than thirty Butchulla people left on K'gari, and they were soon sent away to reserves and missions too. Jack and his wife Alberta (a Nunukul/Ngugi woman from Minjerribah and Mulgumpin) were sent to Yarrabah mission, near Cairns, where they encouraged other Butchulla people to abscond from the mission. Jack spent his last years a virtual prisoner of the state, being moved from one mission or reserve to another, and died at the age of eighty, while living with his younger sister Nora Krotandi at Pialba, within sight of his birthland K'gari but unable to travel there.

Neither he nor his descendants were ever paid the 50 pound reward he had been promised for taking part in the hunt for Ned Kelly.

Looking at the link between Cook and colonialism, Luke Barrowcliffe said, 'I think the problem with Cook is much broader than Cook. The problem with Cook was the British government using him as the vehicle to go around and claim other people's country around the world. It was obviously a very cunning and deliberate tactic of them to grow their wealth and their land assets.

'So to me Cook was the messenger, you know, he was just doing his job. But he was doing his job for the British. So I think that the root problem for me is still the British, and that they've still got an obligation to fix all this mess they made around the world, particularly with Indigenous people.'

Explaining his mob's relationship to K'gari, Luke said, 'It's like owning a house. You know, when you get home and you unlock the door and you walk inside. Coming to K'gari is just like that for us. Every time we come here, it just feels like home and we're supposed to be here, and we're supposed to be maintaining it. We're supposed to be looking after it. And I think if people can understand that, they might start to respect our place and purpose here.'

He said that restoring the island's name of K'gari was definitely a key turning point, a key milestone in reclaiming Country. Though he said that gaining native title was not as beneficial as it is often made out to be. 'Everyone thought, we got native title, we're right now. But nah, it's just a new phase of the fight. We couldn't build a house anywhere. We can put up a tent wherever we want, but we can't build a house.'

Under the Queensland government's *Aboriginal Land Act*, however, Luke has been able to apply for unallocated state land, which he sees as the start of being able to sustainably return to the island. 'Reparation for me is having concrete land that we can live on again, that we can use for commercial enterprise, and we can redevelop our presence, we can revitalise our culture on these blocks. Whereas prior to that, we're restricted to just playing visitors ourselves. We can set up a camp. Stay for a few days, then we've gotta go back home.'

But there will be a lot of work to do on Country as well. Invasive weeds. Trees growing across the midden grounds. Thick ground

Wongari on K'gari

cover that presents a bushfire risk. Over 300,000 tourists a year – with some of them disrespecting Country.

Luke said that one sign that the Country misses the people is in the aggressive behaviour of the wongaris (dingoes). 'You know the troubled wongaris don't have their leaders, because our presence is not back here yet so we can keep an eye on them. They're part of our ceremonial process as well. They're part of our hunting processes. They're part of just our everyday life, so them playing up is just a symptom of them saying, we're missing our proper owners still.'

He also said getting back on Country and practising culture would not just benefit the land, but would benefit a lot of Butchulla people. 'I think it can go a long way to improving the circumstances of all our mob who are lost. They're just lost, and they don't know how to get out of it. I think the ceremonial process just opens their eyes a bit more and gives them a chance to recalibrate their whole thinking of life. That connection to those ceremonial places and the purposes of those ceremonies that were done there.

'All Butchulla want is to live and work and to be able to practise culture on Country again. I'm not asking for that much. Surely it can't be that hard.'

Gooragang (Bustard Bay)
Gooreng Gooreng Country

Wunyungar!
Barrarrbee buhrye gamardin thdou yallarm.
Nallindo ohwhy waybare yearee dullgim.
Gothoo goongoo thungool.
Yungoo burrarns wungmerries wubbarn.
Wunee yoongim ngye boogair.
Woogoo ngye yumgoo nullindoo buhrye.

Welcome to our Country!
Creator God is the owner of this land, this place of shells.
This is our home.
It gave us our meat, our bread and our water, before the white men and white women came.
In the past we were left behind and forgotten.
Now we want to walk together and share what the future holds.[1]

In the A.M. I went ashore with a party of men in order to Examine the Country, accompanied by Mr. Banks and the other Gentlemen ...
Cook's journal, 23 May 1770

After rounding a large shoal north of K'gari, that Cook renamed Breaksea Spit, the crew found very smooth waters, and sailing back towards the land they found the ocean so calm they could see the sand of the ocean's bottom deep below them. Ahead was a smooth, sheltered bay and Cook decided to go ashore there and explore a little and search for fresh water.

It had been not yet three weeks since the *Endeavour* left Kamay but Cook was already starting to look for a place to reprovision their water supplies. The *Endeavour* carried large quantities of drinking water in barrels, and while the water could be stored for many months, it could become quite undrinkable without adding alcohol to make it more palatable. In fact, the men's daily ration of alcohol was one gallon of beer, or one and a half pints of wine that was watered down, or half a pint of spirits watered down.² Needless to say, drunkenness could be quite common among the crew, though generally only punishable if it happened while on duty.³

On the morning of 23 May they took two of the ship's boats ashore. Banks first complained of the chill of the wind, but once ashore complained of the heat, writing that the sun had 'recoverd its influence'.

This was only the second place they had stepped upon the land of this continent, and Cook took note of the sand, grasses and mangroves and judged the land here as 'visibly worse' than that at Botany Bay, with dry sandy soils.

The local people naturally had a different opinion.

Cook took one boat up an inlet to the south of the bay, and while those in the other boat tried to catch fish, Cook found a large lagoon with a freshwater spring where they could fill the ship's casks. Banks, meanwhile, turned his attention to gathering plants and commenting on the wildlife. He wrote: 'On the shore were many birds, one species of Bustard, of which we shot a single bird as

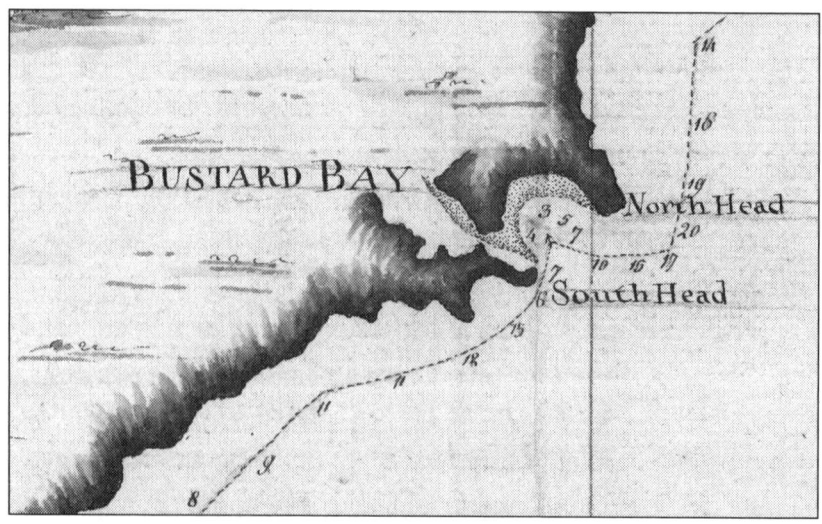

Cook's chart of Gooreng Gooreng Country

large as a good Turkey. The sea seemd to abound in fish ... on the mud banks under the mangrove trees were innumerable Oysters ...'

Cook wrote that while they saw no people, there was a lot of smoke on the west side of the lagoon, indicating their presence.

And present they were. Carefully watching these newcomers to their land. The people whose land this was knew the area as Gooragang – which means 'sandy loam country'. That is, a type of sandy soil that is good for grasses to grow on. It was also an area that was important to the people's songlines, being ceremony Country.

Cook led his party a little further inland, and came across ten small fires in a campground. They looked around and found cockleshells, showing there had been a recent meal eaten there. But the people were gone.

Banks approached the largest campfire and found it was still burning. So he knew the people had obviously seen them coming and hid. He then noted some bark vessels, and correctly surmised that they were for holding water. Nearby the fires they also found many pieces of soft bark about the size of a man. 'These we supposd to be their beds,' Banks wrote. He also wrote that they saw no signs of a house or anything like the ruins of one, but from the ground being much trodden, they concluded that the people had been here for some time, and slept in the outdoors.

And while the people chose not to appear and confront the strangers to their land, the local insects had no such hesitation. Banks described an encounter with the fierce green ants there: 'upon the sides of the lagoon grew many Mangrove trees in the branches of which were many nests of Ants ... These when the branches were disturbd came out in large numbers and revengd themselves very sufficiently upon their disturbers, biting sharper than any I have felt in Europe.'

He was even attacked by a caterpillar. He wrote, 'The mangroves also had another trap which most of us fell into', and described the caterpillar as behaving like a 'wrathful militia' when disturbed, and said the short hairs on their bodies stung more acutely than nettles.

Meanwhile, the men who'd gone fishing were totally unsuccessful in catching any fish, but they were able to return to the ship with the bustard they had shot. It was cooked for the officers and naturalists' dinner, and Banks declared it 'far the best ... that we have eat since we left England'.

And it was this bustard that clearly stuck so firmly in Cook's mind, above anything else they saw that day, because he renamed the place Bustard Bay.

The land that the men of the *Endeavour* thought sandy and barren was able to well provide for the Gurang clan of the Gooreng Gooreng people. Many plants provided foods across the seasons of the year, often things the Europeans did not even recognise as food. The fruit of the mangrove trees, for example, was eaten by being pounded, rinsed and then baked into a damper.

The men employed many methods in the capture of animals and birds for their food, never taking more than they needed. Such lore included the knowledge that booroo (kangaroos) disliked travelling over freshly burned grass, so large areas were burned and hunters then concealed themselves in trees in the small unburnt areas, over which the animals would then travel. Bustards were also captured using fire. A circle of grass was fired around them and as they became confused in the smoke they were easier to catch. All a part of fire knowledge.

Fish were caught on lines using fishhooks made from shells, or in stone fish traps or by using fish poisons. Two of the most effective poisons, plentiful in coastal areas, were cockatoo apple and the red ash. The pulped bark and leaves were placed in the water and the fish were dead in about twenty minutes. The bark of some other trees only stupefied but did not kill the fish.[4]

Gooragang headland and the stream Cook explored

For travelling out onto the reefs to catch fish, the people made canoes from a single piece of bark that had been removed from a paperbark tree. Sharp rocks were used to slowly separate a thick slab of bark, it could then be folded into a canoe, with sticks or twine used to join the ends.

The area where Cook landed, Gooragang, is now the site of a township called Seventeen Seventy. (Yes, really!) It is a popular holiday location, with one of the best ice-cream shops along the coast. But long before that, it had always been a special place to the people of the area, and its stories have been passed down through songlines because it is where fresh water can be obtained and where the old people, or ancestors, crossed over into the spirit world. Today Gooragang is a part of Joseph Banks Regional Park. Named after a man who didn't even spend a full day ashore there and was attacked by insects.

The stretch of coast to the north and south of the township of Seventeen Seventy is these days known as the Port Curtis Coral Coast, and has four Traditional Owner clans: Byellee (or Bailal, to the north), the Gurang, the Gooreng Gooreng, and the Taribelang (to the south).

Traditionally, every few years the clans would travel to the bunya festival further south. Carved message sticks were used to give notification of such festivals, and also allowed the bearer to cross different borders, like a passport. These days the clans still come together for festivals, but the nature of the festivals has changed somewhat.

Festival dancer

In May of each year there is a commemorative festival held at the small town of Seventeen Seventy, with cultural performances and a re-enactment of Cook's landing on the shore. It is fairly popular with the locals and people from around the state. But the 1770 Cultural Connections Immersion Festival, held in September/October is what really brings mob out in big numbers. It attracts some whitefellas, but nothing like the Cook re-enactment festival does. It's a pity. You can learn a hell of a lot about First Nations culture, politics and other issues just by attending events like this.

Held over two days, it features First Nations arts and crafts, and dancers and singers from across the state, sharing their culture and competing with each other. The show-off dances, where the youngsters get to show their best moves, have to be seen to be really appreciated, and they drive the crowds to ecstatic applause. Some of the performers travel over 1500 kilometres to get there, determined to be the best they can be.

After the initial settling in and squaring off, people are very friendly, wanting to know who your people are, and if they find they are married into your mob they might invite you to share a fish with them that they just caught out on the ocean. And that's a welcoming thing too. Then you can pull up a chair and sit under a tree and talk about the different things both your people have gone through.

Under the shade of the large marquee people sit around tables, listening, keen to share their stories and culture. They tell that as far as the name Seventeen Seventy is concerned, there is a lot of renaming of things that needs to happen. And they tell that when Cook landed he was stealing plants and everything.

They also tell that Cook opened the way for tens of thousands of convicts to be sent out. Wave after wave of criminals. And this began the dispossession of their lands. First by squatters. Then pastoralists. Then freehold landowners. Land that is now held in family trusts and is passed down through generations, but is stolen land.

Away from the noise and hubbub of the festival, down along the peninsula by the mouth of the lagoon that Cook travelled to, there is a stone monument to Cook nestled amongst the bush near the car park. It states: 'Under the lee of this point Lieutenant James Cook Landed on 24 May 1770.'

Yeah, nah. Of course it is just a best guess as to where he might have landed.

Down at the water's edge, families play, seemingly oblivious to the monument and the past, just enjoying the present. And then suddenly a dolphin appears in the water there. It makes you think the ancestors are welcoming you. It lifts your spirits, as walking on Country and seeing the animals there coming to check you out often does.

The lagoon, or creek, runs into the ocean at a point where, about 100 kilometres offshore, the Great Barrier Reef begins. The reef then stretches northwards for over 2,000 kilometres. Cook had no way of knowing that it was slowly closing in on him as he sailed northwards along the coast. The reef is a part of the sea Country of all the peoples who live along the coastline to the north, with about seventy Traditional Owners' groups having authority for managing their parts of reef. The Great Barrier Reef in its entirety consists of about 3,000 coral reefs, with over 600 islands and 300 reef islands. But 10,000 years ago, it was almost all part of the mainland and a part of people's traditional Country.

Brent McLellan is the Gidarjjil operations manager for the Port Curtis Coral Coast TUMRA – Traditional Use of Marine Resources Agreement. These agreements are community-based plans for the management of traditional resources. Brent tells that Port Curtis Coral Coast sea Country covers 26,700 square kilometres, which is more than twice the size of greater Sydney. He says, 'Many whitefellas will never understand that sea Country is related to land Country.'

And he explains one of the connections between the two, telling, 'We need to do our core traditional burns on the land – that leads to less detritus going down into the water and the reef. Land clearing leads to more sediment running into the sea. We need to leave this earth better than what we have been.'

There are criticisms that traditional hunting is damaging the sustainability of some species, but Brent McLellan says, 'We don't take near as many turtles as boat strikes and jet skis do.' He adds, 'It is not blackfellas who are doing damage to the Country. We need to keep our culture alive.'

After leaving Gooragang, Cook continued northwards and failed to notice the wide protected harbour where the city of Gladstone

Gooragang

now stands, as he passed by in the dark of night. If he had landed there he would have found large camps on the river, that was later renamed the Calliope River, and the two islands that were renamed Curtis Island and Facing Island.

The harbour area was known as Koongo Yallarm (place of water, place of shells) and provided bountiful resources for the people living there. However, being such rich lands, many wars are said to have been fought over it, between the Bailai and Gooreng Gooreng clans.[5] Like many First Peoples across the continent, they had times of peace and they had times of open conflict.

Neville Johnson is a Gooreng Gooreng Elder, and manager of the Gladstone Aboriginal & Islander Co-operative Society. They are a different clan to those who live in Bundaberg and have a different take on many things, including Cook. Neville sits in the small meeting room of their offices, with several members of his family, all keen to explain the impact that Cook, and subsequent uninvited arrivals, have had on his people.

As he talks, a grandchild comes in to find out what is going on, decides it is too boring for a small child and lets themself be escorted back out.

Neville says that they have a story that when Cook landed, their ancestors met and talked with him and his crew, and had to teach them about the foods and water of the land. 'They had to show them how to fish, and where fresh water was. And they also showed them how to make bread out of a plant there, and they could cut it and make flour.'

The Johnson family: Dale, Margaret, Senior Elder Jacqueline, Minne and Neville

That there can be a difference between stories handed down and those told in the *Endeavour* journals is a consequence of trying to view the complex maze of the past through lenses that have been repeatedly broken by colonisation.

Margaret Johnson says that before Cook even arrived the people knew he was coming. 'There were smoke signals. They were sending out smoke signals and telling people that the white man was coming.' She also says, 'It would have been scary for them to see this big boat coming in, you know. They wouldn't know who it was. Because they used to have their own scar trees where they made their own canoes, to take out to the reef and do their fishing out of – but to see this big ship coming!'

And Dale Johnson, the youngest of those gathered to speak to us – whose traditional name, Thoolgal Biroo, means 'strong warrior' – says, 'I remember Dad telling me that when they come in contact with the white people, Captain Cook and that, all the warriors they wanted to chase them away. But they had a big meeting with the Elders and the Elders said, "No. No, we can't, these people. Look at them. Look at their skin. They're our ancestors. They're ghosts. We gotta help them." That's who they thought they were, you know our ancestors.

'And they [our people] were friendly. They wanted to help them, trade and whatnot.'

Contact

Settlers first began appearing in the 1840s, and Neville Johnson said, 'Before colonisation we lived in abundance. We had more than enough. The food we ate was vastly different to Western society food because you look at the old photographs and people, men, they were lean people, they were very healthy. So they had very healthy, good food.'

And as settlers arrived, he said his people would have welcomed them in at first, thinking they were spiritual people coming back to visit them. 'But then, as it went on, and there was more colonisers coming into the country, the people had seen that the land was starting to get taken off them, gradually, so there was conflict there. Because they cut off their hunting grounds and access to places where they could fish and gather food.'

Records say that settlement was often preceded by terrible diseases like smallpox, which the people had no resistance to. A sympathetic pastoralist and amateur anthropologist, Edward Curr, reported years later, in 1887, that many of the people of the region over forty years of age bore the marks of smallpox, which he said was known as deeum or manboy.[6]

This of course made it easier for settlers to take land. But still the clans resisted. In one incident near Gladstone in 1855, warriors attacked native police troopers on Mount Larcom station. They attacked the station again on Christmas Day, taking sheep and supplies, and killing five station hands, said to be three men, one woman and a First Nations stockman.[7]

Of course there was a brutal reprisal, with the native police hunting down and killing a large number of people across the region in revenge. Such massacres contributed to the First Nations population in Queensland dropping from an estimated 120,000 people to approximately 20,000 over the course of a few decades.[8] And as the people's numbers dropped, the settlers' numbers grew. Lorimer Fison, a Wesleyan missionary, and the ineffectual Protector of Aborigines, A.W. Howitt, wrote in 1890, 'The tide of settlement has advanced along an ever-widening line, breaking the tribes with its first waves and overwhelming their wreck with its flood.'[9]

The Gooreng Gooreng people have very detailed memories of massacres and atrocities committed on their ancestors. Dale Johnson says, 'There is a massacre site down in Bundaberg. They chased the mob down from Gin Gin all the way to Bundaberg. That is a distance of about 50 kilometres. And I heard my uncles say that they shot that many people in the river that day that the Burnett River ran red for three days. And that's the blood of our ancestors.'

You get a feeling that is both chilling and proud to hear a young man like Dale Johnson relay the details of the knowledge that has been handed down to him. It is impressive for a young man to be able to take the responsibility of sitting there and talking openly about massacres and the dispossession of his people, and how this affected his people and how they still hurt to this day.

Margaret Johnson adds, 'We lost our great-grandmother in a bloody massacre. She was murdered. She was only thirty-six years old.

She had a son and a daughter. And the son was our grandfather. His uncle took him on his shoulders and run through the mountains. They chased him, he could hear the horses behind him. He put him in a log, and he says, "Be quiet there, son. Be quiet. Don't move until I come back for you."

'Then he took off. And Granddad said he was laying in the log and he could hear horses jumping over him, you know. And he was only three years old, and he lay there. Yeah, he was scared. And then early in the morning he could hear this whistle. His uncle whistles, "I'm coming to get you." And he waited till his uncle came and got him. Or else he would have been massacred too.

'So, you know, we're a product of that. So that's affected us.'

Neville Johnson continues the truth-telling. 'My father's oldest brother, Bob Johnson, they sent him to Woorabinda, because he used to get around fighting whitefellas all the time. But he didn't want to personally attack them. A lot of wrong things was done to him, you know, and he was purely defending himself from them. But in the eyes of the authorities at that time, Aboriginal men were sent to the mission.'

The Woorabinda mission was established in 1926, over 300 kilometres to the west of Gooragang, to contain First Nations peoples in one location, under the strict guidance of a Christian mission. Although on the lands of the Gangulu and Wadja people, the mission housed people from fifty-two different nations, as far afield as Cape York.

The mission neither recognised nor encouraged traditional culture, including language and knowledge. Over time this led to some lack of clarity over where different people's land boundaries actually lay, and contested spellings of their names. For instance, it is possible to find the Gooreng Gooreng people written as Coorang, Guren Guren, Koreng Koreng and Korenggoreng.[10]

For many First Peoples, one of the tragedies of being sent away from their land has been trying to piece together their past when they come back onto Country. There can be disputes over borders, ownership; resentment over who stayed on Country; conflicting stories passed down along different family lines, and even disputes over who has the right blood lines.

It is painful to watch one clan denigrating another, or disputing their heritage – but that has only happened because of colonial disruption to traditional lives. People are doing their best to put their lives and clan lines back together with patchy information, and a native title legal system that encourages fighting between families and clans.

Margaret Johnson says that back in the bad old days, those people who were visibly First Nations had to flee the area to avoid being killed, but those who had strong South Sea Islander heritage were spared.

Between the 1860s and early 1900s, in another shameful and too often overlooked part of Australian history, over 60,000 men were kidnapped from their Pacific Islands homes and brought to Queensland to work on sugar cane farms. Workers were taken from eighty different Pacific Islands, including modern-day Vanuatu, the Solomon Islands, Papua New Guinea, Fiji, Tuvalu and Kiribati. The practice was called 'blackbirding' – but a more accurate term is slavery.

As Bundaberg was a key sugar centre, and many thousands of Islander men were brought into the country there, intermarriage with local people was inevitable. Looking like a South Sea Islander meant you were seen as a valuable worker, while looking like a First Nations Australian meant you weren't valued and were subject to the brutal and racist practices of the time.

And yes, truth-telling needs to acknowledge that there is a very long history of wars and feuds between tribes and clans, but it also needs to acknowledge that most modern disputes exist as one more legacy of colonisation.

With a large variety of people with diverse languages and cultures being thrown in together on missions and reserves, and English being the only permitted common language, it led to many people's languages disappearing. And as traditional understanding of landscape was informed by a narrative tradition, linking particular features of the natural world to specific stories, to lose the words was to lose the stories, which in turn was to lose the importance of place.[11]

Neville Johnson says, 'There's been a reawakening in terms of speaking language – and dancing and storytelling. It's pretty strong now within the Gooreng Gooreng nation.'

For the people this means that the moon can once again be called narnoonluum, as it was known for tens of thousands of years. And children can be called duppeel once more. Rain can be called boonoo, and fire can be named as boree.[12]

And there is one more important conversation to have, that has been discussed at the cultural connections festival – reparations. Neville Johnson says, 'Our lands and water was stolen by a criminal act of theft from us. It was just taken by brute force to get it, that's the best way to say it, so yeah, there has to be some kind of reparation.

'Like Kevin Rudd said sorry for the stolen generation, but that's only one atrocity. And there's a whole heap of atrocities.'

First Nations Palawa activist lawyer Michael Mansell, who is a guest at the festival, has thought about this for a long time. He says, 'My view is that all the Crown lands of the states should be returned to Aboriginal people without going through a native title process. And 3 per cent of the gross domestic product should be set aside for us. We're 3 per cent of the population.'

He estimates that it would give First Nations people about $60 billion a year, and says, 'I think the upshot is, whatever any final agreement is, it's gotta give back to our people – back to communities – the tools that we can use to make our communities healthy and vibrant and inspiring. And in some cases that's not the case, because white people dominate us and we've got to end that domination and we've gotta make sure the people on the ground have the tools to make their communities happy and vibrant and healthy.

'We've been expected to repair ourselves, and the government just sits aside ... They've gotta take responsibility for getting behind us and healing our people, our past, and creating a future that we think is going to suit us, and we've gotta look forward to the next fifty to a hundred years.'

And our final question put to the Gooreng Gooreng mob is – as in all our discussions – What do you want whitefellas to most know about your mob?

Margaret Johnson says, 'That it took us a long time to get back to Country. We're still battling to have rights to this land. Just let us have our land for our children.'

And Thomas Holden, Warrgamay, Gooreng Gooreng, Gurang, and Taribelang Bunda Traditional Owner, and co-founder of the Indigenous economic development agency Bungal, adds a practical suggestion. 'We want their minds to open up to walk with us. Because we can't rebuild our culture on our own. We can't rebuild what we've lost to injustice on our own. The invitation is there. People just don't know how to do it. So, go to an event. Invite an Aboriginal person into your home. Listen to where we want to go to. Invest in people's business, walk with us, anything.

'Anything.'

Ngari (Hook Island, Whitsundays)
Ngaro Country

Malannandu.   Greetings.

> ... *indeed the whole passage is one Continued safe Harbour, besides a Number of small Bays and Coves on each side, where ships might lay ... I did not wait to Examine it ... being unwilling to loose the benefit of a light Moon.*
>
> Cook's journal, 3 June 1770

Cook had a very pleasant night-time cruise through the Whitsundays, and his journal reflects a rare moment of pleasure at the landscape about him. The name Whitsundays comes from it being 3 June when he was there, or the seventh Sunday after Easter of that year – to wit, Whit Sunday. Comprising over ninety islands, the Whitsundays are actually a part of Australia's largest offshore island chain, the Cumberland group (that Cook renamed after the Duke of Cumberland, a younger brother of King George III). All the islands and surrounding water are protected as part of the Great Barrier Reef World Heritage Area. Some of the islands, famous for their bright blue waters, fringing reefs and rugged vegetation, have also been declared state national parks in their own right.

The Ngaro people, who inhabited the islands of the Whitsundays, have been described as being different even from coastal people, in that they were a full-on maritime people. The Ngaro hunted large marine animals from very sturdy three-piece bark canoes, and sometimes used outrigger canoes. Their domain was the sea and all the reefs and the tidal mangrove systems encompassed by it.[1]

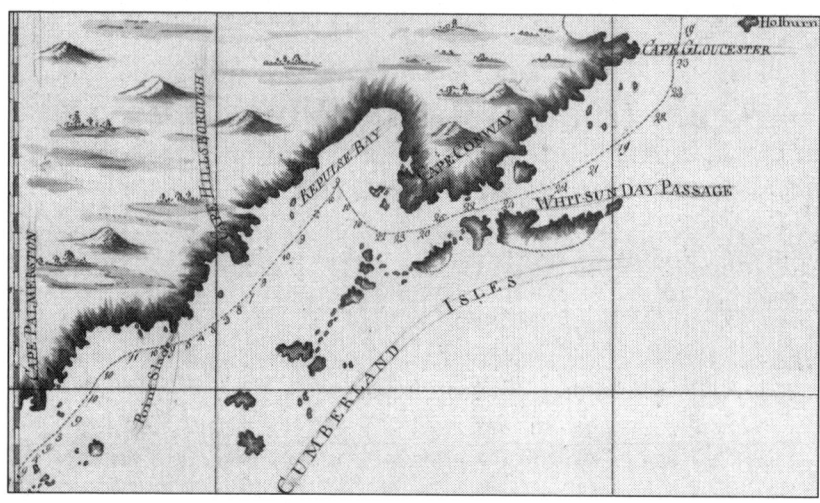

Cook's map of Ngaro Country

Catherine Prior is a direct living descendant of the Ngaro people that inhabited the Whitsunday Islands. She begins by saying that she can't tell too much about the stories of the islands and how they were formed, though she is aware there were lots of stories. This is a common response from people who have been dispossessed of their land.

'We're all from the Whitsundays,' she says, 'but spread out and taken away to all different areas.' She tells that her father was taken over to Palm Island, near Townsville, and her mother was taken there from near Cooktown. They were later able to move to Ingham, where the family grew up – nearly 400 kilometres from their traditional Country and sea Country.

The three members of the Prior family, Catherine, Trevor and Clifford, all live in the Townsville region, which is a little closer than Ingham, only 270 kilometres away from the Whitsundays.

As they talk and feel more at ease they take over the narratives from each other, adding to each other's stories in a way that only family can.

One other sister, Carol, has gone to join her ancestors, but has left her stories with her family. It is up to the men, Clifford and

Trevor, to decide if her story can be shared. But like many people their age, they know their stories need to be collected and shared before they are lost.

Clifford Prior tells that in fact he has never spent considerable time on his traditional land and sea Country, the Whitsunday Islands. He has only been there on day trips, fishing out of Bowen, and come near to the islands. 'But I couldn't tell you what island it was,' he says with a grimace.

Catherine Prior is a part of the seven nations who comprise the Mackay Whitsunday Isaac Traditional Owner Reference Group, who together manage, maintain and protect their tribal lands and sea.

The seven nation members of the reference group are:

Ngaro people – whose Country includes the Whitsunday Islands and the mainland coastlines.
Juru people – whose Country includes lands north of Bowen.
Gia people – whose Country includes the mainland opposite the Whitsunday Islands.
Yuwibara people – whose Country is along the coast south of the Whitsundays, including Mackay down to Cape Palmerstone.
Koinmerburra people – whose Country is south of the Yuwibara's.
Barada people – whose Country is inland from Mackay and west of the Clarke Connor Ranges.
Wiri people – whose Country is north of the Barada.

Despite having been dislocated from her Country, Catherine Prior is active in protecting it. She says, 'I am one of the voices on the spiritual connection that is a link between us and our ancestors. I am an active member of the Reef Catchments Traditional Owner Reference Group and am determined to continue the work of my family to protect, preserve and work on my Country.'

Trevor, Catherine and Clifford Prior

Thanks to the stories of descendants, and artifacts they left behind, we know a fair amount about the culture and lifestyle of the Ngaro, as well as changes to the land they inhabited. For instance, over 10,000 years ago the coast was over a hundred kilometres to the east of where it is now, so the Whitsunday Islands were only formed after that. On one island, South Molle Island, the largest ancient stone quarries in Australia have been found, where a distinctive stone was used to make stone knives – known as a juan – which was traded along the coast.

With more sturdy canoes than many people along the coast built – constructed of three pieces of strong ironbark wood sewn together with a fibrous root – the Ngaro were able to range widely across the islands and out to the reefs.

According to Gumbayngirr/Gamilaroi historian Victor Briggs, 'Along the entire Queensland coast from Hinchinbrook to Dunk Island to the Whitsundays, Aboriginal people were living on these islands in permanent to semi-permanent settlements. These were all canoe people. Though some use of ocean-going vessels was apparent right around the Australian coast, in the north the technology was more advanced and suitable to successful sea voyages to distant lands.'[2]

The Ngaro had also developed a detachable harpoon point, used for hunting animals like dugongs, that would come free from the spear shaft but still have a rope holding it. This meant the animal would not bleed so much, and attract sharks that might take much of the catch. Once they had speared the animal, the hunters would let it tire itself out before bringing it to the side of their canoe.

Thora Nicolson, who was a young girl in the 1920s living on Yara-kimba (Lindeman Island), told that her people's traditional diet included such diverse things as turtle, dugong, flying foxes, birds, yams, wild cherries, Burdekin plums, trochus shells, baler shells, green ants and cockatoos.[3] The islanders were also said to have numbered no more than a hundred – however, researcher Bryce Baker from the University of Southern Queensland, who has studied Ngaro pre-contact history in the Whitsundays, has said that a hundred people would be a conservative estimate when compared with known populations in similar coastal environments elsewhere in northern Australia.'[4]

The Ngaro lived permanently on Whitsunday Island itself, but travelled from there around the other islands. At Nara Inlet on nearby Hook Island, large middens have been found that date back about 2,500 years. Nara Inlet also has a cave where the Ngaro took shelter during bad weather, and they left paintings on the walls that today can be visited as a way of linking back to the past.

Catherine Prior said, 'I would like to talk about my spiritual connection to Nara Inlet and what the paintings there in the cave mean. Those paintings are a spiritual connection with all Ngaro people, and are signs from our ancestors, and that keeps our spiritual connection to those that have gone before. That artwork and everything around there, including the rocks, special places, everything that is on that island, has a spiritual connection, has a meaning for all Ngaro people. Even in the wind, the way the wind blows. So Nara Inlet is a very special site.'

Contact

There was intermittent contact between the Ngaro and European ships in the years after Cook passed by – mostly friendly, until the 1860s, when settlement in the region started increasing. Within twenty years those settlers were forcibly removing people from their lands, stripping them of both their culture and their livelihood.

The earliest people to invade their lands were loggers, harvesting the hoop pine timber that grew on the islands, for use in building in the nearby town of Bowen.

The Ngaro, like their mainland neighbours, resisted.

Professor Bryce Barker, who has researched the history of the lands, waters and peoples of the area extensively, has written: 'There was a realisation that these people weren't passing through anymore – but they were actually encroaching upon the resources of aboriginal people. Then we start getting reports of attacks. A number of attacks were made on shipping, a couple of ships were even burnt and people were killed.'[5] Amongst the ships that were attacked, several of them barely escaped from being taken over, and the schooner *Louisa Maria* was burned when captured in 1878.[6]

The feared native police – labelled by historian Henry Reynolds as 'the most violent organisation in Australian history' – were then called in to clear the people off their lands.[7]

Bryce Barker stated that 'from 1870 onwards, the traditional way of life that had been recorded archaeologically was gone'.[8]

The later the confrontations between settlers and First Peoples occurred, the more violent the confrontation usually was, as the settlers and native police had more access to horses and more advanced guns. Lyndall Ryan, who has been researching massacres across Australia for over ten years, says, 'After the 1860s and the Civil War in America, the Winchester rifle arrives, and other similar big rifles. Not only double-barrelled, they can shoot over a long distance. And so you can kill more people.'

The Ngaro population was destroyed or dispersed – or they were forced into indentured labour, which was often the only way they could remain living on their own lands. Of course a lot of traditional knowledge was lost as the Ngaro were moved to different parts of the state, living on other mobs' lands, eating whitefella rations and catching whitefella diseases. As was all too common elsewhere, they were prohibited from practising their culture and often unable to even practise their own language.

By the late 1890s, almost as if ashamed of the death and destruction they had wrought, Queenslanders started looking for another solution to dealing with First Nations people. The solution was to allow them into townships – but as cheap labour.

The Queensland government turned to the self-styled expert on First Nations people, Archibald Meston. He wrote a report for the government that became the basis of the notorious *Aboriginals Protection and Restriction of the Sale of Opium Act 1897*, that was effectively in force for many decades. The Act had a twofold aim: to control the movement of First Nations people, and to control access to opium. This was surprising when you consider how many employers actually paid their First Nations workers in opium ash – the leftovers of smoked opium – enabling them to have more control over their addicted workforce.[9]

There were many other restrictions placed on First Nations people under the Act, and Carol Prior has left us recordings of some of her thoughts and memories of the impact of living under the Act, which her family have agreed to share. In one recording she says, 'I can remember them coming around home and checking. They'd do this once a week. They'd check the cupboards, they'd check to see that, you know, there was clean clothes, there was food here, that the house was clean. And I never understood it. I never understood until I found out later on that the reason they've done that every week, because we were under the Act.

'When Dad got exempted, Dad and Mum, and I suppose when us kids were too, when we were exempted from the Act, everything stopped. It was freedom. Mum didn't have to get a permit to go downtown, and the permit would say, alright you leave at 9 o'clock, but you'll be back at one o'clock. And they'd come round and check to make she was home just after one.

'You didn't have to report in to the police station. You didn't have to hand all your wages in to the police station. And they'd have to go up to the police station and say, "Can I have £3.00 from my pay please? Or can I have £5 from my pay?"

'And it would be up to the sergeant or whoever was behind the desk to say, "No, I think that's too much for you. I'm only going to give you £2.00."

'When I found out that I was under the Act, it made me very rebellious. I used to wonder why Mum and Dad would get upset with me, because I'd stand up and I'd argue with the police and I'd demand, "How dare you come into my home and check this and that," you know.

'I was just one of those kids. I didn't know. Mum used to get upset. Dad used to get upset and I never understood why. It was only after Mum died and I grew up that I realised being under the Act I wasn't allowed to back answer the police, or question him. No, nothing. I wasn't even allowed to question the teachers at school or anything, you know.

'And I think Mum's worst fear, Mum and Dad's worst fear, was that because I was under the Act I had no rights. I had no freedom of speech. And if I did speak, they'd take me away. At that time they were still taking small children away from their parents. The stolen generation came out of that.'

As their lands slowly became a tourist hotspot, it has become harder for the Ngaro to return to Country, despite the recent increase in demand for cultural tourism.

Catherine Prior explains: 'So they're gonna have the Shute Harbour developments coming up, and there's lots of jobs going there. They'll need people that will be able to work down there. But the problem that we have there is that the cost of accommodation is very high. So it's so hard for people to go down there.'

Her nephew Trevor Prior, who is the former chairperson of Juru Enterprises, agrees. 'You can't stay on Country if there are no jobs.'

Catherine is also worried about the impact of tourism on her Country, with half a million visitors coming to the islands each year. 'A lot of the islands, they're being destroyed by man-made tourism, and when the cyclone came through [Cyclone Yasi in 2011] it just destroyed the lot. And we had to go see – there's middens we had to check, we had to see what happened with all the fish places, if they were destroyed after the cyclone.'

Trevor Prior explains the connection to Country they still maintain. 'We went on a camp to the Whitsunday Islands and

The Whitsundays, looking towards Hooke Island

camped on the islands and they had a helicopter and I spotted a fish trap from the air. So that chopper landed on the beach and me and my brother walked through the mangroves, and there was that fish trap – not a big one – just coming out from the mangroves, just enough to, you know, get a few fish.

'And while we were there, a big trevally just jumped in. Me and my brother were just standing watching this splashing around, and then it jumped back out again.

'And I went back and told Dad about it, and he said, "That's the old people telling us welcome there. That's our blood connecting us to the land."'

Catherine Prior has had her own spiritual encounters on the islands. 'I went to the island to get sand. I was walking in ankle-deep water and a stingray came and stared at me.' She said she wanted whitefellas to understand that this is how their spiritual connection exists with their old people. 'When we go into the bush and all the hairs rise down your arms – because they want us back home.'

And then Clifford tells a story. 'A lot of my friends and white people, they don't understand that. I've got a Fijian friend. We went fishing one night, and we had to come up the hill to the car, and had no torch. I said, "Stop there." With the lighter he flicked the light and right in front of him was a brown snake standing up, ready to strike. People don't understand that we can get the feeling. We feel it.'

Catherine says, 'You see, that brown snake was our mother's totem. And our mum was taken away.' She adds, 'I said I want to go back to my mother's Country. And so we did. And it was interesting, because when we first got there those cockatoos met us.'

Clifford Prior takes up the story. 'And the whitefellas there said, that's strange, those palm cockatoos there at this time of the year. Because we were there. And they come out of the blue, big flapping, and landed right next to the big bus we were in, squawking and carrying on. And the bus driver, he said, "Look here, they're welcoming you back home on Country." And when we left, they were all there, squawking, saying goodbye to us. And that's what we believe, the old people are welcoming us back on Country.'

They share these stories so that people better understand their connection to the land and animals – even when they are living away from their Country – and how it defines who they are, and will always be.

In her recording, Carol Prior says, 'Ngaro means to me that we are saltwater people. We are Aboriginal people. We lived off the land. We lived off the sea, and in particular the sea. My grandfather was a seafaring man, that's in everybody's blood to go out and fish and hunt and gather off the sea. And that's everything.'

She also said of her culture, 'I wasn't alive when Granddad was. He died before I was one. But it's been passed on to my dad. My dad passed it on to his children, and even today my youngest daughter, she makes cast nets, throws the cast nets, and she loves the sea. All my children love the sea. My grandchildren, they're all hunters and gatherers, they live off the land, and they live off the sea.'

Thul Garrie Waja (Cleveland Bay)
Bindal & Wulgurukaba Countries

Wadda Mooli.   Welcome.

This bay, which I named Cleveland Bay appeared to be about 5 or 6 Miles in Extent every way. The East point I named Cape Cleveland, and the West, Magnetical Head or Island …' smoke in several places in the bottom of the bay.

Cook's journal, 7 June 1770

The area that Cook renamed Cleveland Bay – most likely after John Cleveland, a secretary of the Admiralty, but perhaps after the Cleveland Hills near his home in Yorkshire – has likewise several different stories about it.

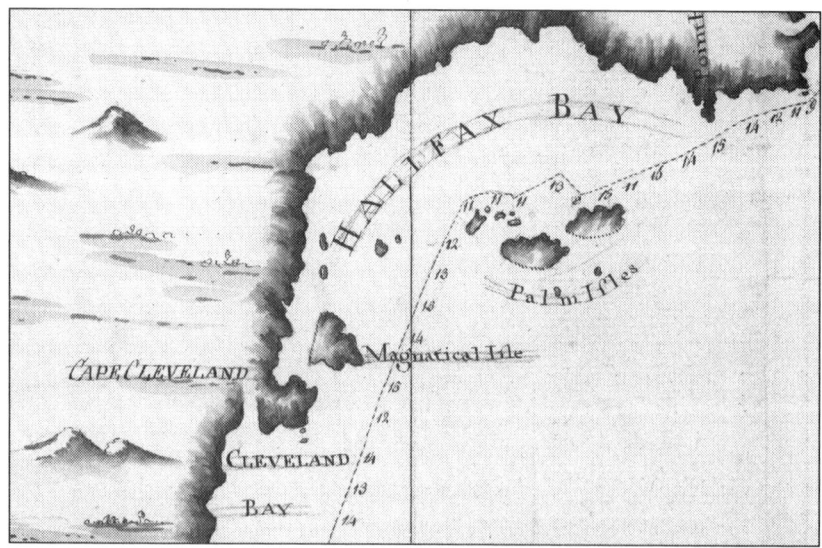

Cook's chart of Bindal and Wulgurukaba Countries

One story is told by Eddie Savage, a Bindal Traditional Owner who works as the Indigenous student support advisor at James Cook University in Townsville. He takes visitors to the top floor of one of the student accommodation blocks at the university so they can look across to the city and the mountains looming behind the campus. He points out where the Ross River is and the key parts of the landscape. Then he tells the Bindal Creation story of the two brothers Mandilgun and Yunbenun.

'They came down to this area, crossing Galbidera [Ross River], and they decided to have a bit of a rest. So one of the brothers went for a swim in the river. He came out on the other side of the bank and decided to lie down and looked over the Galbidera. He then became the Creation story for Mandilgun [Mount Stuart].'

Eddie indicates the large red rock of the mountain nearby and shows us where to look to see the shape of Mandilgun reclining in the rock. His head. His shoulders. Eddie is joined today by his mother, Dorothy Savage, his sister Dorothy Hellyer, and his two nieces, Maekeira Hellyer and Chelsea Purcell – who have come along to hear what Eddie Savage and the two elder women have to say, as they don't often get to hear these stories.

Eddie Savage continues the story, telling that Mandilgun's brother, Yunbenun, then decided to go further away, and he had a bit of a rest and decided to lay down in the ocean. He looked back over towards his brother and he then became the Creation story for Magnetic Island.

'So the two brothers were sitting down, resting, having a bit of a yarn. And they seen some pebbles laying around, some red pebbles. So they decided to start throwing the pebbles towards each other, not hitting each other. The pebbles landed in the middle of them and became Cootharinga [Castle Hill].

'They are actual landmarks, and you can really see how that story and that creation could have happened, Mandilgun throwing rocks, landing in the middle.'

Eddie Savage says that while there were different boundaries, along watercourses and mountains, it has always been a shared Country for the different tribes of the region. But a lot of precise knowledge has been lost, like from many places along the coast where people were forced off their land when European settlers invaded the land. The Bindal are now working hard to restore their stories and language and culture, and a resultant sense of pride in who they are.

Eddie Savage stresses the importance in his people knowing they were the first in nearly everything, with a culture dating back over 60,000 years. 'If we were navigating by the stars, we were the first astronomers. If we were making stone axes out of rock, we were the first stone masons. So everything that we've done would have been the first because we were the first peoples.'

First Nations people find it galling to know they have such long connections to Country and yet need to rely on the written words of relative newcomers to validate that connection to Country. This is particularly true when trying to achieve native title, and needing to produce records proving an ongoing connection with the land.

Eddie Savage says, 'I must prove to them that we've got connection. Why isn't the onus on them to show that we haven't got connection? We've got connection hundreds of years old, longer than settlement, and yet that's still not enough proof for your connection.'

Dorothy Savage adds, 'The one thing that colonisers or invaders did, they were good at documenting, and so we rely on a lot of their documentation – even though it's not all the truth. We know it's not the truth when we hear the oral history stories, but we got to rely on some of it, you know, that they've documented.' And, she says, colonisers documented both good and bad – including 'evidence of the slavery and how they treated our people under those Acts'.

One of the earliest sources of information on the Bindal people is from the testimony of James Morrill, an English shipwreck survivor who lived with the people for seventeen years. He had been shipwrecked off the coast of Queensland in 1846, and with the other survivors drifted for forty-two days on a raft before eventually being washed ashore near Cape Cleveland, just south of current-day Townsville.

Three of the survivors died shortly after, due to their ordeal, but the remaining four were taken in by the people and cared for. Morrill stayed with the tribespeople until he heard stories of white men coming up from the south. Then he had a serious decision to make.

Eddie Savage says, 'And so those white people run into him – another white man, you know, living with our original people. And so that actually gave us a lot of information because as time went by we'd lost a lot of our language. But it was actually recorded because when these white people run into this other white fellow they started asking questions. What's the name of the group? And they started getting the name of the different plants, the different animals, which is really helpful for us.'

Morrill's accounts relate many aspects of Bindal culture, from the weather to the burial rituals. He told, for instance, that every aspect of the heaven and earth could be explained, and thunder and lightning were the manifestation of evil spirits. He described how the Bindal cremated the dead, keeping the ashes for twelve months before burial. He even described the ornaments they wore: necklaces, armlets, girdles and headbands.

Eddie Savage says that Morrill's stories have let them retrieve a lot of their culture. 'Because we were put into missions and not allowed to speak language. And that's why our language is lost. Because it was forcibly taken from us.'

The people of the area here have not only lost their language, but too often have lost their voices – with a scarcity of historical narratives told by the local people, and a heavy reliance on whitefellas telling their stories.

For a visitor to Townsville it can be hard to find First Peoples' voices. There was the Aboriginal and Torres Strait Islander Cultural Centre but it has closed down, which is a pity, as every second small town along the coast has a small museum extolling the virtues of their pioneers, with maybe just a corner devoted to largely out-of-date information on the original inhabitants. Townsville's Queensland Museum Tropics notes that all their best First Nations exhibits are in the museum in Brisbane. Even the archives relating to Townsville are seemingly dominated by whitefellas telling the stories – though we should acknowledge that some of those whitefellas, like Professor Henry Reynolds, were amongst the first people anywhere truth-telling about colonial conflicts, in books such as the *The Other Side of the Frontier* and *Why Weren't We Told?*

Bindal Elder Dorothy Savage says of Morrill, 'And when the white people came this way, he only lasted another year or so, after, you know, living seventeen years with our people.'

When Morrill returned to 'civilisation' in early 1863, it was partly because he feared what the encroaching white men would bring. He even had a proposal for sharing the land. He wrote that the Bindal people's last wish to him was: 'with tears in their eyes that I would ask the white men to let them have some of their own ground to live on. They agreed to give up all on the south of the Burdekin River, but asked that they might be allowed to retain that on the other [side], at all events that which was no good to anybody but themselves, the low swampy grounds near the sea coast.'[1]

His proposal was ignored and a prediction that he made about the fate of those who had looked after him for so many years came true. He had written: 'I was obliged to tell them that there were a great many people, many more than themselves, and plenty of guns, and that if they went near they would be killed before they got there. I told them the white men had come to take their land away.'[2]

European settlers, with their fixation on land borders, have long been driven to define the tribal borders of all First Peoples of the land, often ignoring the fact that some lands were culturally shared. One of the first attempts to do this on a national scale was by Norman Tindale. Around the Townsville area he mapped five different peoples. They were:

Bindal people – who lived on the plains of the lower Burdekin.
Wulgurukaba people – who lived on the plains of Cleveland Bay, and on the offshore islands.
Warakamai people – who lived on the coastal plain of Halifax Bay.
Nawagi people – who lived in the rainforest of the northern ranges.
Warungu people – who lived on the tablelands and ranges to the west.[3]

However, the boundaries that Tindale gave have proven highly controversial, and no one agrees with them completely. This is consistent with how the country's past was so often recorded by settlers – haphazardly and then inevitably contested.

Contact

The earliest European visitors to the Cleveland Bay region, such as J. Beete Jukes in 1847, described the people as 'the most friendly and communicative we have yet seen on the coast'.[4]

However, in 1860, when George Elphinstone Dalrymple encountered people on his expedition to the Burdekin River, he interpreted the friendliness of the people quite differently. He wrote: 'Some blacks came down and we gave them biscuit and tobacco, etc., being kind and civil to them, which they seemed to appreciate. They, however, began to feel us all over, and especially the Botanist ... smacking their lips and giving other unmistakable evidences of their relish for human flesh, and a desire to gratify it. More blacks came down; they attacked us with stones and spears, when we were necessitated to fire upon them, repulsing them with loss.'[5]

The crew on board their ship, the *Spitfire*, then fired the ship's gun at a group of men approaching the vessel. This shooting was confirmed by James Morrill, though he gave a different view of events. He said that a group of men had been yelling and waving to attract the attention of the Europeans because they wanted to tell them a white man was living with them. In response the Europeans opened fire, killing one man and wounding another.

Tragically, this set the tone for future contact. Author and historian Peter Bell wrote: 'From that time, irrational fear spread through the new arrivals, and the European occupation of the North Kennedy district was conducted like a military campaign. Nearly all Europeans carried firearms, and unprovoked violence became regarded as normal behaviour.'[6]

Violence was met with violence, and some estimates are that up to 30 per cent of European settlers at this time were killed.[7] So of course the settlers called in the Native Mounted Police.

Professor Noel Loos from James Cook University, who has been a pioneer of writing on black–white relations, has written that the cost of such protracted struggle must have been very great for both races. 'But especially for the Aborigines. Rarely, of course, was the cost of the European invasion of Aboriginal land chronicled with an Aboriginal perspective.'[8]

But it was not always inevitable that the same tragic story was going to play out in this region as played out along the Queensland coast. Bruce Breslin, writing in his groundbreaking work on conflict in the Townsville-Bowen area, *Exterminate with Pride*, said that for several years in the first days of contact, both white and black had shown that they could share a common fireplace. 'This campfire shed not only light but also the possibilities which could be ignited

Magnetic Island from the mainland

in people's hearts: peace, strength and friendship. It was during this brief – all too brief – period that there seemed to emerge a glow from the fire.'[9]

But sadly the smoke from the guns of settlers, that Morrill had feared would be turned on his friends, would ultimately prove a more realistic metaphor for black-white relations.

A key part of the story of the Townsville region is the story of the two offshore islands Palm Island and Magnetic Island. And while most people are familiar with Magnetic Island as an idyllic tourist destination, the more troubling story of Palm Island is much less well known.

Magnetic Island lies so close to the mainland that First Peoples tell of their ancestors wading most of the way out at low tide and swimming the remaining distance. Ferries run regularly to the island from the port in Townsville now. On the island, you will find not only places named for Cook (Mount Cook, the highest peak on the island, and Mount Endeavour), but also places where

Chelsea Purcell, Maekeira Hellyer, Dorothy Hellyer, Eddie Savage (standing) and Dorothy Savage (seated)

the Wulgurukaba lived and thrived. There are many shell middens, pigment art, fish traps and stone artifacts spread across the island.[10]

Palm Island, by comparison, is much harder to get to, and its history much more confronting.

Dorothy Savage said, 'It was one of the most notorious penal settlements that was set up, it was likened to Alcatraz, but worse. A lot our people were removed there. My dad was removed there, along with his mum and grandparents.'

Under the 1897 *Aboriginals Protection and Restriction of the Sale of Opium Act* the Queensland government granted itself the power to have any First Nations people within any district in the colony removed to a reserve anywhere else in the colony. This meant in practice that people could be – and were – sent far away from their traditional lands.

Dorothy Savage said, 'We've got all these different missions and reserves that are now communities. And that's where our people were removed to, but from all over the place. Palm Island had about fifty-six different tribes sent there. All different languages. Today they call themselves the Bwgcolman – which means many tribes. The Manburra people [of Palm Island] gave them permission to call themselves Bwgcolman.'

She said that people were moved to Palm Island after the mission at Mission Beach was knocked down by a cyclone in 1918. 'A lot were sent to Palm. So many people were sent there. But many of our females were removed to work on farms and stations, and that was the slave trade of our people. It was also the start of our fair-skin babies. A lot of our women, our grandmothers and great-grandmothers, were raped and a lot of fair-skinned babies come out of that.'

Palm Island became a reserve in June 1914, and between 1918 and 1972, almost 4,000 people were sent there, from as far away as Brisbane and Cloncurry. Palm Island also had dormitories for children under five years of age, who were taken from their parents. These dormitories did not close until 1975.

Palm Island is one of sixteen islands in the Palm Island Group, and several of the other islands have their own terrible histories. Nearby Fantome Island housed people suffering venereal diseases, tuberculosis and leprosy. It did not close until 1973.

First Nations activist Burnum Burnum wrote in 1988 of a visit he had made to the leprosarium, 'I had the harrowing experience of greeting and shaking hands with a number of old friends whose hands were half missing. In a real sense these people were never to be seen again on mainland Australia because of the stigma attached to the disease, and the shame and attention their physical appearance attracted.'[11]

Nearby Eclipse Island was used as a punishment location, where people could be exiled to, on a diet of bread and water.

The more you learn about Palm Island's troubling history, the more shocking it can be. For instance, in 1883 nine men were kidnapped from Palm Island by a circus agent and were taken to the

USA to be live exhibits in the Barnum & Bailey Circus. Most of them died obscure deaths overseas, but one of the men was later identified as Kukamunburra (or Tambo) when his mummified body was found in the basement of a funeral parlour in Cleveland.

Cleveland Bay to Cleveland USA!

His body was repatriated to Palm Island in 1994 and laid to rest with full ceremonial rites.[12]

In 1930 the island's punitive superintendent, Robert Curry, went berserk, killing his two children and burning down several of the island's buildings. He had been described as a harsh overseer, keen on public humiliations, and had increasingly been drinking after his wife died in childbirth the previous year. His erratic behaviour, fuelled by paranoia that he was going to be sacked, included accusations that he had assaulted colleagues and flogged a female inmate.

On the day before his crazed attacks he had written a letter to the Chief Protector of Aborigines, John Bleakley, stating, 'I am going to revenge those who have injured me, and I will make them cry for mercy. I am just as sane as you are, so don't think otherwise.'[13]

Then, in the early hours of 3 February, wearing only a red bathing suit and armed with dynamite, petrol and revolvers, he drugged his eleven-year-old son Robbie and nineteen-year-old stepdaughter Edna, and dynamited the family home in which they slept. He then shot and injured the reserve's doctor, C.M. Pattison, as well as the doctor's wife, who Curry had been feuding with. He then proceeded to set fire to the homes of other staff and blow up the reserve's main buildings.[14]

He was only stopped when a Palm Island man, Peter Prior, shot and wounded him fatally.

Although he had acted under instructions from the Assistant Superintendent, Thomas Hoffman, Peter Prior was then charged with Curry's murder and spent several months in jail before the case was finally dismissed. He wrote of his time in prison: 'when I finally dozed off to sleep, I would see Mr Curry's face and it was always the

Cape Pallarenda with Palm Island in the distance

same dream. Even now, I can see him lying on the beach in pain and just staring at me.'[15]

Journalist and author Chloe Hooper, who has written about more contemporary violence on Palm Island, observed, 'In northern Australia, we did not have official slavery or segregation, but we did have racial atrocities of our own, and we did have, like the Americans, a violent, sometimes genocidal frontier. For years, we denied this reality ... Our present may be more complicated than we let ourselves believe, but our past is also a long way from being past.'[16]

Violence and deaths have been too much of Palm Island's history, but organisations like the Palm Island Community Company, are focused on the future, working to deliver ready access to the range of human and social services that most Australians have easy access to. And Palm Island, which is one of the largest First Nations communities in Australia, surely deserves a better future than its past.

Eddie Savage says that the hope for the future lies with the younger generation, who are learning their culture through dance groups and using song to relearn and revitalise their language. He also says they have been getting Elders back on Country and sharing stories more.

And Dorothy Savage, who has taught social work students at university about the true history of the area, says, 'It's about knowing about the atrocities that happened. Australia is still a hidden history, not telling the truth about what happened. So I'd like to see the truth-telling in education. And let's start using our own resources written by our mob in the schools.

'We do a lot more cross-cultural awareness, because reconciliation action plans are now part of a government policy. And that's probably a good thing, because they have to do cross-cultural awareness training. So that's the future for us. That's where we want these young ones, because we're not gonna be around forever. We want them to pick up that baton now and start doing what we're doing. It's an opportunity.'

Eddie Savage says he wants to see more cultural awareness happening in primary schools, and the younger generation agree with them. Eddie's niece Maekeira Hellyer says, 'We need truth-telling of the real history behind Australia. Growing up with Indigenous background we've been taught what Captain Cook really did.'

Eddie Savage also says that while there are increasing discussions about what really happened in the past, 'There should be more reparations for past atrocities that have happened to our people. Intergenerational trauma is a big word, but when you live and can see the changes not happening to your children because of what has happened – that's what the acknowledgement should be about.

'That's not to say we shouldn't get off our own arses and be working towards our own self-determination. But you know, if this didn't happen back then, or if our stolen wages [were paid] to our people, how many lots of land we could have bought – which would just change all the dynamics of your own people, your own families.

'These are things people should know.'

Munamudanamy (Hinchinbrook Island)

Bandjin & Girramay Countries

Nyurraji janyja bani buralaygu nganajinu mijagu girramayja.

Come now and see our Country belonging to the Girramay people.

> *This point I have named Point Hillock on account of its Figure. The Land of this point is Tolerable high, and may be known by a round Hillock or rock that appears to be detached from the point, but I believe it joins to it.*
>
> Cook's journal, 8 June 1770

Unbeknownst to Cook and Co., the point of the land that he renamed Point Hillock was part of a large island. In fact, Europeans did not discover that the place they were to name Hinchinbrook Island was an island until 1843.

Cook then continued renaming the landscape as if it was all an entry in Britain's Who's Who. Rockingham Bay was named for the Marquis of Rockingham, Charles Watson-Wentworth; and Cape Sandwich was named after the Earl of Sandwich, John Montagu. Of interest, the name Hinchinbrook was not given until 1863, and supposedly because the Earl of Sandwich lived at Hinchinbrook in England.

Cook and Banks saw people on a rocky islet near the shore, staring at the ship, so he renamed that chain of islands the Family Islands. The people were members of the Girramay people, whose Country was the land around present-day Cardwell, opposite Munamudanamy, or Hinchinbrook Island. And the people living on the island were the Bandjin.

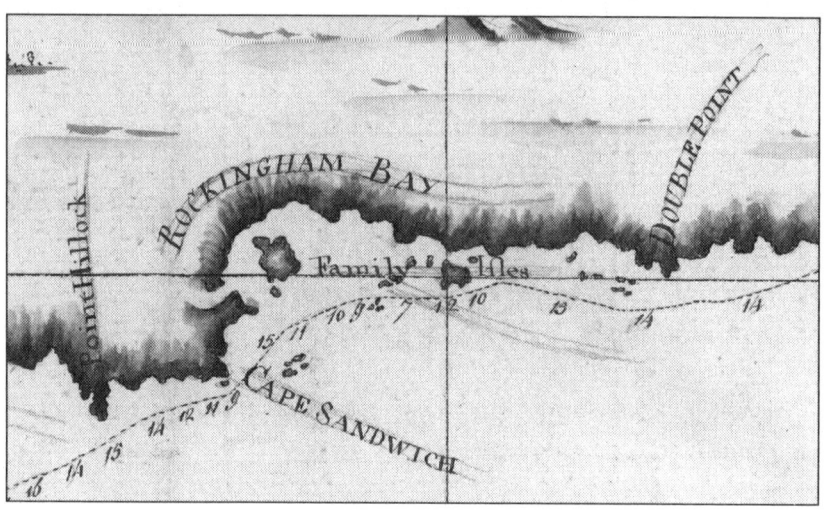

Cook's chart of Bandjin and Girramay Countries

They have numerous stories that tell how their landscape was formed, including the stories of the half-man, half-eel Girroo Gurrll, or the carpet snake Gubal, who formed the channel between Munamundanay and the mainland. But Munamudanamy is more than the island, as it encompasses the sea, mangroves, rivers, swamps, forests and mountains of the land, each of which have their own names and stories.

Hinchinbrook Island was believed to have been able to support a comparatively large population, estimated at about 400–600 people.[1] It is now protected as a national park and managed by the Bandjin and Girramay Traditional Owners.

Phil Rist is a Traditional Owner of the Nywaigi people, to the north of Townsville, and is one of the co-founders of the Girringun Aboriginal Corporation, located in Cardwell. You can see the island renamed Hinchinbrook from his office.

The organisation represents the interests of nine tribal groups of the region: Bandjin, Djiru, Girramay, Gugu Badhun, Gulnay, Jirrbal, Nywaigi, Warrgamay and Warungnu. Phil Rist says, 'We're very, very grassroots. We're not a land council or Indigenous Health centre or anything else.'

Phil Rist

He talks with calm authority and knowledge, and says, 'Our strength is land and sea management. We've got a pretty big range of programs, with a lot of resources. Arguably we've more resources than National Parks, we've got boats and other vessels and vehicles and we've got about twelve rangers.'

He also says, 'Of the nine groups that we have, six of them are saltwater people, and they have come together under strong leadership and they've determined with the Elders to put together an agreement about how they hunt turtle and dugong in the marine environment. When they are involved in that management it's better because it's coming from the people, you know, it's not government putting it on us. So it stands the test of time.'

Then he tells a story about how his organisation got its name and what it means. 'The Queensland government wanted to give the national park here a name – Lumholtz National Park. And he [Lumholtz] was with the Oslo Museum. He heard about this tree-climbing kangaroo, and he said, "No, that can't be right. There's no such thing as a tree-climbing kangaroo." And so he was interested. He came here to look for that. He spent about four or five years in the upper Herbert River area looking for the tree-climbing kangaroo. He found it – so one of the two species of tree-climbing kangaroos is named after him.'

Carl Lumholtz was in Australia between 1880 to 1883, spending significant time with the people of the Herbert-Burdekin region of Queensland, and the tree-climbing kangaroo that carries his name is of course the Lumholtz tree kangaroo.

Phil Rist continues, 'But while he was there he wrote this book, because he spent a lot of time with mob back then. And the book was called *Among Cannibals*. And I think that's where Pauline Hanson jumped on that, saying, "You are all cannibals!"'

And he clarifies that there were some isolated practices that could be considered cannibalism – though not as it is widely understood in popular culture, nor in the sensationalist commentary of the day. 'It was a witchcraft thing,' he says.

'So he saw this stuff, so he wrote that book and the government wanted to name this national park Lumholtz, and in that book he called us the lowest form of human being on the planet. Uncivilised people. Nothing more than monkeys. And things like, this race will soon be eradicated from the face of the Earth. Not knowing that we've been here for thousands of years. And we were very civilised in our way, you know – not your whitefella way, our way – which enabled us to live and survive and prosper.

'We had a big meeting here and said, "No way we are going to have our place named after this mongrel." So they put our name, which is Girringun, which means "mythical leader". A long twelve-year battle, and a lot of those Elders that were around when we first started this battle, they are all gone. But there was one old fella left, and the idea, the aspiration, was always to go to that waterfall, where David Attenborough stood.' For a 1994 documentary, David

Attenborough had stood at the top of the Kennedy Falls, about 30 kilometres inland from Cardwell, and stated he was surrounded by the Lumholtz National Park.

'We wanted to go back to that same footprint where he stood, and chuck that name out and put our name there. This one old fella was left that was involved way back then. By this time he was very frail, old, and we had to carry him through the rainforest on our back. Us younger fellas took turns to carry him, followed by a huge entourage of government people.

'And he just couldn't make it. He was too frail. He said, "I can't go anymore. I can't go on." He wanted to get to that same footprint there where Attenborough stood. That's what all the Elders before him that was involved in this wanted. To go there to that spot. But he just couldn't do it.

'And he said, "Put me down here." So we pull up in the middle of the rainforest. It was drizzly and it was eerie – right in the middle of the rainforest, he sang it out, loud as he could in his own language, and took that Lumholtz name off and put our name on it, Girringun National Park.'

Phil smiles at the memory of it.

Hinchinbrook Island from Cardwell

Contact

This is a story of both pain and healing.

After Cook there were several encounters with the people of the region – and all were reported as peaceful. In 1848 the explorer Edmund Kennedy landed just north of Cardwell for his ill-fated expedition northwards. Reports on the expedition stated, 'The natives remained friendly'.[2] Then in 1861 the Queensland colonial government opened up the district for leasing land. For a time, peaceful relations continued. It was even reported that the people of the region often fed starving Europeans trying to get established at Cardwell.[3]

Phil Rist recounts one of the incidents that changed things. He says, 'First contact was very friendly around the area. Just straight out here, there's an island, the whitefella name is Goold Island, and they got some big oysters there. And they are so big you could put one in a sandwich. And it's well documented in local books here as well that there was an understanding between the Traditional Owners of the day and the early settlers, but these fellas, these white people, they went there and they just went overboard with oysters, went crazy. And that started a big fight and they killed some of them whitefellas there.

'But then they brought the native police in, and their response was swift and very brutal. But they didn't take the time to understand why these lot were wild – cranky – because, you know, that's their tucker.

'It's like anybody. If I went into somebody across the road, into their house, and went looking back in the fridge, what they gonna do to me? Same thing. Uninvited and helping yourself, taking too much.'

So peaceful contact turned to violence.

The people began resisting the continued invasion of their lands as more and more settlers arrived, and once more the native police were brought in, establishing a camp at Cardwell in 1864.

Only three years earlier, in 1861, the Queensland Legislative Assembly had held an inquiry into concerns about excessive violence by the native police, which may have curbed their outrages but the committee found that any attempts to disband or change the force would 'destroy its efficiency'.[4] As David Marr points out in his excellent book *Killing for Country*, each inquiry held into the native police 'was designed to ventilate disgust and take no action'.[5]

That the force continued dealing out death and destruction was clear when the missionary Reverend E. Fuller came to Cardwell in 1874, hoping to establish a mission on Hinchinbrook Island. Reverend Fuller – described mockingly in the press as 'that zealous seeker after aboriginal souls' – did not have a great track record for success. He had been at K'gari, before the mission there was abandoned. Then he had moved to Lake Weyba south of K'gari, but 'during the whole time of Mr. Fuller's stay there not one black ever put in an appearance'. So then he moved to Cardwell, but after three weeks of scouring Hinchinbrook Island he was reported to have not seen 'even a solitary aboriginal'.[6]

The *fuller* truth tells that Fuller 'found only women and children all the men having been shot by the Native Police a few weeks prior to his arrival'.[7] Yet seven years before, in the interior of the island, the captain of the steamer *Black Prince*, Captain Major (yes, really!) and his party counted some forty or fifty huts spread out over about half a square mile.[8]

Records are scarce, but there are some indications as to what happened on the island, through reports collected by the Frontier Conflict and the Native Mounted Police in Queensland project, a collaborative research project by several universities funded by the Australian Research Council. One of the reports, from 12 February 1874, reads: 'A few days before our arrival at Cardwell an attack had been made on the blacks of Hinchinbrook Island; a tribe had been massacred, but for some reason or other a little boy and girl had been saved.' The girl referred to was described as being 'about six or seven years old ... and was handed over to one of the police to be cared for. The first night he had her at the police camp he brutally ill-used her in the sight of his fellows.'9

The history of the Native Mounted Police in Queensland is one of the darkest chapters in Australian history. From about 1849 until about 1904, around 1,000 First Nations people were recruited into the Native Mounted Police to hunt down and kill other First Nations people – a policy the British had used in other colonised areas like India and South Africa. Led by white officers – often ex-military – a band of between six and fifteen troopers would ride down the people they were hunting, or surround them in the dark – and then 'disperse', 'dispatch' or 'collide with' them (read: 'kill'). While many records were destroyed, researchers have used improved access to digitised documents and non-official reports to find more clues, and now estimate that the Native Mounted Police were responsible for over 60,000 deaths.[10] That is almost the same number of Australian soldiers who were killed in World War One.[11]

How can that not shock the nation – blackfella and whitefella alike? How can we not commonly know this? How can there not be memorials to those killed in small towns all across the country, like there are to those who fell on foreign shores?

Sixty thousand fathers and sons and brothers and daughters and mothers and wives and grandparents!

Sixty thousand.

The Native Mounted Police project states that there is no official staff file for any individual First Nations members of the Native Mounted Police, even though they were paid members of the Queensland Police Force. A few names exist, but they were often European names given to people when they joined – often just a first name too.

Jonathan Richards of Griffith University, who has spent many years researching the native police, said that in addition to the scarcity of records, 'violence against Indigenous people during the colonisation of Australia is a subject that many prefer not to confront'.[12]

Others who have conducted serious studies into the force (and this is not a task for weekend Google warriors, as you really need to be a dogged sleuth to hunt and sift through the scant records to find much information) describe them as 'a government-financed paramilitary force tasked with protecting "settlers" and subduing Aboriginal resistance'.[13]

Historian Bill Rosser used more direct language: 'Led by white officers, and equipped with horses, authority and guns, this band of murderous little bastards was the perfect killing machine!'[14]

But a key question that is not well addressed is, why did so many young First Nations men join the force and become such 'perfect killing machines'?

The answer seems as complex as the story of the native police itself, though it is clear from the high rate of desertion that many young men had no wish to remain in the force once they had been recruited. There is evidence that many of those recruited may have been living between worlds already, since kidnapping children was so common on the Queensland frontier (often done by the native police), after their family had been killed. And as these children grew older they may have been more susceptible to coercion or compulsion to join.[15]

It can be a very confronting issue for First Nations people to come to terms with, as it was mob killing mob. Gamilaraay and Kooma man Boe Spearim, creator and host of the podcast *Frontier War Stories*, says, 'It's harder than you think – don't get me wrong, they did some really horrible things, they massacred and killed and they tracked their own people, you know, like, they did it. And that's the frightening thing about it.

'But this is one of the tricky things because a lot of our mob, we pride ourselves on our people, and what our people have done for our Country. And a lot of our mob have them deadly stories of the trackers, of grandfather, he walked hundreds of kilometres and found them little white kids or the black kids or whoever. Or they tracked some prisoners hundreds of miles away, in the rain, in snow or whatever.

'It's a tricky thing because a lot of our mob were trackers in our family, and also some mob were quiet because they knew them other mob were a part of the Native Mounted Police. And I'm sure they are feeling as bad or as sorry as any mob that knows their family was a part of the Native Mounted Police.

'I think the Mounted Police was one of the most horrific organisations, because a lot of blackfellas went and signed up to be a part ... as they were the last survivor of their mob. Some of them were kidnapped, some of them were promised trinkets, grog and women, and were coerced. And then they tried to run away as well. And we know what happens when blackfellas don't go along with them [government] – they steal our kids and put them in dormitories and boarding schools.

'And no matter how close you get to the colony, whether we as black folks are running from it or working within it, we're always going to be victims of it.'

Complicating things even more, Lyndall Ryan, the lead researcher in the massacre maps project says, 'There's a number of cases where some of the white officers took Aboriginal women and produced children, but the officers end up staying there. And so you've got families where members of the family are both victims and killers. And I think that's incredibly hard. But it's part of the Australian story ... Oh, it's a dark story, but it's important to tell.'

A sugarcane grower living just outside Cardwell, John Ewen Davidson, whose property was attacked twice by First Peoples, recorded an eyewitness account of the Mounted Native Police in action in 1876. He wrote, 'Some blacks were seen, pursued and shot down; it was a strange and painful sight to see a human being running for his life and see the black police galloping after him and hear the crack of the carbines; the gins and the children all hid in the grass ... One little girl took refuge under my horse's belly and would not move: of course, I took no part in these proceedings, that being the duty of the police: it is the only way.'[16]

And Phil Rist says of the Cardwell area, 'There was a high presence of native police here at that time, because there was a lot of conflict between our people and settlers. And they had a big camp down there on the other side of the creek there, on my Country. They sent for them to come up from down Brisbane way, and they came and set up a huge camp there. But there were other camps as well, but that was one of the main bases.'

He said their presence led to a lot of massacres. 'So the two go hand in hand, where we have a strong native police presence, there's massacres, you know. We've had a lot of massacre sites around here as well, and stories associated with those massacres.'

Hinchinbrook. Mission Beach. Murray River. Mission Beach again. Dunk Island. Mission Beach a third time. Cardwell. Mount Farquharson. All known sites of massacres or Native Mounted Police killings – and all within an hour of Cardwell.

It *is* a dark and very complex story, but it *is* a necessary story to tell as part of truth-telling.

That is the story of pain. But there are stories here of healing too. Phil Rist tells how Country can heal you. 'It's almost miraculous,' he says. 'This old fella, a really senior Elder, we'd been planning this cultural heritage survey for many months. And this old fella is getting very sick, sicker and sicker. And anyway, I started getting worried. I said, "Oh man, I'm not too sure whether we should take this old fella."

'I went to see his family. I said, "I'm getting bit nervous about this. I think we better leave him behind, at the hospital or something."

'And you know what his family said? "No, no, no. Take him. You can't leave him behind now. You gotta take him." And they said, "You have no worries. You watch him."

'We had to physically carry him out from the caravan that he was in, and put him in the four-wheel drive. He's sitting, and he slumped down in the other front seat beside me, and I said, "Oh man, I'm getting a bit touchy about this. I don't want to get bloody growled at or bashed up by his family if something goes bad."

'We had to travel like two and a half to three hours over dusty corrugated road to get to where we were going to camp, and there was about three or four vehicles, and he was stuck there beside me.'

Then Phil smiles. 'The change was miraculous. One moment he's sitting there half dead beside me, next he's grabbing all the front, and is up like this, you know, talking about the Country we've gone back to.

'And he looked at me laughing. And when we finally got to the spot where we were going to camp, he was fully alert. And where we was camping, on top of the riverbank, there's a long way down into the river and you got to follow a cow path down to get there.

'He jumped out of that vehicle. Jumped out, taking off his clothes and heading down to that creek. By the time he got down into the sand in the middle of the river, he was stripped naked, singing to the fellas, "Make a fire. Come on, make a fire. Go and get me black bream and turtle and all that."

'And he's sitting there and he's singing and that, and we had to go down and get him, night-time coming down, and we thought, I better go down get this old fella, getting cold, you know. Bring him up here to camp. So we had to go down, and it took us an hour or so to convince him to come up for feed.

'And so that's what Country means to people. It was miraculous to see that. Healing places. Healing waters here.'

And as Phil tells the story it makes you want to stay longer, and go through his Country that he's talking about, and visit those healing waters. But it is good to just listen to him talking, because he's talking about strength and culture and healing, and all his ancestors. Talking about empowering his people. Because they've had a lot of sorry business in that Country, so it's good to know they have sacred places for healing. Because in our culture we talk about certain places of healing, healing waters, and mountains.

And the thing that Phil Rist most wants Australians to know, after all the complexity of the past, is really quite simple: 'It's not about race, it's about need. If we agree that this is the oldest living continuing culture in the world, so how do we protect that?

'In fact, that's everybody's responsibility, not just the blackfellas'.'

Girringun Badu figures on the foreshore in front of Munamudanamy (Hinchinbrook Island)

Djilibirri (Cape Grafton)

Gunggandji, Mandingalbay, Yidinji & Irukandji Countries

Wanjarra.   Welcome.

> *An Island tolerable high lies about 2 miles from the point of the main between which we went with the ship and were in the middle of the channel at noon, where we had 20 fathom water. The point land we were now abreast off I called Cape Grafton …*
>
> Cook's journal, 9 June, 1770

To the Gunggandji people, the large headland that Cook renamed Cape Grafton has always been known as Djilibirri, which means 'barramundi head'. The Gunggandji have lived there since the time of the Dreaming, which is reflected in their stories that recall a time when megafauna and giants roamed the earth.

Cook had renamed the headland after Augustus FitzRoy, the 3rd Duke of Grafton, who had been Prime Minister of England when the *Endeavour* set sail in 1769. Unbeknownst to Cook, FitzRoy had since stepped down, amongst criticism of his leadership, and the current prime minister was Frederick North, 2nd Earl of Guilford. But whether it was renamed Cape Grafton or Cape Guilford, it didn't matter to the Gunggandji people – it was always Djilibirri to them.

Cook and Banks and the other naturalists came ashore here quite late in the day, looking for water, plants or people, and they climbed up the stony peak of the cape to examine the land. They saw the spires of smoke further away, indicating that people were nearby,

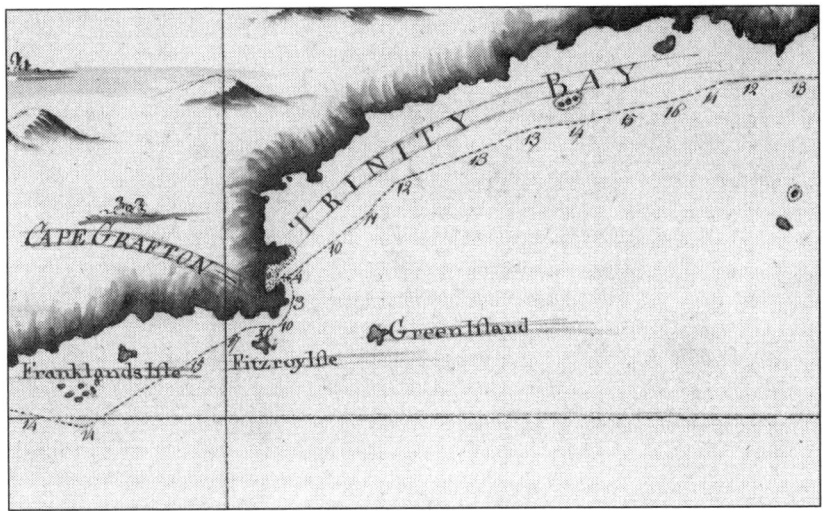

Cook's chart of Gunggandji, Mandingalbay, Yidinji and Irukandji Countries

but once again they were being watched by people who chose not to be seen.

Cook wrote: 'We hardly advanced anything into the Country, it being here hilly, which were steep and rocky, and we had not time to Visit the Low lands, and therefore met with nothing remarkable.'

Banks added a little more detail, and included seeing a man on the shore: 'The Countrey about them was very stoney and barren and it was almost dark when we got ashsore; we made a shift however to gather 14 or 15 new plants after which we repaird to our boats, but scarce were they put off from the shore when an Indian came very near it and shouted to us very loud; it was so dark that we could not see him, we however turnd towards the shore by way of seeing what he wanted with us, but he I suppose ran away or hid himself immediately for we could not get a sight of him.'

The men of the *Endeavour* had landed near the current community of Yarrabah, which, although only 50 kilometres from Cairns, is largely unknown to most people who visit the region today. Yarrabah was once a mission, and like many missions and reserves, became

1817 sketch of Djilibirri (Cape Grafton)

the home of people from all across the state who were removed and sent there. This resulted in many different peoples calling Yarrabah home, though it was not their traditional homeland.

Alfred Gray, who prefers to go by the name of Touché, is a proud Gunggandji man who works with the Gunggandji-Mandingalbay Yidinji Peoples Prescribed Body Corporate Aboriginal Corporation, telling cultural stories to invited visitors. He arrives near the end of the day, still wearing ochre on his face from a cultural lesson he has been giving, and he pulls up an old tractor tyre to sit on. The nearby foreshore is half hidden by trees, and the whispers and giggles of young kids down the bank behind the trees show they have a more relaxed attitude to possible crocodiles than visitors do.

He says, 'We've got like sixty to seventy different nations that live in Yarrabah here today. But at the end of the day, there's only one true owner of this Country and it's Gunggandji people.'

Listening to Touché is like hearing from a person much older, as if you might be talking to one of his ancestors – passing on their cultural stories and their wisdom and knowledge of their Country. His deep history of connection to Country goes beyond the rising of the seas 10,000 or so years ago and he says that his family came from way outside the continental shelves. 'We lived way outside there. And we were the only ones that have a memory of that event in the region. The other mob, like my dad's tribe, they only been here like three thousand years ago.'

Gunggandji Creation stories tell of a time when giants walked the earth. 'Well, that's one of our Creation stories in there. When the sea rose. When now, when one of the giants came from inland, they were looking for wives. So he came out onto the continental shelf, far, where one of our fathers lived. One of the giants. And he had two daughters. So the tribesmen he came out and he asked their grandfather for a wife. Or two. So grandfather said, OK, then you can have both my daughters. These are now your wives. So take them in and look after them.

'But as they were coming in from out there on the journey, coming back in, the giant got hungry and thirsty and he wanted something to eat and drink. Then the wives offered to give him something to eat and drink. But being a man, he didn't want the women to save him. He wanted to save his own self, and the law was already laid then upon him not to touch anything in the region, because everything here belonged to his wives.

'But yeah, he came to one of our sacred pools. Then one of the fish bit him. And he struck out at that fish, a protector of the planet. But by him striking the fish, he killed the protector. And then when he killed the protector, our father was way outside and he felt the pain, felt something wasn't right, and he knew that one of the protectors was killed. So he sent in the great flood. To punish the giant and both his daughters. So he drowned them. The tide caught up to them out here.

'But the giant managed to get up onto the mountain, then he started running up to the highest peaks. And then he started, like, making all the big fires and collecting all the granite, all the big granite boulders, making them super red hot. Like, not just on this mountain range, but from way down. He threw them into the sea to stop it rising.'

Touché says that this time, that is known as the Dreaming to many, is known in his family as Bulurru. 'That's the time of the Creation stories. And that's when all the Creation beings were still around. But they were the last of the beings that had those superpowers. That was when their times were coming to an end.'

The land under the sea is still a part of Gunggandji Country, and the people still care for sacred sites and Dreaming tracts that have long been underwater.

The offshore islands near Cairns were a part of the mainland as recently as 10,000 years ago, and were regularly visited for ceremonies. With his European eye, the ship's artist Sydney Parkinson described the offshore islands as 'so many heaps of rubbish'. For the Gunggandji, however, islands and individual land formations can have significant importance. And while every place on their

Alfred 'Touché' Gray

Country has some cultural significance, some places have special spiritual values associated with them.[1]

Pointing to a small island in the bay, Touché tells that it has a story linked to a giant ancient shark. He says the small island is the child and when that shark came in it just smashed the channel open, between the mother headland and the child island. But the umbilical cord is still connecting mother and child, because a spring runs under the ocean and comes out and feeds the child. 'So yeah, the umbilical cord is still underneath. Still connected.'

He explains that everything was giant-sized in the Bulurru times, and the animals were all megafauna. 'Like you got the biggest machine they got on the planet now, they dwarfed them. The biggest machines you got in the mines, they make those machines look small, because they can move and create mountains.'

According to the Gunggandji, culture is intimately linked with the land and sea Country, and the survival of their ancestors over thousands of years depended on their knowledge and management of Country. This included deep and intimate knowledge of important animals and plants and how to use them sustainably, how to hunt and gather, how to adapt to the seasons, how to survive cyclones, how to manage fire, how to process poisonous plants to make them edible, and how to treat wounds and sicknesses with bush medicines.'[2]

Cook, of course, saw none of this. Though he would very soon be forced to look more closely at the land about him, and consider how it might sustain a people, when needing to live off the land himself. But that story is coming very soon …

Touché has a different take on Cook than many First People. He says, 'Joseph Banks should have been the bad guy. Captain Cook, he told everybody about all of us, what he saw. But Joseph Banks, that bloody prick, he went back to the motherland and told them, "No one there."'

Touché says it is important to keep culture strong. 'We're not just singing and dancing, just for no reason. We're singing and

Cape Grafton and the child island beyond Yarrabah township

dancing for our songlines.' He still speaks the old tongue – the first language of the region – and says he has been taught by the old people. 'Words can travel right across the country. Everybody got their own words, but they go right across the Countries because of trade.'

He also says the ancestors had stories about people coming from the stars and the oceans. 'We don't need the scientist to tell us human life come from up there, you know? Like they said life form comes from the stars and it came out of the ocean. We already know that. We didn't need David Attenborough to come and tell the story.'

However, Touché feels that only a small percentage of people are really keeping culture and knowledge strong in the face of the distractions of the modern world. The lights of Cairns lie just across the bay, and can of course be very attractive to some.

He says that while he observes the proper season for hunting dugongs, which is the wintertime, there are a couple of idiots in the community. 'They just go and kill, kill, kill, and fill up their freezer and won't share.' He said if it was tribal times they'd be punished harshly.

There were five other tribes that shared similar language and Dreaming stories about the Creator god Bulurru. They were three rainforest peoples to the west, the Djabugay, Buluwai and Ngadjan, and the Yirrgay and Yidindji saltwater peoples to the north and south of the Gunggandji.

These tribal neighbours shared boundaries, marriages, trade, ceremonies, celebrations, sacred sites, resources, knowledge, traditions, rites and lore.[3] While there was some animosity with people further away, the good relations with those who lived nearby allowed culture and arts to thrive, expressed in ornate tribal dress, elaborate stories and ceremonies. Gatherings were held that provided a chance for marriage, trading and settling disputes, as well as socialising. At such gatherings bodies were often ceremonially decorated, and amongst the rainforest clans it was common to decorate the body with moistened white ash. Also, pieces of shell were delicately carved and hung with twine to make decorative necklaces.[4]

Amongst the six tribes, people were classified into one of two moieties (a particular social division), that were explained in a Creation story. There were two argumentative brothers, Damarri and Guyula, who were responsible for creating parts of the landscape and establishing the law that guided who a person could marry. There are many stories about the brothers, including how Damarri lost a leg to Ganyarra the crocodile, and his blood gave birth to all the wet totems and water creatures.[5] When this happened, Damarri called to his wife to run for her safety, and he lay down as the Whitfield Ranges and his wife became the coastal ranges. And the brother Guyula became the white-bellied sea eagle that is seen as a protector of the region.[6]

The first brother, Damarri, represented the Gurubana moiety (guru means 'good' and bana means 'water' or 'wet', thus 'wet season'), while Guyala represented the Guruminya moiety (minya means 'meat') or the dry season. Stories of the two brothers' conflict explained the wet and dry seasons and the existence of plants and animals, as well as guiding the choice of marriage partners from a particular group or area.[7]

Proceeding on from Djilibirri, Cook charted the wide bay to the north, naming it Trinity Bay – it being Trinity Sunday. He had crossed into the lands of the Yirrganydji (Irukandji), a coastal seafaring rainforest people.

Jeanette Singleton is an Elder of the Irukandji people and says that her traditional Country goes from Cairns to Port Douglas along the coast. She tells, 'I have heard a couple of stories about Captain Cook, on his way going north he pulled in at Cape Grafton. They came into the bay and had a look and hopped back into their boat after they got a bit of fresh water and that.'

His arrival was told in a dance, and she said, 'There is an Elder that I know who came down one day from around Mossman and he saw our mob all painted up and dancing and doing a dance about Captain Cook now going up on the *Endeavour*.'

The Irukandji people (from who the deadly Irukandji jellyfish gets its name) have about twenty clan groups, who live across the wet tropics and sea country. Because the reef and the rainforest provide an abundance of food and raw materials, clans were able to sustain themselves in relatively small areas, unlike those who lived in the drier regions west and south who needed much larger areas to live in.[8]

The Irukandji people moved across their land following seasonal food sources and were both rainforest and saltwater people. The waters of the rivers and ocean yielded kuyu (fish), ngawuyu (green

Jeanette Singleton

sea turtle), duyun (dugong), julkay (pipi) and julwa (black mangrove mussel). On land they hunted dulpil (wallabies), kanyal (goannas), jarruy (birds), jama (snakes) and various birds. Their diet also included many fruit and vegetables, including mundimay (long beach yam), yiwurra (black bean), padil (cycad), and various nuts and berries.[9]

Towards the end of the dry or winter season (gurraminya minya, roughly from May to October), vegetation would be fired and burnt off. This stimulated new growth, providing fresh pasture which attracted many of the animals on which the Irukandji fed.[10]

Contact

European settlement was slow to take off in the Cairns region, often because early explorers, such as Edmund Kennedy, described the rainforest of the region as impenetrable tangles of economically useless timber.[11] European eyes again.

As settlement slowly grew it was highlighted by difficult relationships between gadja (Europeans) and the bama (people). Bêche-de-mer, or sea cucumbers, first brought Europeans to the region, for collecting and selling to Hong Kong. The Northern Protector of Aboriginals, Walter Roth, described the impact of bêche-de-mer gatherers as 'one long record of brutal cruelty, bestiality and debauchery: my heart bleeds at what has come to my knowledge'.[12] There were attacks on both sides, with the expected outrage in the colonial press about barbarism and savages.[13] There was little understanding, or willingness to understand, by the Europeans that they were clearly trespassing on the lands of the bama, who had strict laws around entering a land uninvited.

The surveyor J.F. Mann wrote a decade or two later, in 1883: 'many a man has lost his life by unconsciously infringing their rules – such as walking into a camp without first obtaining leave. This may be considered equivalent to a person walking into a stranger's house and sitting down without being asked.'[14]

In 1872 the trickle of settlers had become a storm. In that year William Hann announced he had found gold to the north, at Palmer River. It triggered an almighty influx of settlers. Cairns sprung up as a small access port to the inland goldfields, as well as access to the prized red cedar trees of the rainforests. Further clashes between the newcomers and the bama over land and water and other resources was inevitable, as more townships and farms were established across the region.[15]

After many horrific years of violence and disease, the population of the bama of the region was estimated to be only a few hundred people, spread across several groups. Many had died during violent 'dispersals' by the native police, who were responding to complaints by settlers about alleged 'depredations' by the bama.

Touché says, 'But a lot of the tribes in there, well, my father's tribe, well, we were one of the ones that got massacred, my father's tribe, because we had a war band that were fighting for the other smaller tribes. So my dad's family, we paid the ultimate price. Like, we're not the only ones that got massacred, but we got massacred right down to only like three to four family members left.'

As occurred all over the colony of Queensland, people were removed from their homelands and incarcerated at the Yarrabah mission. The name is believed to come from a Gunggandji word for the creek running down from the Wambilari ranges (Murray Prior Range) into a fresh waterhole.

The mission was established by the progressive Anglican priest John Gribble in 1892, although he died soon after and left the running of the mission to his son Ernest. And while he was Ernest by name, he was unfortunately a fanatic by nature. He implemented a strict regime of timetabling people's days, believing that idleness was an enemy to be defeated. But in denying people their traditional lives and making them dependent on the mission's meagre rations, he was taking away the very activities that had kept the people busy day to day. Like many missionaries of the era, he believed the First People to be a dying race and that the best path for them was paternalistic segregation.[16]

The managers that followed Ernest Gribble were no improvement, and Yarrabah became 'a barely disguised prison'.[17] Not only were people from different tribes and clans forced to live together, but all men and women had to live in separate quarters, and children were raised to behave like white children.

Jeanette Singleton, who grew up on the mission in Yarrabah, says, 'The first mission to open up in Queensland was in Yarrabah in 1892. A lot of people got taken. Some of them got sent to Palm Island to Cherbourg, to all around the state then.'

And Touché says, 'Then what the government done when they started splitting us up, you know, taking us off Country like, they took us three or four thousand miles away from home, thinking we're not going to get back there. But what the biggest mistake they've done, they gave us a greater range. They gave us more Country. Because the new one [Country] they sent us to, we all grew up and we all we regrouped and our numbers grew in those places they took us to. But the memories of the place we came from was always there, so we always linked back. So everything all interconnects once again.'

He also says, 'We've got to respect both our parents because we got two parents, but from them we've got grandparents. So we've got to love and respect our parents and their parents, their grandparents. That gives you ties to those clans and tribes. And that's what makes our songlines greater.'

But Touché is critical of those who live on a new Country without knowing the stories of that Country. 'And another thing, my brothers, today we've got so-called Elders. Just because they have an age on me, some of these people, they're like, "I'm an Elder." And I'm like, "OK, I respect you, but you're not an Elder." If they don't know their story, songlines or their dances, they're not an Elder to me.'

He says there is a correct way to learn culture properly. 'There are a lot of gammon [fake] black people who learn from a book, which is ridiculous. A book don't talk or dance to you. It doesn't. It cannot.'

Touché!

But he also acknowledges that unfortunately a lot of people can only get knowledge from what is written, as they no longer have Elders they can learn from.

Jeanette Singleton tells us that her grandparents met in Yarrabah. 'And that's where my grandmother and grandfather were sent to. They met over in Yarrabah. But we came out of Yarrabah in 1956. I was ten years old. They kicked us out. The whitefellas kicked us out.

'To be honest with you, this is how it happened. A few of the men in the village were coming together and they were starting to put pressure on the white people to do better for us. They were pretty strict on us, wanting to put us in a dormitory. But my father never put us in a dormitory.

'In those days, living on a mission, the white men were treated like gods. What happened was, my uncle was a butcher, and he decided that on this particular day, he decided he'll give the best cuts of the meat to the community and give them [the white men] what they normally give us. Well, it didn't go down so well.

'That caused a big row among them. He was an Englishman, the captain, they called him Captain Wilcock, and he kicked us out. About twenty families. But we also realised there what they done to us, we were coming back to our own traditional Country of Cairns.

'Because the government came and then six years later took over the mission from the Anglican church. The government put in a superintendent and we formed our own community council. And the chairperson all those years was my uncle.

'Over at Yarrabah, if you fought with any of the white staff over there they sent you away to either Palm Island or Woorabinda, or Cherbourg. I've seen a couple of families I was very close to who were told to pack their bags and I've never seen them again.

'To go from Yarrabah to Cairns you needed to get special passes for a day trip, and if you didn't catch the boat back when you were meant to, then the police could come and lock you up. They had the authority to do that.'

Jeanette Singleton says she does not think that many people in Cairns know the history of Yarrabah. 'Not really.'

Yarrabah today is home to up to 5,000 people but has only 400 houses, which has led to chronic overcrowding and associated health and social risks.[18] It also had one of the highest Yes votes in the 2023 Voice to Parliament referendum – 76 per cent, despite Queensland recording the lowest Yes vote of any state in the country, at 31 per cent. Late in the day children are playing on the streets, often riding horses around barebacked, laughing and waving as they gallop past. You wouldn't know they have such high unemployment and health problems within the community.

A vital part of Jeanette Singleton's history that has been reclaimed is a breastplate, given in 1898 to her grandfather, known as Billy Jagar, that was lost for many years. While today such breastplates – or king plates, as they can be called – can be considered divisive and a patronising symbol of colonialism, if you were given one by the government back in the day, you were held in high regard as a person of knowledge and culture.

Jeanette said, 'Well, when they [white men] came he was twelve years old and he lived all his life on the Cairns esplanade. There were sections of Cairns that were purely for the white people. If you were an Aboriginal you had to be out of there at five o'clock, and they lived in these camps.'

Walking along the far end of the Esplanade earlier, you got a feeling that something happened there many years ago, and that formed a connection when Jeanette Singleton told how that is where all the people used to camp.

She also told, 'That area near where the airport is, is where the mouth of the Barron River was, and then around about 1940s a cyclone came and changed the whole course of the river.'

The breastplate is kept in perfect condition by Jeanette, and is engraved: Jagar, King of Barron, 1898. 'The story is that the breastplate went missing at some point and it was picked up by a US marine in the Second World War and they took it back with them to the States.' And it was there for sixty years, passed down through the family.

Cape Grafton from the northern end of the Esplanade, where Billy Jagar's camp would have been

The Barron River

'In about 2000 a woman was inquiring about the breastplate and asking how far Cairns was from the Barron River. She rang the museum and that's how she got put on to me. And I spoke to her on the phone, and I said to her, "Oh, you got my breast plate."

'She said, "Well, I couldn't keep it anymore because I knew it belonged to you."'

After explaining the significance of the breastplate it was agreed it would be handed back, which was done in a ceremony in 2005.

Jeanette Singleton also said, 'And to me, I'm glad it was Captain Cook that came. Why? Because he brought the Bible with him. And regardless of what happened, the man on the cross was the one that gave me my freedom and every other race in the world.'

Touché has a different philosophy, grounded in culture.

'Well, in Yarrabah we talk about a word that translates as "one fire", but it also means "one people". So just say we're sitting around this fire now. Then more people come. So what we're going to do? We're going to expand. Make that circle bigger. So everybody got a place.'

Jagar's breastplate

And what does he want whitefellas to know?

'We are all the human race,' he says. 'We love talking and storytelling. That's all we want. That's all the children want, my brothers. They just want to sit down and get told a story and the story can be two minutes, three minutes, five minutes, five hours long. It doesn't matter, as long as that happens with someone who's showing them love. And we all of us got a special gift to offer to our friends and family and to our mum, to our dad.

'We all got a gift to offer.'

Kulki (Cape Tribulation)
Kuku Yalanji Country

Yalada.　　　　　　　　Welcome.

The Shore between Cape Grafton and the above Northern point forms a large but not very deep Bay, which I named Trinity Bay, after the day on which it was discover'd; the North point Cape Tribulation, because here began all our Troubles.

　　　　　　　　　　　　　　　　Cook's journal, 10 June 1770

On the morning of 10 June, Cook had weighed anchor and headed north again. They measured the depth as they went, as was their custom, with one man throwing out a lead weight on a rope. It had been a good method for knowing if the amount of water below them was tending to increase or decrease, though it did rely on a certain amount of luck. And on the evening of 10 June their luck ran out.

For the past few weeks they had been successfully charting their way northwards, not realising the vast corals and shoals of the Great Barrier Reef were slowly closing in, boxing them against the land like a large fish trap built by the giant ancestors. On this night, shortly after Cook and Banks had turned in for night, the linesman casting the lead weight to measure the depth found it was a safe 17 fathoms (about 31 metres). But barely had he gathered in the line to cast again when the ship struck the edge of a reef.

Cook's journal, written after the event of course, describes a calm and ordered reaction, with crewmen taking down the sails and putting out the ship's boats to examine the reef in more detail. But Sydney Parkinson captured the anxieties of many of the crew when he wrote: 'We were, at this period, many thousand leagues from our native land, (which we had left upwards of two years,) and on a barbarous coast, where, if the ship had been wrecked, and we had escaped the perils of the sea, we should have fallen into the rapacious hands of savages.'

The crew could feel and hear the grinding of the ship below as the swell thew it back and forth on the sharp coral. Cook, in his nightshirt initially, ordered the ship's boats out to check the depth around them and then ordered everyone to bring down the sails to prevent the wind pushing them harder onto the reef. The boats reported deep water on most sides. That was promising. They had an opportunity to drag the ship off. So he dispatched the ship's longboat to carry the anchor to a distant point and set the men to winding it back in, hoping to pull the ship free.

The ship had two winches, the capstan and the windlass, and both were turned by sheer muscle power. To wind the anchor chain or ropes, several sailors needed to insert a thick wooden handle into one of the square holes on the central axis, then they would push

Cook's chart of Kuku Yalanji Country

until their muscles felt like they were snapping. As it turned, one sailor would remove his handle while the others kept theirs in place, and he would move his handle to a lower hole and continue the turning.

But the ship would not move.

Worse, the tide was going out. They needed higher water to float free.

Cook then ordered his men to lighten the ship, by throwing overboard everything that was not vital for their survival. Ten tonnes of iron ballast. Six cannons. Most all of their drinking water. Old stores. Anything.

As the ship was taking on water, they knew there was a hole in there somewhere and everyone joined in taking turns at the pumps, even the officers. By daylight they could see land about 40 kilometres away. A long distance for almost a hundred men with only three boats, most of whom couldn't swim. By the following evening, when the tide was back in, Cook estimated they had thrown overboard 'about 40 or 50 Tuns weight'.

Was it enough?

As the tide rose again the water started to overtake their efforts to pump it out of the ship. Banks gave up and started packing what he thought he might save, preparing himself for the worst. He had good reason to worry, for the rush of water into the ship meant that even if they got it off the reef it would undoubtedly sink.

The men put their backs into the capstan and windlass again, straining to pull the ship free. Muscles bulged. Sweat ran freely. Desperation added to their efforts. And slowly, slowly, some good fortune returned – the ship was dragged free. But they still had the leak to contend with.

Luck was with them again as one of the men, young midshipman Jonathon Monkhouse, told how he had been on a ship in the North Atlantic which had sprung a leak and been saved by horse and sheep shit. The process, called fothering, was to make a bandage out of a sail filled with dung and unwound rope, and lower it over the hole. This was carefully done and the crew found the flow of water into the ship diminished greatly. Banks, perhaps more describing his own mood, said the men on board went 'in an instant from almost despondency to the greatest hopes'.

But they still had to face that barbarous coast and find a place to repair the ship.

The *Endeavour* had struck the reef in the waters of the Kuku Yalanji people, who live in the rainforests from just north of Port Douglas up to the Annan River, south of Cooktown, and as far inland as Mareeba, Chillagoe and Lakeland. One of the most well-known parts of their land, Cape Tribulation, is called Kulki by its people. It is the end of the line for many travellers heading north, as the road becomes the Bloomfield Track and is only passable by four-wheel drives. It carries you on to the small settlement of Wujal Wujal, nestled deep in the rainforest by the Bloomfield Falls.

Talking with the Elders in Wujal Wujal – back before the whole community had to be evacuated due to floods in late 2023 – they

Weary Bay, Kuku Yalanji Country

tell that their ancestors would have been aware of the *Endeavour* out there on the reef, as it was in their fishing grounds. As bits of flotsam from the ship would have washed up along their shores, most probably around Weary Bay, they would have wondered what they were, and then tried to see if they could be of any use to them.

The Kuku Yalanji people are divided into five main clans. The traditional story tells that the original family got too big, so five brothers went to different places, creating the five clans. In their telling, the land and sea were created by the Ngujakura, ancestor beings, who went into the ground after forming the mountains, rivers and forests – where they still live. To the Kuku Yalanji, while some places are sacred, all of their Country and sea Country is important, particularly waterways, as they are paths of Yirrmbal the Rainbow Serpent, and keeping them clean is a part of one's obligation to manage Country.[1]

The eastern Kuku Yalanji's lands and waters were rich in resources, with access to reefs, shallows, islands, beaches, fresh water, tidal creeks, mangroves and swamps. They also had access to lowland rainforests and open woodland forest. Each of these environments provided different resources that were used by the people on a permanent or seasonal basis.

The Kuku Yalanji had up to twelve varieties of spears, that were classified by the number of prongs, the nature of the prongs, what type of barb or stone tip was used, and what the spear shaft was made from. The main hunting conducted at sea was for turtles. This was the domain of men only and generally took at least two or three men. One would paddle the outrigger canoe, while another stood on the prow with a harpoon of up to 3 metres long in his hands. When a turtle was sighted the man at the prow would have to hit it in a soft spot, such as the neck or tail, and the other man would jump into the water and turn it over and bring it to the surface.[2]

Kuku Yalanji warrior with shield and wooden sword

Another aspect that defined the Kuku Yalanji was their large wooden swords and ornate shields (kun-juri), the latter being made from the wide, above-ground roots of a rainforest fig tree.

This coastline of Kuku Yalanji Country contains some of the largest relatively undisturbed tropical lowland rainforest left in Australia. Mossman Gorge is a key landmark and the background to the gorge is Manjal Dimbi (Mount Demi), which means 'mountain holding back'. According to the Kuku Yalanji's stories, the large, human-looking rock represents the ancestor spirit Kubirri, who came to the assistance of the Kuku Yalanji when they were persecuted by the evil spirit Wurrumbu. Kubirri still holds back the evil spirit, who is in The Bluff above Mossman River, and in English Kubirri is known as the Good Shepherd.[3]

The Kuku Yalanji had a rich culture, well suited to the unique landscape they lived in. And while Kubirri might have been able to protect them from the evil spirit of Wurrumbu, they had little to protect them from the coming of the white men.

Contact

The first recorded Europeans to come ashore on Kuku Yalanji land were with Captain Phillip Parker King, who visited the area in 1819. His ship, the *Mermaid*, anchored in Weary Bay, and master's mate Frederick Bedwell was sent to examine the river there. King wrote how the canoes they found were very different in construction to the canoes further south: 'Mr. Bedwell was sent to examine the opening, which was called Blomfield's Rivulet ... Near the entrance upon the bank of the inlet several huts were noticed, and near them Mr. Bedwell found a canoe; which, being hollowed out of the trunk of a tree, was of very different construction to any we had before seen; its length was twenty-one feet ... an outrigger, projecting about two feet, was neatly attached to one side, which prevented its liability to overset, and at each end was a projection, from fifteen to twenty inches long, on which the natives carry their fire or sit.'[4]

The next recorded visitor was not until over fifty years later, when William Hann arrived in 1872. He had been commissioned by the Queensland government to explore Cape York, to assess its potential mineral and land resources. On his journey he renamed the Palmer, Tate and Daintree rivers. But it was the Palmer River that was to cause the Kuku Yalanji much grief – for one of Hann's party discovered gold there.

That led to one James Mulligan leading an expedition back to the area in 1873, and he reported that the sandbars of the river glittered with gold. It triggered a massive gold rush. By the end of that year government officials and prospectors were flooding the region, along with a detachment of the feared native police.

Conflict between the miners and the Kuku Yalanji began almost at once, and a party of ninety-three miners was attacked as it set out to reach the Palmer River from the Endeavour River. The miners had no notion of, nor interest in, seeking permission to cross the lands of the Kuku Yalanji, nor any qualms about shooting any animals for food – or any people who threatened them.

The skirmishes culminated in a pitched battle between approximately 150 warriors and the miners at a site on the Normanby River now known as Battle Camp. A newspaper of the day published the following account: 'Blacks surprised us at daybreak, about 150, all were armed; got close to the camp before anyone heard them; great consternation; shot several; they ran into large waterholes for shelter, where they were shot.'[5]

Within a year, over 5,000 Europeans and 2,000 Chinese were working the Palmer River. But the gold there didn't last long, playing out by about 1880, so many of the newcomers then cleared land for farms. And things went the way they had all along the coast, with native police aggressively attacking the local people while settlers cleared the land.

The thick uncleared scrub of the rainforests provided a good refuge for the Kuku Yalanji, but it contained insufficient food for them, and in 1878 the police commissioner reported that from the Mulgrave to the Mossman rivers, 'the natives [were] literally starving'.[6]

The land suffered as well, as the people were unable to effectively use fire management, knowing that the smoke would give away their positions to troopers. They also let the grass grow long to better hide in it.

First Nations author Victor Steffensen has written on the problem this has caused, which has been growing over recent decades. 'Because there is so much fuel, the fire is hotter than the soils and trees can bear. The wildfire rages at the wrong time of year, with massive loads of dead vegetation to feed its greed. Everything on the ground is burnt to a cinder, nothing but black, burnt ground to be seen.'[7]

And then, when the violence against the people had run its course and numbers were drastically reduced, a mission was predictably proposed as a way to ensure the people's survival. For the Kuku Yalanji it was a Lutheran-run mission on the Bana Yiri (Bloomfield River). It can hardly have been called a success, though, for while up to 120 Kuku Yalanji people lived there at various times, not one person was baptised or converted. Indeed, one study of the mission used the title 'A Case Study in Failure'.[8] The old mission site (in fact it was the last mission in Queensland to close, and not until 1987) is now the township of Wujal Wujal, which means 'many falls', being close to sacred women's falls.

Also, as occurred across most of Queensland, people were taken off Country and moved to distant missions, which led to disconnection with culture and Country, and the ongoing impacts of that.

Talking with workers from the Jabalbina Yalanji Aboriginal Corporation, which represents the interests of the Eastern Kuku Yalanji, it is stressed how important it is that the young people know their deep history, and what happened to their Elders.

One of the workers, Alex, tells that his grandfather was taken to Palm Island when he was three years old. He had an older sister who followed him a couple of years later, and that enabled him to one day reconnect with his family.

Jabalbina means 'for our ancestors', and the purpose of the corporation is to make the ancestors proud. One of the Jabalbina Yalanji Aboriginal Corporation's many focuses is working with troubled youths, reconnecting them with their culture – where the justice and social welfare systems too often mirror the practices of the past in taking children away from their families and Country. Many of the young people have been in and out of detention, but Jabalbina's programs are designed to enable local communities to deliver locally designed solutions and support young people to turn their back on crime, and to reduce antisocial behaviour. This includes running cultural workshops and taking people camping in the Daintree. On one recent camp, that had the theme of nutrition for the body, mind and spirit, the participants explored where jalun (sea) and bubu (land) met in the mangroves of Cooya Beach. They got themselves a feed of crabs and periwinkles and had kangaroo burgers on the beach.

Jabalbina also manages programs looking after Country. Alex said they had teams up in the Daintree who were replanting native vegetation, to get back to their old ways.

As a registered cultural heritage body, Jabalbina works hard to preserve and protect both bubu (land) and jalan (sea). This includes informing visitors to sacred places, such as Kija (Roaring Meg Falls) and the Bouncing Stones, that they are women-only sites and men are not allowed to go there. They also request that no photos or videos of these places be taken, and that any visitors delete any images of these places they may have uploaded to their social media accounts.

Jabalbina has also been a part of the purchase of protected and at-risk rainforest properties that are home to several endangered species, like the cassowary and the Bennett's tree-kangaroo. When land is purchased it is owned and managed by its Traditional Owners.

However, there are some aspects of reclaiming culture that are more difficult. For while the Kuku Yalanji language is widely spoken, there are still some gaps in knowledge that have been lost with the passing of Elders. We are told that this is one of the impacts of Cook and colonisation. Some people have lost language, and some people have lost culture – and we are told some tribes have even become extinct. These are not easy things to know, but again are things that more Australians need to know.

Whalumbal Birri (Endeavour River) Guugu Yimidhirr Country

Wanhtharra nyundu!   Welcome to our Country!

In the A.M. 4 of the Natives came down to the Sandy point on the North side of the Harbour, having along with them a small wooden Canoe with Outriggers, in which they seem'd to be employed striking fish, etc.

Cook's journal, 10 July 1770

The Guugu Yimidhirr people of the area around Whalumbal Birri in northern Queensland have come to tell a different story about Cook than many of the First Peoples of Australia. To them he has, in recent years, come to be seen as a man who ultimately, despite transgressing several laws and protocols, showed respect and took part in a reconciliation with them. And the story of how they got to that is as important as the event itself.

It should be told first that despite spending forty-eight days on Country, and having the opportunity to meet the bama (people), Cook had actually not intended to stay there that long. But after repairing the hole in the *Endeavour*, contrary winds kept him there long enough to not just establish some relations with the Guugu Yimidhirr people, but to both offend and appease them – and then learn from them.

It leads to the question of how he might have been remembered by other First Nations people if he'd had the opportunity and time to learn a little more about them.

The *Endeavour* had hit the reef about 40 kilometres out at sea, and after temporary repairs it took them five long days to make their way northwards to a sheltered river that some of the crew had found. Cook renamed it the Endeavour River, which he described as being 'very narrow, and the Harbour much smaller than I had been told, but very convenient for our Purpose'. But to the Guugu Yimidhirr people, whose land it was on, it was Whalumbal Birri, and had been formed by a mighty serpent called Yiirambal.

According to their stories, Yiirambal began its travels from the north, creating rivers and streams in the deep tracks it made. The bama were happy because water ran through their Country, making green grass and bush foods with berries, and yam vines, in abundance.

As Yirrambal travelled it found it was getting hotter, and it needed shade, but it couldn't find anywhere to hide from the heat. As it moved, looking for shelter, its mighty tail pushed up dirt, making the hills and ranges. Yirrambal then dived into the earth, and each place it surfaced became a lagoon or waterhole, a river or a stream. Then, heading out to sea, it created the great river Whalumbal Birri.[1]

When the bama see a rainbow they know they are connected to water through Yirrambal, and the rivers, streams, ranges and hills that it made now mark the boundaries for each clan group. Different clan groups can actually have different stories of Yirrambal, as they also have different sacred areas where they believe it still resides. To Cook and the men on the *Endeavour*, however, the river was a safe haven where they could mend their ship. They were pleasantly surprised to find the land around the river was not as hot as would be expected in the tropics, thanks to sea breezes that blew regularly from the south. They also found the land contained plants the botanists identified as edible, though they sometimes got that a little wrong. And importantly, they found people who were willing to greet them rather than oppose them.

Guugu Yimithirr Traditional Owner and Bama historian, Alberta Hornsby, said that people of her grandfather's generation had commonly believed that Cook was responsible for killing and raping their women, which was an understandable belief, considering the way the history of colonial expansion was told, ignoring the bloody dispossession of First Nations and making Cook the hero.

However, in 2008 the late Eric Deeral – a Gamay Warra clan leader of the Guugu Yimidhirr – and his friend and Cook enthusiast, John McDonald, began to take a closer look at the *Endeavour* journals. They methodically examined entries from a cultural perspective and found something more complex than was commonly accepted.

Alberta said, 'Myself and a small group of Guugu Yimidhirr bama became involved in these discussions and it became obvious to us that there was much more to the Cook story than anyone had known in the past.' She said that the journals actually reflected elements of cultural governance of place and Country, law and lore, beliefs and customs – which were the prevailing forces behind the undisturbed landing that Cook encountered.

'The journal accounts recorded the places, the sightings and contact by Guugu Yimidhirr bama, and recorded the exchanges of language, including an attempt to record the names of men, use of the throwing stick, demonstration of spear throwing, exchange of food, and use of plants.'

The journals also recorded a hostile incident – over turtles – which finally led to a reconciliation at a place now known as Reconciliation Rocks. 'We were amazed by what we read, and now understood this part of history not just as a history of Cook, but also our history as well. Studying the journals allowed us to get a glimpse of the thinking behind European exploration of the time, and an opportunity to understand Cook.'

This all fed into the annual re-enactment of Cook's landing, held each year in Cooktown. Alberta Hornsby said, 'It is only

Cultural historian Alberta Hornsby

through the efforts of the Cooktown Re-enactment Association that we have promoted a revised history, based on our research. Our re-enactment of this event attempts to reflect the truth.'

So Cook and his crew brought their ship into the Endeavour River and started examining the land and looking for the best place to mend the ship. Importantly, they were able to find fresh water from a nearby creek, and the river supplied plenty of fish to help feed the roughly one hundred men on the ship. It is worth noting that at this point in the voyage they had several sick people on board, some showing early signs of scurvy, which the fresh food diet quickly alleviated.

When the crew tipped the ship over to repair it, they were amazed to find a piece of coral the size of a fist lodged in the hole ripped in the wood. This piece of coral had prevented the water entering too fast, and, combined with the padded sail the crew had lowered over the hole as a bandage, had enabled the ship to stay afloat. After ten days the ship was repaired, but now they needed favourable winds for a safe passage to freedom.

Banks wrote that in exploring around them he found the frames of houses of the people (who he called 'Indians'), but no signs of the people themselves, though the crew had sighted their footprints in the bush.

The bama, however, kept a very close eye on these strangers.

Word had already spread to the Guugu Yimidhirr bama from the Kuku Yalanji bama to the south, who had watched the *Endeavour* working its slow way to shore. Trade between the two peoples was common and there was also intermarriage, which meant messages passed easily between them – including the stories of this strange ship.

When the *Endeavour* came ashore on the banks of the river, the Guugu Yimidhirr – like all the people of the east coast before them – tried to fit what they were seeing into their existing understanding of their world. Hence they wondered if they were seeing

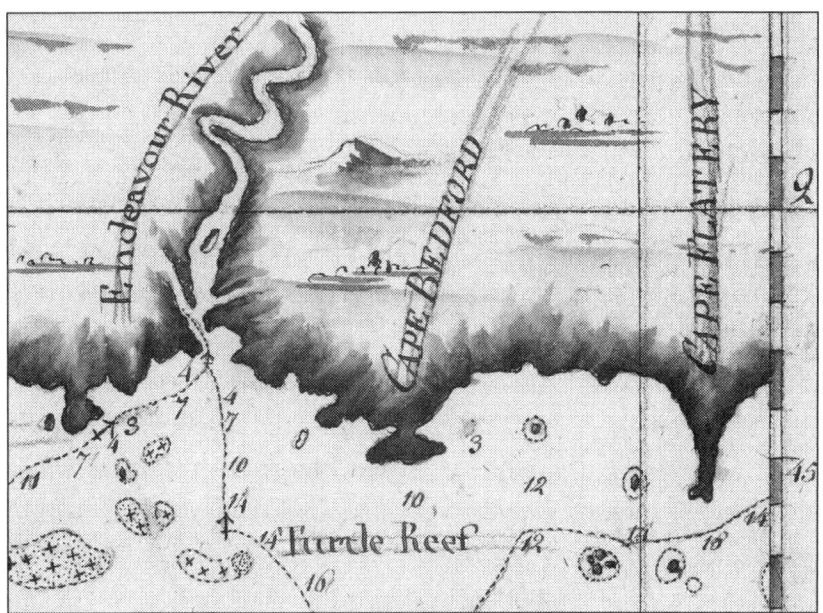

Cook's chart of Guugu Yimidhirr Country

their ancestor spirits come back to them.

Alberta Hornsby says that in the bama's oral history, their ancestors came from the west in the form of the masked plover and wallaroo, and when they died they travelled to the east – and the bama are awaiting their return. She says the bama understood that the spirits became white in this journey, and so thought it was possible Cook and his crew were those returned spirits. So they hid and observed, she says, watching to learn more about these strange spirit people. Were they good or bad spirits? Should they be watched or speared?

Fortunately for Cook he had only briefly beached his ship on the northern shore of the river before moving it to the southern shore. He did not know that he had now set up camp on an area known as Waymburr, which was a place of ceremony and peace. A place where blood was never to be shed. The north shore had no such requirements, and the bama often conjecture what the crew's fate might have been had they landed there, and had the bama decided they needed to be chased away or punished for transgressing laws.

To the bama, understanding what type of spirits or people these visitors might be was central to knowing what to do about them, for the bama were governed by the spirits of the land, animals, water, life and death.

In the Dreaming time of Creation, the bama could speak to the animals, and retained many close links with them. Animals such as mirrgi (owl), who was never far from the people, always telling them if others were coming to their Country, or if there had been a death amongst the bama. And for those that lived near the coast, whose totem was the white cockatoo, that bird told them where foods were, such as gangurru (eastern grey kangaroo) or balinga (echidna).

However, there were many less benevolent spirits. Wuji, for instance, was a fearful spirit and was the guardian of sacred areas.

Or Maargami-ngay, which dwelled in dark or remote areas and loved to steal children. If it managed to steal a boy, it would change him, causing his teeth to grow sharper and his ears to grow larger. His only hope would be if a clever man managed to recapture him and would be able to change him back by using the correct magic, such as rubbing him with right leaf that had been warmed over a fire.[2]

Another spirit, the Manu-galga-thirr, could be seen at night because flames and sparks flew off it as it moved. It would often come into a camp and eat the coals of dying fires, but could be scared away by bright light, so fires were always kept up to keep the Manu-galga-thirr away.

One of the most feared spirits was Yigi, who also dwelled in the darkness. It had long pointy yellow teeth and lots of fingers and toes with long sharp nails, and if you were out after dark Yigi would certainly chase you, and if it caught you it might even eat you.

Today when the bama celebrate the annual Endeavour River festival – a night of traditional singing and dancing by the river just on sunset – a tall figure dressed as Yigi walks on stilts amongst the performing children, waving long arms with sharp nails, scaring them back to the safety of campfires.

Whalumbaal Birri/Endeavour River

So the bama watched and waited, to determine what type of spirits these beings on the ship might be. If they were ancestors, how was it that they did not seem to know which food was good to eat and which was not? And how was it that they so easily broke laws? Had their journey from the lands beyond addled their memories, or was there some other reason?

It is likely that the bama eventually came to view the newcomers as people, as they called them Wangarr (white people), but a different kind of people than they had ever seen. And they wondered, as all the First Nations people along the east coast did, When will they go away?

The bama had a complex seasonal calendar, given to them by Yirrambal the rainbow serpent creator, that told what foods were available at what times in what locations, and what foods needed to be avoided until their proper time. This ensured that food was always available to those with the knowledge, and that no resource would be over-consumed at the wrong time – such as when an animal was with young. Young boys were taught all aspects and protocols of their culture when they were initiated into manhood, being led by a mentor who would then guide them through manhood after the initiation.

But these newcomers – clearly adults – did not seem to know any of the things they should have known. Their clothing also made it hard to see if they had initiation scars on them.

Some of the foods the bama ate that the Europeans did not know how to cook properly included yams, which they cooked too fast, making them inedible. The bama cooked them on slow fires. Similarly, cycad nuts gave the Europeans diarrhoea and vomiting, while the bama knew to pound the nuts with stones and then put them into string bags and soak them in water for five nights, to wash out the toxins. The bama also ate the larvae within ants' nests, which the Europeans did not even remotely consider as food.

The bama watched the visitors cook meat differently, putting it over a fire rather than cooking it in the ashes. Nor did they lay fish on top of hot rocks to cook them.

It was eventually apparent to the bama that they would need to get closer to these strangers to better understand them.

Alberta Hornsby also does tours of the Cooktown Botanic Gardens, where there are samples of the trees and bushes that Jospeh Banks collected and Sydney Parkinson drew. She explains the bama's uses of each, and how often the British failed to know what was edible, or safe to eat.

She shows a dilby, which she says is 'like a custard apple, but tastes bitter to whitefellas'. Then there is the bambubul (weeping ivorywood or tennis ball tree), with a fruit like a tennis ball. 'Very tasty – limey-lemony, peary, peach-something. But it has a lovely pungent smell.'

She shows there are three types of native banana trees, though all have lots of seeds in them. One curious plant is the dugunyja (*Morinda citrifolia*, or cheese fruit), which you need to eat before it gets ripe and stinks too much like old cheese.

Alberta Hornsby says that looking at Parkinson's drawings, it is apparent that some plants had fruited earlier in 1770 than they normally would have done. Perhaps due to lots of rain, but it meant the British had more food they could find.

On 10 July, the crew of the *Endeavour* saw four of the bama standing on the far side of the river from them, and watched as two of the men paddled across on a very small outrigger canoe. The crew beckoned them closer and offered gifts of cloth, nails, paper and beads – which the bama showed little interest in.

But then a small fish was thrown to them.

Banks wrote that they expressed the greatest joy imaginable at this and indicated they would fetch the other two men. While the ship's crew might not have known it, they had enacted a part of bama custom, providing food, which was both an offering of peace and an act that would demand reciprocity.

The bama landed on the same side of the river as the ship, and the Tahitian navigator, Tupaia, went to them to try and talk to them. However, he was no more able to understand them than he had been able to understand the people at Kamay – Botany Bay.

The men, bama and British, then sat on the ground together and the British noticed how agitated the bama became if anyone walked near their spears. After unsuccessfully attempting conversation, the British invited the men to go onboard the ship with them for a meal, but the bama returned to their canoe and paddled back across the river.

Cook wrote in his journal that one of the men was 'something above the Middle Age, the other 3 were young', and all their limbs seemed small. He also noted that some part of their bodies had been painted red and one had his upper lip and chest painted with streaks of white. This was a clear sign the men were all initiated and were painted for an official meeting with the British.

Cook wrote: 'Their features were far from being disagreeable; their Voices were soft and Tunable, and they could easily repeat any word after us, but neither us nor Tupia could understand one word they said.'

The next day, two of the same men, with two new men, came back to visit. Cook wrote that one of them had a bone the size of his finger through a hole in the septum of his nose, and upon examination they found all the men had such holes, both in their noses and ears. They also wore bracelets on their arms made from hair.

The men, all now being a little more comfortable in each other's presence, examined each other carefully, fascinated by each other's clothing and adornments. The Guugu Yimidhirr men demonstrated remarkable patience with the Englishmen's inquisitiveness as they examined their bodies. Banks went so far as to spit on his finger and rub it on a man's skin to see if dust was hiding a different coloured skin beneath.

In Banks' account he stated that the name of one of the men was Yaparico and he had brought with him a fish, which the botanist supposed correctly was in return for the fish they had given the men the day before. Reciprocity.

The journals tell that over a period of ten days the bama came to visit the Europeans six times, each time bringing new people. Eventually they even went onboard the ship and Banks wrote: 'they venturd on board the ship and soon became our very good friends'. It was noted that the only women the British saw, however, were on the northern shore of the river and they never came over to the crew's camp.

Cook, Banks and Sydney Parkinson wrote detailed descriptions of the bama, and Parkinson said that though of a diminutive size, they ran very swiftly, and were very merry. He wrote, 'They had flattish noses, moderate-sized mouths, regular well-set large teeth, tinged with yellow. Most of them had cut off the hair from their heads; but some of them wore their hair, which was curled and bushy, and their beards frizzled.'

He also said they had initiation scars on their chests and hips, and some were painted with red streaks and others had white streaks on their faces. The women, who he only observed on the far shore

The Endeavour *beached for repair at Whalumbal Birri (Endeavour River)*

through a telescope, he said had feathers stuck on the crown of their heads, fastened by a piece of gum.

Parkinson also took a great deal of interest in the bama language, and compiled a word list of 120 words. He described their language as not harsh, and said they articulated their words very distinctly. He also said that in speaking they made a great motion with their lips, and said *tut, tut*, many times, but he could not determine what it meant.

Banks' insights were a bit more disappointing. As one of the main scientists on board – or 'experimental gentlemen', as they were called by the crew – he might have been expected to have a more observant eye for the types of science the First Peoples of the continent had mastered.

Chris Matthews, a Quandamooka man from Minjerribah, is the Associate Dean of Indigenous Leadership and Engagement in the science faculty of the University of Technology Sydney, and has said that First Nations knowledge was often misunderstood or underestimated. He said of the British scientists, 'They looked physically at the people and didn't have the capacity to know what they were seeing.'

However, the journals also show that it greatly amused the bama to see that while they could easily repeat words in English, the British had great difficulty in trying to pronounce any of their words in the Guugu Yimidhirr language. Even simple words like: tocaya, 'to sit down'; wonananio, 'asleep'; yeiye, 'is it this?'; hala, hala, mae, 'come here'.

On 18 July Cook wrote that he went into the woods with Mr Banks and Mr Solander, and met with five of the bama. He said that although they had not seen any of these individual people before, they came to them without showing any signs of fear. Two of them wore necklaces made of shells, which they seemed to value, Cook said, as they would not part with them.

Later Cook wrote: 'I do not look upon them to be a warlike

people; on the contrary, I think them a Timerous and inoffensive race, no ways inclined to Cruelty.'

The men of the *Endeavour*'s first proper sighting of a kangaroo happened while at Whalumbaal Birri, though they struggled to describe it, needing to use common European animals for comparison. Cook wrote in his journal: 'One of the Men saw an Animal something less than a greyhound; it was of a Mouse Colour, very slender made, and swift of Foot.'

And when Cook saw one, he wrote: 'I saw myself this morning, a little way from the Ship, one of the Animals before spoke off; it was of a light mouse Colour and the full size of a Grey Hound, and shaped in every respect like one, with a long tail, which it carried like a Grey hound; in short, I should have taken it for a wild dog but for its walking or running, in which it jump'd like a Hare or Deer.'

When Joseph Banks saw the animal, he wrote: 'In gathering plants today I myself had the good fortune to see the beast so much talkd of, tho but imperfectly; he was not only like a grey hound in size and running but had a long tail, as long as any grey hounds; what to liken him to I could not tell, nothing certainly that I have seen at all resembles him.'

Banks had his own greyhound, that he brought along on the *Endeavour*, chase one of the animals, but said that it was unable to catch it as it hopped into tall grass that slowed the dog down while the animal leaped over the tops of it. He also stated that they were surprised to see that the animal jumped on only two legs, not four. And the print of the foot, when seen up close, was described as being like that of a goat.

On 14 July the men finally managed to shoot one of the animals and they were able to examine it in more detail. Banks wrote that to compare it to any European animal would be impossible, as its front legs were so short as to be of no use in walking, and its rear legs were extremely long, allowing it to jump seven to eight feet (up to 2.4 metres).

Continuing their study of the animal, in the manner they studied many of the new species of animals they encountered, Banks wrote, 'The Beast which was killd yesterday was today Dressd for our dinners and provd excellent meat.'

And Sydney Parkinson wrote that it tasted like a hare, but with a more agreeable flavour.

And while the word gangurru has been adopted in English as 'kangaroo', it actually only refers to the eastern grey kangaroo; other types of kangaroos have different names. For instance, the eastern grey male is known as dhulumbanu, a female wallaroo or euro is galbaala, and a male wallaby is a galgarrunggul.

Relations between the British and the bama were going well, but considering how many breaches of protocol the British were inadvertently making, it could not last. Shortly before the crew were ready to leave the Endeavour River, the journals tell, a group of bama visited the ship once more and were shocked to see a dozen or so large sea turtles in nets on the deck, that the British had caught out on the reefs.

The bama were greatly agitated at this, as it was not the right time for hunting turtles and taking that many would leave a large impact on resources. Also, as it was a sacred animal, there were proper protocols for hunting them that had to be observed. For instance, when a turtle had been caught and was being cut up, the men would chant all night until the first light of day, and women were not allowed to witness the butchering.

Knowing that the Europeans had broken several taboos, the bama felt it was their duty to release the turtles. This is not how the British saw it, though.

Cook's statue at Cooktown

Cook wrote that the following day, 19 July, ten or so men approached the ship carrying a large number of spears. They came onboard and using signs indicated they wanted some of the turtles. When this was refused them, one of the men became very angry and tried to drag a turtle to the side of the ship, only being stopped by the ship's crew. Cook wrote, 'being disappointed in this, they grew a little Troublesome, and were for throwing every thing overboard they could lay their hands upon'.

The bama then went ashore, determined to follow protocol and punish the newcomers. One grabbed a burning stick from a fire there and ran around setting the grass aflame, threatening to burn all the goods the men had ashore. Fortunately for the Europeans, most of their goods had now been packed aboard the ship, in preparation for departure, and the main damage done was the death of a small pig.

The bama then tried to burn the grass close to where the ship's fishing nets and some cloth was laid out to dry. The British grabbed their guns and fired small shot at one of the men, who, being hit, dropped his burning stick and 'ran nimbly to his comrades who all ran off pretty fast'.

The British knew the man had been hit because they saw a few drops of blood on some of the linen he had run over. Cook then led a small party into the trees to follow the men, chasing them along the river's edge. They soon met them coming back towards them, armed with a handful of spears each. It was a tense moment, and Cook said that not knowing the bama's intention he had his men seize whatever spears they could. This alarmed the bama so much, as a clear act of aggression, that they made off again. Cook followed them for about half a kilometre until they caught up with them once more. The two groups were both armed, and waited to see who would act first.

The late Eric Deeral has told the bama's side of the story: 'Our bama were so confused and angry that they set fire to the campsite. Then they heard a loud bang and saw a puff of smoke. One of the men could not believe that something invisible punctured his leg and blood started to flow. They all ran away. Before going back to their camp, our bama lit more fires to warn other clans that something had gone wrong.

'Ngamu Yarrbarigu, an elder of the clans, called all the members together to discuss the day's events. A strategy was agreed upon. Ngamu Yarrbarigu and a number of men would visit the strangers' camp the next day and every effort would be made to make peace, because our bama now knew that the visitors possessed a spirit which was more powerful than they had experienced.

'Next morning, before our bama left camp, a customary ritual was performed by the elders. Each man was wiped with sweat from the armpit of the elders and our women chanted, "Ganhil gunday." This was for them [the men] to be protected, to practise self-control and to leave camp with a blessing. When our bama confronted the strangers we each had four spears. The elder Ngamu Yarrbarigu carried one spear which had no barb. Our elders were afraid to do anything that might result in the spirits of our departed ancestors being upset, in case Cook's mob were indeed wangarra or reincarnations of our ancestors. And so with this doubt and fear in their minds they used discretion, decided against any rash actions.

'Ngamu Yarrbarigu said to Cook's men: "Ngahthaan gaaai thawun maa naa thi hu. We come to make friends."

'Sensing that the strangers were not sure of their intention and did not understand what their leader Ngamu Yarrbarigu said, our bama then put their plan into action. They withdrew to an outcrop of rocks, where it is possible that more bama were positioned. There they placed their spears on the ground and sat down. At this point Cook may have become aware that his life was in danger – however, diplomacy was used by both sides. It may be that the caution on the part of the Guugu Yimithirr saved Cook's life.'[3]

Now a quite remarkable thing happened. Even though the British had just broken one of the strictest taboos, in shedding blood on the land of Waymburr – and should have been punished for it, easily triggering a conflict that would have led to many deaths on both sides – cool heads actually prevailed.

The little old man known as Yaparico came towards the British, calming the agitated warriors. Being the elder of this area, he walked out in front of the British with a broken spear, wiping sweat from his armpits and blowing it towards Cook. According to Guugu Yimidhirr lore, marking Cook with his sweat would mean the spirits would believe he was one of them, and would look after him and keep him safe. Yaparico also called Cook 'Towun', which is something like 'a friend'. Cook had the presence of mind to understand this symbol of peace and had his men hand back the spears they had confiscated.

Both sides then sat on the ground and mutual respect was established.

Reconciliation Rocks is today a monument to the first act of reconciliation in Australia between the British and First Nations peoples. But the bama point out that reconciliation had in fact been happening there for many thousands of years, as different groups came to the land known as Waymburr to settle disputes.

This is a very important story for the Guugu Yimidhirr people, as it contributes to negating the myth of *terra nullius*. It demonstrates that there was a law of the land and how people should behave on the land. So this is a story that Guugu Yimidhirr people would like all Australians to know.

However, Alberta Hornsby has said that not even all the Guugu Yimidhirr are aware of the story. 'We are all just learning this part of history 250 years after the event,' she said.

On 20 July 1770, after nearly seven weeks, Cook felt they could finally leave the Endeavour River. But as they sailed out – only to encounter a change of winds that held them near the river mouth a few more days – the bama set fire to the land where they had been camped. Banks wrote: 'all the hills about us for many miles were on fire and at night made the most beautiful appearance imaginable'.

The bama were not seeking a spectacle, however, for the British did not understand that they had fired to the land to cleanse it, particularly of the desecration of intentionally spilling blood on Waymburr.

Contact

The bama were not to see any more Europeans until explorer Captain Phillip Parker King, arrived at the Endeavour River in 1819. He wrote in his journal that the bama had noted one of his men who had a very fair complexion, and urged him to take off his clothes and reveal if he was a man or a woman. The sailor took off his shirt but would not take off his trousers, which caused offence to the bama and led to an altercation and the firing of a musket to chase the bama away.

One more misunderstanding that threatened to end the peace earlier established by Cook.

Later European visits were more disastrous for the bama, and when gold was discovered at the Palmer River, over 150 kilometres inland, the township of Cooktown sprung up in a few short weeks in 1873, as miners arrived seeking to hit it rich. The sudden influx of settlers led to the type of dispossession and scarcity of the people's water and foods that accompanied such rapid settlement elsewhere along the east coast, as well as protracted conflicts and the death on both sides.

The goodwill established between Cook and the bama was long gone.

The European and Chinese miners failed to understand that they were intruding upon the land of several different language groups, and saw every one of them as potentially hostile. This led to pre-emptive attacks which of course led to retaliatory attacks.

The township of 'Cooks-town' grew rapidly to 4,000 people, with several thousand having trekked to the nearby goldfields, often heavily armed and ready to shoot at any of the local people attempting to oppose them coming onto their lands. In 1875 the *Cooktown Herald* wrote of the ongoing conflict: 'the natives, wholly ignorant of the terrible power of fire arms and confiding in their numbers, showed a ferocity and daring wholly unexpected and unsurpassed. Grasping the very muzzles of the rifles they attempted to wrest them from the hands of the whites, standing to be shot down rather than yield an inch. This was the beginning of a series of attacks that at first were daringly open; but as the knowledge dawned on their minds that the white race had a fatal superiority of weapons, these attacks became stealthy, cautious, and only made at great advantages of numbers and situation.'[4]

By 1877 there were approximately 17,000 European and Chinese miners on the Palmer River goldfield, and while numbers are sketchy at best, it has been estimated that over six years a minimum of seventeen European and Chinese miners were killed, and at least ten more were wounded. In addition, at least 133 horses and sixty-seven bullocks were speared over the same period.[5] There are no accurate records for how many bama were killed, but based on the activities of the native police it was likely in the hundreds. The native police maintained an active presence in the area for over thirty years, and many bama captured on the goldfields were sent to Palm Island, Yarrabah and Cherbourg.

Memoirs of the day refer to even officials being 'in frequent peril from the blacks, who were constantly on the watch, ever on the alert, and a very strange cannibal lot'.[6]

The reporting of the time was similarly sensationalist, and continued for so long that the official centenary history of Queensland ridiculously put the numbers of Chinese killed and eaten by local people on the Palmer River in the thousands.[7] Demonising the bama made it that much easier to justify the acts of violence being carried out against them.

And then, almost as suddenly as the rush had started, the gold began to run out, and by the mid-1880s the number of miners ran out too. But the damage had been done.

Cooktown, now a supply port for the pastoralists and settlers of the region, was, like most towns in Queensland at the time, strictly segregated. The local people had to be out of the town by nightfall, and back on the other side of Boundary Street – a street which still exists by that name in modern Cooktown.

A temporary reserve was set up on the northern shore of the Endeavour River in 1879, and in 1886 a German mission was established north of Cooktown, at Cape Bedford, by Johann Flierl. He had actually been on his way to New Guinea, and only stayed one year until he was replaced by George Schwarz, who remained at the mission – called Hope Vale – for over fifty years. He was affectionately called Muni [black] by the bama.

The first recruits to the mission, and the first converts to swap their traditional beliefs for Christianity, were girls from the surviving clans. Then young men seeking wives joined them. But by the early years of the twentieth century children were being sent to the mission from as far as Bamaga at the top of Cape York. Other children who were deemed to be of mixed blood were sent away, as were any children caught living in the bush. Some were even brought to the mission by their parents, who were unable to care for them in their traditional way.[8]

In contrast to most missions of the time, at Hope Vale the missionaries used the Guugu Yimidhirr language and the mission did relatively well – until World War Two. One day in 1942 the Department of Native Affairs suddenly ordered the evacuation of the Hope Vale mission. It was supposed by the authorities that George Schwarz, being German, would naturally be giving support to any Japanese soldiers that landed in Queensland, and that he might also solicit the help of the bama in this. He was arrested, and over 250 bama were sent south to the Woorabinda mission. In a colder climate, far from their traditional homes, nearly ninety people died in the first months there.

By the end of the war, the Guugu Yimidhirr survivors started returning to their land, and from 1949 rebuilt a community at Hope Vale. It still stands today, a short drive from Cooktown, and the Guugu Yimidhirr language is taught in the schools and is widely spoken. And in mid-June each year the Hope Vale community come into Cooktown to participate in the re-enactment of Cook's landing on their Country, which they have had input to, and to tell that story of the first act of reconciliation between white and black Australia.

Pajinka (Cape York Peninsula) Gudang-Yadhaykenu Country

Mita dju.   Greetings.

The same sea that washed the side of the ship rose in a breaker prodidgiously high the very next time it did rise, so that between us and destruction was only a dismal Valley, the breadth of one wave ...
Cook's journal, 16 August 1770

Making its slow way thorough the reefs and shoals, the *Endeavour* stopped at the island the Dingall people called Jiigurra – which Cook renamed Lizard Island, after the number of lizards there – to climb the highest point and search for a safe passage out to sea. He eventually found a thin channel that is now called Cooks Passage, and contemporary navigators with GPS and modern charts marvel at how he managed to make his way safely through it.

In fact, it was a close thing that he made it out at all and was not wrecked a second time. Having finally made their way beyond the reef into the open ocean, Cook and his crew found that they were actually not free from the reef's perils after all. Having travelled northwards for four days, Cook decided to move closer to the land in order not to miss the hoped-for passage between New Holland and New Guinea. However, during the night a strong current pushed the ship close to a dangerous reef.

With no wind to move the ship they put the two workable boats out to try and tow the ship clear. Cook stated: 'we were in the very jaws of distruction', and Banks wrote 'a speedy death was all we had hope for'.

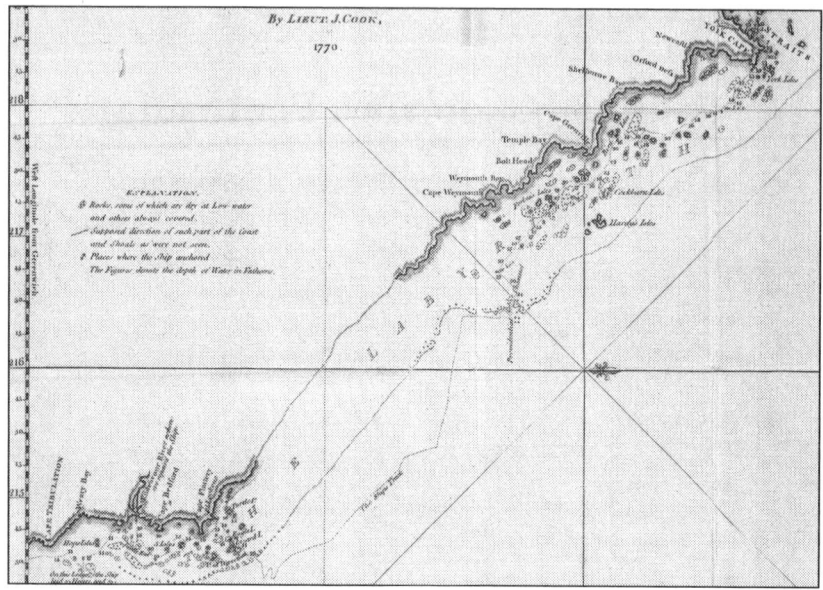

Cook's chart, showing a gap where he sailed outside the reef

But where bad luck had led to Cook striking the reef offshore of Cape Tribulation, today good luck was with him. Just as 'distruction' seemed imminent a light breeze sprang up – enough to move the ship 100 metres or so from the breakers. And they soon caught sight of a passage through the reefs.

They were safe, but back inside the reef, about 300 kilometres north of Lizard Island. In front of them were the lands and waters of the Wuthathi people – sandbeach people who lived on one of the most dazzlingly white stretches of sand along the coast. Their origin stories tell of their totem, the diamond stingray – yama – which was washed up on the shore and flipped onto its back during a storm, exposing its pure white belly.

The *Endeavour*'s charts show a long gap between Lizard Island and where they came back inside the reef – so Cook missed seeing and charting the lands of other people, including the Koko Ompindamo, the Yintjingga, the Ompeila and the Koko Ya'o.

Wuthathi land runs for about 70 kilometres along the coastline, and the people are known as the Pama. They are descended from the bird, fish and animal people that created the landscape and lore during their Dreaming time, which they call the Story Time.

Cook continued sailing north, passing the lands of the Yadhaykenu (Yadhaigana) and Andooyomo, before approaching the tip of Cape York – Pajinka – the land of the Gudang people. According to early anthropologists, trying their level best to distinguish between peoples who often traded and intermarried and spoke each other's language, the Gudang and Andooyomo got along very well – even with the Kaurareg, the closest Torres Strait Islanders. But, anthropologists have stated, the Gumakudin and the Yadhaykenu had fearsome reputations.[1]

Nearing the top of the cape, the *Endeavour* was picking its way slowly through so many shoals and reefs that Cook stated there were too many to properly chart. On one small island they saw trees and empty huts. Cook wrote that he supposed it was occasionally inhabited by the people on the mainland who would have come over to hunt turtles.

And then, finally, they reached the top of the continent. Cook renamed it Cape York, after King George III's younger brother, Prince Edward, the Duke of York and Albany. Their journey along the east coast – a path that Cook had not particularly preferred to take – had ended up taking them four months. Ahead of them now was a short trip to Batavia where they could repair the ship. But Cook had one more task yet to perform, which involved a flag and a flagstaff.

Nicholas Thompson Wymarra is a proud Gudang-Yadhaykenu man who has been handed down cultural authority for the Gudang-Yadhaykenu nation. He explains that the two tribes, once enemies, amalgamated as a matter of survival. He says, 'Our tribe is the Gudang-Yadhaykenu nation of the east and west coast of the

Nicholas Thompson Wymarra with the Gudang-Yadhaykenu land and sea Country behind him, including Wymarra Rock

Cape York Peninsula area.' He says, 'For our family, they say we are separate, but still one people – Gudang-Yadhaykenu.'

Today he is standing at the small settlement of Injinoo, one of five small settlements near the tip of the cape, looking to the islands to the north that are a part of his people's Country. He points out several islands, including the island that is known to his people as Thunadha – which has different names for other peoples of the region, and which Cook named Possession Island. It is good to have him there as a guide and to provide a welcome. An earlier visit to a remote part of the cape, approached from the sea, had a very different feeling, with no one providing a welcome onto the Country. Standing on the remote beach there, close to the most northern tip of the country, keeping an eye on a crocodile lurking in the nearby creek, it felt a little unsettling. Then it suddenly started to rain. That was clearly understood as the ancestors telling it was time to go.

Nicholas Thompson Wymarra tells that the small communities on the cape are home to several different peoples, including those who come from a little further south, and Torres Strait Islanders. Just behind the small headland is an old cemetery.

'That goes back to the 1800s, so our great-grandparents are there, and lots of aunts and uncles.'

He says that the many deaths that happened in the early twentieth century were put down to causes like the Spanish flu. 'But that flu was at the end of World War One, and this was 1913 when our families were there.

'But the most important thing for families, our high priority, is to identify the unmarked graves, because our loving late old people are coming out of their graves.'

He tells that the old people had to endure hard times when the colonist settlers arrived on the cape. 'If they spoke their native tongue they got punished. We are only just now starting to pick it up. Back then our grandfathers and great-grandfathers, if they tried to speak their native tongue they got all their rations taken off them – their flour and tobacco, blankets, everything – just from speaking their native tongue. And they got forced to worship the bible, to study and be educated and go to school.'

The tip of the cape, Pajinka, at the far right, with Thunadha (Possession Island) in the foreground, High Island in the centre, and Peak Point behind that

He says, 'Our families, we are the survivors – most of our old people, my grandfather, my great-grandfather, wanted to get away from all that.'

He points out landmarks as he talks. 'Our Dreaming is the salt- and freshwater ipi [water] Dreaming, which is all part of the rich ecosystem that we've got throughout our islands and the tip of Cape York Peninsula. And part of our Dreaming is the rainbow serpent or rainbow snake, and one of our totems is urruvu – the sand goanna.

'Throughout the islands we have the turtle rock formation, and also the green frog sitting on the back of the rock formation of the turtle at Peak Point. And the turtle with the green frog on the back of it represents the ecosystem, the rain, rainy season and the climate.

'The actual Peak Point there is the sand goanna urruvu. That's all part of our Dreaming and our blood stories. The rainbow snake created all the islands and the riverways, coming in and out of the land. And our land goes all the way around the cape to the east coast. We've got all our marine resources. I say our area's a rich ecosystem – turtles, dugongs, sand goannas, fish, crayfish, so everything is in that area there. And the rock formations represent the marine resources that we have around, which is all a part of our hunting magic and part of our stories.'

Contact

After Cook had passed by, the people at the top of the cape witnessed several other ships pass by over the years, before vessels seeking pearls, trochus and sea cucumbers started visiting their waters. But the most notable early contact with the peoples of the top end, that was deemed worth putting in the history books of the day, was the failed expedition of Edmund Kennedy in 1848.

Kennedy was born on the Channel island of Guernsey, and had come to the colonies as a man with a mission – and that mission was to make his mark on the colonies. He got himself appointed leader of an expedition that would explore an overland path to the tip of

Cape York from Rockingham Bay, around current-day Mission Beach.

The expedition was not a success – by any measure. After two months the men and their carts and supplies had only travelled about 20 miles. So Kennedy decided to push on alone with his young companion Jackey Jackey (whose real name was Galmarra, and who was most likely a member of the Wonarua people, near present-day Newcastle).

Kennedy and Galmarra made their slow way along the coast, travelling through the lands of the many sandbeach people until, very near the tip of the cape, they trod uninvited onto the lands of the aggressive Yadhaykenu. Kennedy and his horse were speared and Galmarra narrowly escaped to join the rescue ship *Ariel*. He told his rescuers how the local people had been trailing them through the scrub, with their destination just in sight, until 'a good many blackfellows came behind in the scrub, and threw plenty of spears, and hit Mr. Kennedy in the back first ... They went away then a little way, and came back again, throwing spears all around, more than they did before; very large spears ... he said, "I am very bad, Jackey; you take the books, Jackey, to the captain" ... I then tied up the papers; he then said, "Jackey, give me paper and I will write," I gave him paper and pencil, and he tried to write, and he then fell back and died ...'[2]

As in many cases, the failed expedition was hailed as heroic, and Kennedy as a hero. Galmarra, who provided one of the few exploration narratives recorded by a First Person in the nineteenth century, saw his testimony become incorporated into colonial storytelling – some of it sensationalised of course.[3] As historian Maria Nugent has said of his public recognition, 'It is often at moments of crisis that Indigenous people become visible in the records of exploration.'[4]

Galmarra was rewarded with 50 pounds and a silver breastplate, and his story became a part of the narrative of the faithful native guide, rather than the story of the resourceful First Nations person using his knowledge to survive when all others fell behind or died.

He never collected the money and never wore the breastplate.

The next major contact was in 1864 when the colony of Queensland had just broken from New South Wales and decided it needed to establish a trading centre at the top of the cape. It also wanted to counter the recently established French colony in New Caledonia. The chosen location was renamed Somerset, in honour of the late Edward Seymour, the First Lord of the Admiralty and 12th Duke of Somerset. It was also, ultimately, to be a failed venture, and also characterised by violence and death.

John Jardine was appointed the settlement's first – well, just about everything. He was appointed police magistrate, Commissioner of Crown Lands, and district registrar. And twenty-five Royal Marines were initially appointed to help protect the settlement too, though two of them were speared by hostile locals. So clearly relations with the local people were never going to be great.

John Jardine wrote that the spearing of the two marines had been 'met with severe and just punishment'. Colonial shorthand for yet another massacre.[5]

John Jardine's two sons entered whitefella folklore in 1865, when they brought a mob of cattle overland from Rockhampton. This was praised by some as 'one of the finest droving trips in the annals of Queensland'.[6] But it has been condemned by others as violent and destructive. The ten-month cattle drive resulted in so much violence that Frank Jardine boasted of some eighty notches on the stock of his rifle, representing First Peoples he had killed.[7]

Frank Jardine, who was baptised Francis Lascelles Jardine, and who might be considered a violent psychopath by today's standards, later became police magistrate at Somerset and oversaw some of the worst times there. When in 1868 there was an attack on his cattle station at Vallack Point, he is said to have organised a retribution where over thirty people were killed.[8] He even had a band of his own native police, though when some of them deserted in 1871, taking with them arms and stores, he hunted them down and is said to have shot two of them dead.[9]

Anthropologist Nonie Sharp, who worked with the people of the cape for nearly twenty-five years, wrote: 'Frank Jardine was a man of violence, of this there is no doubt. He himself boasted of the notches on his rifle accrued during his overland journey to Somerset; he confided in Dr Cannon of his admiration for those squatters who used poisoned flour as the "final solution" to the Aboriginal problem; he had his personal "native police" at his command until he eventually killed two of them in cold blood.'[10]

Constable Ginivan, who came to Somerset in mid-1867, said of Jardine that he was terrorising 'the Aborigines with the assistance of his private "troopers".'[11]

And Gudang-Yadhaykenu man Nicholas Thompson Wymarra said, 'For the missionaries, for Frank Jardine and the troopers, they see us living our own traditional lore as something wrong. As evil. Our old people always stood their ground and fought for what is good for us.

'One of the stories that I'd like to share is a group of our family members, seventeen family members, females, males and kids – one day, there was a dispute about the use of a stone axe head. Because of the troubles, Frank Jardine and the missionaries couldn't control our late families, our ancestors – they shot them. The whole seventeen of them.'

To add to the injustice, the skeletal remains were stolen and taken away to a museum in Germany. However, they were eventually repatriated and buried at nearby Pulu (Somerset).

'In October 2014 we did the repatriation of skeletal remains from Charité Medical University in Berlin, Germany, returned to Australian soil – the so-called Great Southern Land. But they were returned to their traditional lands at Pulu on the Cape York Peninsula.'

Nicholas said, 'On Cape York Peninsula there has been a lot of bad and horrific and terrible dark history. Our heads, our skulls, our skeletal remains were seen as commodities. Neighbouring tribes turned against one another, just for the fight for survival to gain rations.'

Frank Jardine's reign of terror and division over the people at the cape was demonstrated when, in 1869, the crew of the pearl cutter the *Sperwer* were murdered by Torres Strait Islanders of Muralug (Prince of Wales Island) while trading in the area. This happened only 30 miles from Somerset, and adding to the hysteria in southern cities was the story that the wife and son of the captain of the *Sperwer* had been kidnapped by the Kaurareg people of the Torres Strait.

The whitefella story goes that the Gudang people informed Jardine of the killings and he decided to lead a retaliatory raid on the islanders. The blackfella telling is that Jardine enlisted the aid of his Native Mounted Police and the crew of another vessel that he had whooped up ready for violence. As in many massacres, there were no written records kept, but according to Jardine's son, Bootles Jardine, a great slaughter of Kaurareg took place on Muralug.[12] No sign of the captain's wife and son was found. Not surprising, since they had been in Melbourne the whole time.

Even more shockingly, Jardine admitted that the killings might have been greater except for the presence at Somerset of two missionaries, Frederick Charles Jagg and William Kennett, who – again according to whitefella stories – worked hard to form close relationships with the peoples of the cape and to mediate the violence.

However, as Nicholas Thompson Wymarra tells, it is well known that Kennett took a young Gudang woman with him back to Dorset in England when he left the cape, along with a wallaby and many artifacts. 'That late female ancestor of ours had a very distinct shell necklace. We have photos and pictures.' For there is a photograph of her from a school in Symondsbury, where Kennett ended up teaching. The caption reads: 'So sad and far from home.'

Nicholas Thompson Wymarra visited Symondsbury in 2014, and heard the story of the woman living in a strange country, taken away from her traditional lands. He said that living in that cold climate, over the years she became very depressed.

'One of the senior members of that community can remember his grandfather telling him a story of the late old lady, our ancestor from Somerset, falling into great depression and sitting on the top of the church. And for the members of that community to see a black silhouette on the roof of the church, they saw that as something bad – an evil spirit. So that dark silhouette got shot at.

'But they're saying that they shot the wallaby.

'On the side of the church in the schoolyard, the school students and their families and any visitors coming there, there is always the story of the famous rock wallaby from Australia.'

But Nicholas is not convinced that it might be a wallaby buried at the church. It is a mystery that Nicholas would like to travel back to Symondsbury and solve, investigating what or who lies in that grave.

One of the less violent stories relating to Somerset occurred in 1875 when a French shipwreck survivor was brought into the settlement. He had been living with the sandbeach Uutaalnganu people (also known as Night Island Kawadji) for the past seventeen years.

The man, Narcisse Pelletier, had been a fourteen-year-old cabin boy when the ship *Saint Paul* was wrecked in 1858, near New Guinea. The crew abandoned 300 Chinese passengers – who had been on their way to the gold diggings – to a grisly fate at the hands of local tribes on a small island, and headed to the mainland in one of the ship's boats. They abandoned Narcisse there in turn.[13]

He was fortunate to be found by the friendly Uutaalnganu, who renamed him 'Amglo', and even initiated him into their tribe, making traditional scars across his arms and chest. Worimi historian John Maynard said that when he was found by members of the Uutaalnganu, he offered up a small metal cup he had and the people took this 'as right protocols of trying to connect as a gift'.[14]

He settled in well and became a valued member of the tribe. In 1875, he was found by the crew of the *John Bell* and they forcibly brought him aboard the vessel, threatening to kill his Uutaalnganu family and chaining him so he would not escape. They took him to the closest settlement at Pulu (Somerset).

A report in the Rockhampton paper *The Capricornian* of the time read: 'Narcisse, however, states that the sailors laboured under a misconception, and that neither did the natives wish him to go, nor did he himself wish to leave. In fact, at the time, he would much rather have returned to his tribe, but that both he and the blacks were afraid of the guns in the boat.'[15] When he arrived at Somerset he was described as being restless and uneasy, and as sitting like a bird on a rail watching everyone in a frightened way.

And upon being returned to France and reconnecting with his French family, he opted for the isolated life of a lighthouse keeper. But he had his story recorded, which provided Europeans with some understanding of his other family and life with them.[16]

Eventually the hopes and dreams for a prosperous settlement at Somerset were moved to Thursday Island in the Torres Strait, which was a safer harbour, and also added to the Queensland government's claim over those islands.

Nicholas Thompson Wymarra said, 'Somerset was supposed to be like Singapore, but Thursday Island became the hub. It had a safer harbour so everything went to Thursday Island. That was only in the 1880s, and my great-grandfather was there.'

He also said that his great-grandfather at one time speared Frank Jardine, 'after all that, you know, the massacres and everything that was going on there'.

For the people of the cape, too much of their recent history is dominated by the Jardine years. According to the Reconciliation Australia report, 'Recognising Community Truth-Telling', it is clear that these events and subsequent actions against the people of Cape York and the Torres Strait Islands have had a lasting, intergenerational impact. For instance, the Gudang had enjoyed a close relationship with their Torres Strait Islander neighbours to the north, often based around trade, but when the Gudang were seen as aligning themselves with the settlers at Somerset, relations soured. It ultimately did little good for the Gudang people, for by 1875 'official opinion was that the Gudang tribe had become extinct'.[17]

But Nicholas Thompson Wymarra said, 'Yeah, nah. That's why we are here to tell the story. We are the last Cape York Peninsula frontier warriors, and we make up the Gudang-Yadhaykenu combination. We're the survivors.'

And as a step towards getting beyond the darkness of the past, in 2022 the formerly named Jardine River National Park was renamed Apudthama National Park. It is being managed by the Gudang-Yadhaykenu, as well as the Atambaya and Angkamuthi native title holders from further to the south, in partnership with the Queensland government. Apudthama means 'everybody'.

When asked what he felt most Australians should know about his people, Nicholas Thompson Wymarra said, 'They need to know the real story. Acknowledging and respecting our cultural beliefs. We just had a group come through here, all the way from Sydney, they came all the way up here to Cape York. And they come up here and they got a bad name, like hooligans, wrecking campsites, and their goal was to make it to Cape York, and when they got there, bloody arseholes went and dacked their pants, six of them bloody standing there with their pants down, facing the other way showing their arses. So it caused a big uproar that did.

'That's the reason why Uluru is the way it is. They warned us, you know. Told us that with all these tourists coming through there would be disrespect and stuff like that.'

Nicholas also says that it is incorrect to consider his people custodians of the land. 'We are not custodian owners, we're not native title Traditional Owners, we are sovereign First Nations people of Injinoo!

'We are the last Cape York Peninsula warriors.'

Thuined (Possession Island)
Kaurareg Country

Aieh Wal Manin Nithamun kauraregau gagaith.

We welcome you to Kaurareg land and sea Country.[1]

> *Having satisfied myself of the great Probability of a passage, thro' which I intend going with the Ship, and therefore may land no more upon this Eastern coast of New Holland ... I am confident ... [this coast] was never seen or Visited by any European before us.*
>
> Cook's journal, 22 August 1770

There should be no surprise by now that oral histories don't always agree with what has been written, but the implications of the distance between oral telling and recorded history at Thuined (Possession Island) are really quite significant.

In short, did Cook plant a flag there and claim the whole east coast of Australia for King George III, or didn't he?

On 22 August 1770, Lieutenant James Cook stated in his journal that he'd landed on a small island nestled just offshore of Cape York, and 'now once more hoisted English Coulers, and in the Name of His Majesty King George the Third took possession of the whole Eastern Coast from the above Latitude [38] down to this place by the name of New South Wales, together with all the Bays, Harbours, Rivers and Islands situate upon the said Coast'.

But that is not the story told by everyone. According to Waubin Richard Aken, Kaurareg cultural historian and a rightful owner, 'Cook cooked the books.'

When the *Endeavour* came alongside that small island, Thuined, Cook wrote that they saw ten men on the shore, most armed with spears – but one with a bow and arrows. Waubin Richard Aken says that man was one of the Torres Strait Kaurareg people, as only the Torres Strait Islanders used bow and arrows. Cook then wrote that as they came near the shore in the ship's boat, they expected the people 'would have opposed our landing; but as we approached the shore they all made off, and left us in peaceable possession of as much of the Island as served our purpose'.

It was at this point, Cook wrote, that he hoisted English colours and took possession of the whole east coast of the continent. But Waubin Richard Aken disputes whether he was able to come ashore and plant the British flag.

Waubin Richard Aken, who has a Bachelor of Law and Management degree from Deakin University, tells that before Cook arrived in the Torres Strait there had been fire and smoke signals from Adhai (Crab Island, on the western side of Cape York), letting all the clan groups know a strange ship was travelling along the

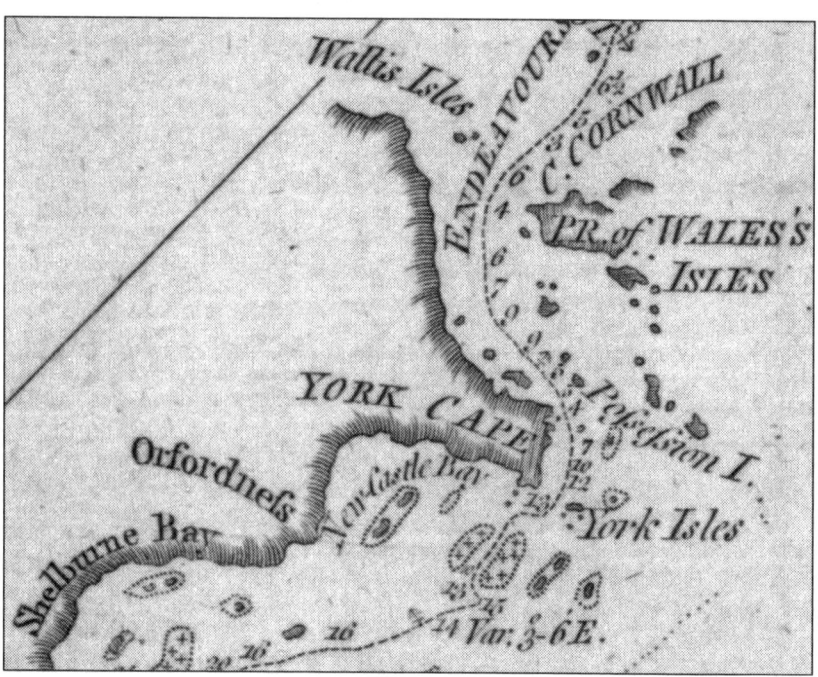

Cook's chart of the top of the continent showing Thuined (Possession Island)

east coast. He says that smoke signals and the message stick were 'a blackfella internet'.

And he says that if Cook and his crew had actually landed on Thuined there would have been 300 warriors waiting for him and he would have certainly been speared for violating Kaurareg sovereignty. He says Kaurareg's Djirrudjirru Kernge Kuiku Mabaigal – orange-foot people – came out on the northeastern side of the hills, that Cook didn't see, and would have violently opposed his landing.

Cook wrote in his journal that, having ascertained the 'great Probability of a passage' before him, and having 'took possession of the whole Eastern coast', he then 'fired 3 Volleys of small Arms, which were answer'd by the like number from the Ship'. But Banks, who accompanied him ashore, makes no mention of that ceremony in his own journal.

Sydney Parkinson, third major journal writer on board the *Endeavour*, confirmed that Cook went to the top of a hill and, 'seeing a clear passage, hoisted a jack, and fired a volley, which was answered by the marines below, and the marines by three vollies from the ship, and three cheers from the main shrouds'. But this has been seen as describing the relief felt at finally finding a clear passage ahead, rather than claiming possession of the whole eastern side of the continent, which Parkinson does not actually mention.[2]

Those who support the idea that Cook did not actually land on Thuined suggest that his journal entry about claiming the land was added much later, either in Batavia (Jakarta) or back in England. And this could have been done by Cook himself, realising he should make a claim to pre-empt the Dutch (or French, or somebody else), or it could have been inserted by the man who wrote up Cook's journey for publication, John Hawkesworth, at the instruction of the Admiralty. There is even speculation that, since Cook never named any territory as 'New', the New in New South Wales is evidence that the passage was written by Hawksworth.[3]

It has also been suggested that both Cook and Parkinson's journals could well have been amended by the Admiralty, but Banks, being a private citizen, would not have had his journal changed.

So we contacted the National Library of Australia to ask if the journal they have in their possession (as manuscript item number MS 1) was written by Cook or not, they replied: 'This item is indeed in Cook's hand, including corrections and rub outs.' But the Library also stated that 'it isn't possible to know exactly when these edits were made by Cook', and that 'other versions of the journal ... were done by a clark/scribe'.

But what about the ship's logbook, in which hourly entries were made as actual events occurred? Cook's log, also held in the National Library, has a passage that reads: 'The Cap'n with the Marines arm'd in the Pinnace and Yawl went ashore to examine the Country

Cook's journal of 22 August 1770, which states, 'Notwithstanding I had in the name of his Majesty taken possession of several places upon this coast I now once more hoisted English colours and for the name of His Majesty King George the Third took possession of this whole Eastern Coast from the above Latitude down to this place by the name of New South Wales ...'

and view the coast from one of the Hills. Saw several turtles and when we came too it was high water – we found the tide of ebb … At 6 Possession was taken of this Country in his Majesty's Name G [King George III] and this was announced from the shore by firing vollies and answered from the ship with Colours flying: the whole concluding with 3 cheers.'[4]

But the National Library catalogue entry for the logbook states: 'Manuscript copy of the log of the *Endeavour* … attribution of which is difficult … considered anonymous … It seems to be a fair copy done some time after the original.'

And to quote that old advertisement, 'But wait! There's more!'

There is also an argument that, in claiming the land, Cook would have been in clear contravention of his orders, that stated: 'You are also with the Consent of the Natives to take Possession of Convenient Situations in the Country in the Name of the King of Great Britain: Or: if you find the Country uninhabited take Possession for his Majesty by setting up Proper Marks and Inscriptions, as first discoverers and possessors.'

So if Cook did not seek the consent of the people of the continent, and just made a captain's call that the land was effectively uninhabited when it clearly wasn't, then perhaps that makes his claim invalid, as he went against his orders.

Waubin Richard Aken says that Cook's claim in his journal is a make-believe story, but even if it wasn't, it is certainly unwarranted, based on false pretences of sovereignty without rightful consent.

Visiting the island of Thuined is difficult, not just because it is so isolated, but because the northwestern side where Cook claimed to have landed is surrounded by many underwater rocks. It is difficult to get a boat ashore there, even one with sonar – and even then only at high tide – so travelling there makes you wonder how a wooden ship's boat might have fared trying to find a path through the rocks.

Before setting out to the island, Waubin Richard Aken performs a welcoming ceremony that involves water, not smoke, as water creates life. But it makes you feel the old ancestors of his people are watching you and will ensure you have safe passage over the waters to reach the island. He tells that a water ceremony is done through seasonal hunting using either fresh water or salt water. Fresh water comes from an underground aquifer, coming from Migi Daudai (Papua New Guinea) and running through the western Torres Strait all the way to the Great Dividing Range on the mainland. So it is the same water you can drink in Normanby station west of Cooktown.

He says Thuined is 'unique in a way that only certain people come here for ceremony, according to their bloodline, people come here, not any Kaurareg, just the right people with apical ancestry [ancestors at the tip of the known family tree] come here. And not women. No women allowed in this place. It's very unique this place.'

Walking along the beach of the island there is a mix of bleached turtle bones and washed-up plastics, and on one small bluff a concrete plinth with a plaque on it that reads: 'Lieutenant James Cook R.N. of the "Endeavour" landed on this island which he named Possession Island and in the name of his majesty King George III took possession of the whole eastern coast of Australia from the latitude of 38° South to this place. August 22nd 1770.'

A second plaque on the side of the small monument says that the plinth was built with financial assistant from the Queensland government as a bicentennial project, after the original cairn had been vandalised.

The Kaurareg might dispute whether it was the land or the cairn that had been most vandalised.

Walking on the beach gives a weird feeling, like the ancestors are watching really closely, making you wonder if you should be on the island, of if you shouldn't stay there too long. It is hard to describe it, but undeniable.

Waubin Richard Aken rests as he walks along the beach back to the boat, looking first at a path in the sand made by a turtle crawling up the beach, then he turns and points out to the channel that separates the island from Horn Island and Prince of Wales Island to the north. And he adds to the arguments that Cook did not land here, as the Kaurareg's knowledge about the currents and tidal systems in this area of Thuined tell that there is no close place to anchor, and ships will float away immediately from the islands.

'Now you see where the *Endeavour* was, but when you look out here there it's hard to anchor. I know a couple of navy boats had the same problem, with patrol boats trying to anchor up here in Thuined/Possession Island. They tried to anchor but they couldn't – the tide was dragging them.'

The implications of Cook having never really claimed the land are pretty significant, though perhaps overruled by Governor Arthur Phillip later claiming the land at Sydney Cove in 1788. Yet Governor Phillip's actual instructions from the British government have long been missing and so it is not known exactly what he was instructed to do, but the journals of those in attendance at the ceremony on 26 January 1788 make it pretty clear he was claiming all the land that Cook had charted.[5]

So what does it all mean? Well, it probably means that because most people cherrypick the information that agrees with their biases and opinions, different readers will conclude that the arguments support their own point of view on the matter. So we will leave all discussion of whether Cook landed at Thuined or not and sail on.

Interestingly, Cook's arrival is actually not that big a deal for most Torres Strait Islanders, not when compared to another European arrival. The event that far outweighs Cook's sail-by occurred in 1871

when missionaries arrived – an event so important in Torres Strait culture that it is referred to as the Coming of the Light.

The light, or missionary religion, is widely held to have come to the Torres Strait on 1 July 1871, when a former slave ship, the *Surprise*, arrived at Erub Island carrying a band of missionaries and their families from the London Missionary Society. These missionaries had just been ejected from the Loyalty Islands and New Caledonia by the French government, and were looking for a new place to set up. But they had actually been preceded in the Torres Strait by the Society for the Propagation of the Gospel, that had been based on Muralag Island (Prince of Wales Island) since 1865, building houses, a school and a church, and teaching the word of God there.

The London Society missionaries were led by the Reverend Samuel McFarlane and the Reverend Archibald Wright Murray. Clan elder and warrior, Dabad, is said to have met the missionaries, ready to defend his land and people. He walked into the water and McFarlane met him and dropped to his knees and presented Dabad with a bible. Dabad accepted it and the light had arrived.

The importance of the Coming of the Light – known locally as Zulai Wan, or Bi Akarida – cannot be overstated. The religion soon spread across the islands. It was adapted very easily into existing cultural beliefs, and depending on your point of view, it heralded an end to much of the cultural violence across the islands, or it heralded an end to many cultural practices. Or a bit of both. Prior to the arrival of the missionaries the Torres Strait Islands had seen a lot of tribal warfare between different peoples, as well as attacks on Europeans.

Waubin Richard Aken said, 'That's when the war stopped. So we forgot about our head-hunting and stuff and started going to Church.'

The next significant arrival was the 1898–99 Cambridge University anthropological expedition led by Alfred Cort Haddon.

Over several years he collected – some might use the verb 'appropriated' – about 2000 objects along with photographs and reams of notes on culture and customs. Haddon felt that the artifacts needed to be saved from destruction by the zealous Christian missionaries, who were prohibiting the use of traditional sacred objects.

Waubin Richard Aken said that some of the artifacts taken by the Cambridge expedition have since been returned, but Kaurareg artifacts are still under negotiation. 'The different islands have different perspectives about bringing it back. We Kaurareg, we are just finalising our tribal position on it. As a cultural historian I need to know the position of my clan, and my family responsibility.'

And again, the irony is that while missionaries and anthropologists and other Europeans took away a lot of the people's culture and practices, they also recorded a lot of it, so that stories of the creation of the islands are still told. Though in the Torres Strait

Thuined (Possession Island)

there is still a lot of oral knowledge as well. The Creation story of Thuined, for example, was recorded in the 1970s when Sarou Billy sang the song to story collector Margaret Lawrie. He told her that the words had been sung originally by Norinori, the sacred snake ancestor (tabo augud). The story goes:

'For many years Norinori, a big snake, lived at Paira (Cape York). Norinori did not obtain his food on land. Instead, he used to lie watching in the sea and, when he saw a canoe, swim out to it, sink it, and swallow all the people who had been aboard it. And then he used to sing:

Tabo ngai ad (ia),
(A) kai ad (ia).
Wa, tabo ngai ad (ia),
(E) (a) kai ad (ia) O!

'(I am the sacred ancestor snake. Yes, I am tabo [snake], great ancestor, sacred ancestor.)'

The day came when Norinori decided to leave Paira and go to Thuined. There, too, he obtained his food from the sea, sinking every canoe that came near and swallowing its people, afterwards singing his song. From Thuined the ancestor snake went on to Zuna (Entrance Island), from there to Muralag (Prince of Wales Island), and from there to Ngurupai (Horn Island), to Waiben (Thursday Island), and then finally to Kiriri (Hammond Island). And at each island he left offspring.[6]

Waubin Richard Akin said that the Kaurareg know that Norinori is the rainbow serpent snake, and one of his children is Waubaki, that lives in Kuipidh Creek on Ngurupai (Horn Island).

He says, 'Our stories are real stories … they come from this Country. They are not from somewhere else and they are not from comic books. This is what we need to tell the truth about. It doesn't matter if it offends the hearts and minds of people, but brings society to respect our cultivation of our knowledge and the implementation of spiritually sustainable development systems.'

Torres Strait Islanders believe in a Creation time, similar to the Dreaming, which is known as Bipor Taima (Before Time, or Kaipha Kulai Thonar). In the Bipor Taima the ancestral heroes came to the Torres Strait, and created the islands, the people, the animals and plant life. They also gave laws to the people.

Waubin Richard Aken said, 'Our plants and animals were created, even mother earth, sky, stars, mountains, rivers and waters were created first, before we came into existence, we got to respect them first. Without them we wouldn't survive on the land.'

Other Creation stories tell of the Kaurareg warrior Waubin, who is believed to have travelled from central Australia to the Torres Strait and lived on Muralag with a number of his Ippilies (wives). He roamed the island hunting, and fighting with other warriors.

One key story tells of Waubin's final battle, and is connected to a hill known as Waubinin Mabauzi Lag (meaning 'Waubin walked down') and Waubinin Malu ('the sea of Waubin'). Waubin was fighting a warrior, Badhanai, who was very short, and in the battle Badhanai darted beneath Waubin, slicing off his right leg with his bamboo knife (upi). The blood from the wound then flowed down the hill Waubinin Mabauzi Lag, into a waterhole at Rabau Nguki, and from there it was carried out to sea. Waubin said to his wives after the fight that they must leave Rabau Nguki, but a reddish tinge is still visible in the sea there. And as far as the blood spread it marked the territorial boundary of the Kaurareg people.

At Waubinin Mabauzi Lag vegetation will not grow, and there are also very fast flowing tides at Waubinin Malu that were created by Waubin when he walked into the sea that protects Muralag.[7] Ippili Reef is his wives. After the fight he sat down in the ocean and turned to stone – the small island now known as Hammond Rock – and he protects his people by sending strong currents around Muralag.[8]

Waubin Richard Aken

The Torres Strait Islands are actually extremely diverse in culture and languages, and Cook passed by only the southernmost group of islands, which was one of the five major island groups. In total there are over 250 islands of varying sizes. The people are not the same as those of mainland Australia, but are Melanesian, being more related to the people of Papua New Guinea.

Having said that, the people of the islands have long intermarried and traded not just amongst themselves, but with people from Asia, including Macassar (the island of Sulawesi), Timor Leste, and across Melanesia to the Solomon Islands, as well as with people from mainland Australia. And anthropologists have concluded that Torres Strait Islanders came to the islands much later than the people of Australia came to the land to the south, arriving only about 9000 years ago.

However, Waubin Richard Aken, says it is scientific racism to say his people had only been there for 9000 years – or even 65,000 years, demonstrating the conflicts that can arise between scientific beliefs and traditional beliefs.

He said, 'Our people were here since time immemorial.'

The island of Thuined, where Cook's engagement with this continent ends, was important to many different peoples of Cape York and nearby islands, including the Kaurareg, Gudang-Yadhaykenu, Ankamuthi, and some other clan groups, and is known by many different names. To the Gudang-Yadhaykenu it is Thunadha, and to the Kaurareg the island has two names – it is called Thuined in the time of the southeast trade winds, and it is called Bedanug in the time of the northwest monsoons.

Waubin Richard Aken says, 'Sagerau thonar (the eastern wind) blows from April to November, making the seas rough. But there is malu aidhal and lagau aidhal (plenty of seafood and food on land). Hunting always happens near Thuined when birubiru (kingfisher birds) appear, and with the arrival of gaenhauw (Torres Strait birds) travelling from Migi Daudai (Papua New Guinea) to the northern part of Khai daudai (Australia). September is waru sisari (green turtle) mating season.

While the island has many names and seasons, and can be quite different in each one, Cook only saw it for a single moment, and was unable to appreciate its moods and seasons, as those who had lived there since time immemorial did. Likewise, his charts and journal capture only a fleeting view of the whole east coast, compared to those who lived there and knew the lands and waters deeply.

And yet, as Cook sailed away from Australia, writing up an overview of his thoughts, he recorded something quite insightful, showing he was perhaps starting to see beyond the lens of European perspective after all. He wrote: 'From what I have said of the Natives of New Holland they may appear to some to be the most wretched People upon Earth; but in reality they are far happier than we Europeans, being wholy unacquainted not only with the Superfluous, but with the necessary Conveniences so much sought after in Europe; they are happy in not knowing the use of them. They live in a Tranquility which is not disturbed by the Inequality of Condition. The earth and Sea of their own accord furnishes them with all things necessary for Life.'

Contact

Much of the early contact between Europeans and the Torres Strait Islanders did not go well. William Bligh, having sailed through the strait after being thrown off the HMS *Bounty* by mutineers in 1789, returned on board the ship *Providence* in 1792. Like Cook he renamed several of the islands, including Darnley Island (Erub), Stephens Island (Ugar), and Mulgrave Island (Badu). And like Cook further down the east coast, Bligh shot at people. He killed or wounded three Erub Islanders in a canoe after misinterpreting a peace offering and opening fire on them.[9]

In accordance with traditional customs, this violence led to payback, and the following year an officer and four seamen from the merchant vessel *Shah Hormuzear* and the London whaler *Chesterfield* were killed and then ritually dismembered during a visit to Erub Island.[10]

So fearsome were the Torres Strait Islanders thought to be by Europeans that it reached a point where seeking a passage through the Torres Strait was described as 'a dangerous exercise for European mariners', both because of the many unmapped reefs and also because of the 'resident Indigenous communities who had acquired a reputation for brutal attacks and cruel treatment of castaways'.[11]

And then, in 1834 things escalated significantly. The ship *Charles Eaton* was wrecked near Raine Island in the northern Great Barrier Reef and the survivors set out in a ship's boat and two rafts. The ship's boat eventually made it to Batavia, but those on the rafts were not so fortunate. They were met by a large canoe of Torres Strait Islanders, who took them to Boydong Island. They might have thought they were saved, but all the adults were clubbed to death and beheaded. Only three children were spared, and one of those soon died. The two surviving boys, John Ireland and the captain's son, William D'Oyly, lived with their captors for a few months, before being traded to visitors from Mer (Murray Island, home of land rights activist Eddie Mabo) for a bunch of bananas. The people of Mer treated the two boys with kindness, renaming them Wak and Uass. The boys lived with the Mer islanders until they were rescued two years later, in mid-1836.

The rescuers were told by the Mer islanders that the attackers had come from Auridh Island, and, full of colonial fury, the crew went there, but found the island deserted. However, they found a small hut with a ceremonial mask made from a turtle shell, surrounded by about forty human skulls. These were taken to Sydney and identified as European, the victims of the *Charles Eaton*. There was sensationalism, there was outrage, there was racist stereotyping.

When Torres Strait Islanders were eventually asked for an interpretation of events, they explained this was one of the more extreme practices of the followers of the cult of Kulka, one of four Creation brothers. A further explanation has been provided by Torres Strait Islander artist Janice Peacock, who wrote that Torres Strait Islanders would only claim castaways who they 'recognised' as either friends or as family members. Otherwise they were killed, usually by beheading.[12]

There is also a story told to the anthropologist Charles Haddon, who spent several years in the Torres Strait. He recounted that a man named Pasi had told the missionary the Reverend MacFarlane, probably in the late 1800s, that people who had been in the water, like shipwreck survivors, were considered dangerous, and might make puripuri (harmful magic) and harm people while in that crazed condition. Haddon recounted that Pasi said, 'The salt water spoils his face and eyes, the sun blisters him so that his face comes different, his head comes another way (he is not in his full senses), that's why we kill him.'[13]

More (and more very cautious) mapping and exploration expeditions followed through the Torres Strait, including Captain Owen Stanley on HMS *Rattlesnake* during the 1840s. The voyage of the *Rattlesnake* made several interesting discoveries, but none more so than one day in October 1849, when some of the sailors were washing clothes in a stream on the cape, and a woman in a grass skirt approached them and in halting English told them she was a white woman and a Christian who had been living with Torres Strait Islanders. After the sailors had overcome their surprise, they took the young woman, Barbara Thompson, on board the *Rattlesnake*. There she was able to tell how she had been shipwrecked near Ngurupai (Horn Island) and had then lived for five years with the Kaurareg on Muralag (Prince of Wales Island).

Janice Peacock wrote that Barbara Thompson had been very fortunate to have been found by a Kaurareg man, Peaqui, who believed her to be the markai (returned spirit) of his own deceased daughter Giomi.[14] And as Giomi, Barbara slowly learned the language and ways of the Kaurareg, and remained with them for nearly five years, but unlike Narcisse Pelletier, she always longed to return to her own people.

Like Eliza Fraser's story, news of Barbara Thompson living with the Islanders stirred up the wild fantasies of some in the popular media of the day, and her leaving of the Kaurareg has sometimes been depicted as escaping a life 'with savages under the most primitive conditions'.[15] But on board the *Rattlesnake* Giomi/Barbara Thompson related her story to the ship's artist, Oswald Brierly, providing extensive details of the Kaurareg's life and customs. Though the name of the people is more accurately spelled in English as 'Kawalgal', it was transcribed as 'Kaurareg', which has stuck over time.

Barbara told how the mainland Gudang were constantly going back and forth to the islands, and there could be large changes in their relationships with the Kaurareg, due to misdeeds or misunderstandings. But with other groups, like the Gumakudin, relations were invariably hostile. And she described how raids for capturing women – or even men – from an enemy tribe could end in marriage. She told how there had been an attempted raid by a party from Badu Island, to capture her and take her to marry a man named Weenie, a Frenchman who had settled among them, who she thought to have been a runaway convict. She also told Brierly that the Kaurareg pitied the white fellows, who they thought had no Country of their own and therefore had to roam about on their ships searching for provisions.[16]

Waubin Richard Aken said, 'Every time when a sailing ship went pass, they painted her [Barbara] with charcoal – black – so they wouldn't recognise her. She was one of us. She did a book about our language, which is important for us now for current generations. And recording all the language is very important, and it is for us to revitalise it and start speaking it and try and put it in through the education system.

'We thank her too for her knowledge and wisdom and understanding of the psyche of the Kaurareg – how we do things here.'

In 2022, two of Barbara Thompson's descendants returned to the Torres Strait to meet with the descendants of the Kaurareg she had lived with. One of the descendants, Glynis Hatch, said that they were warmly welcomed. 'People would come up to us and hold our hand and say, "You share Barbara's blood." We cannot stress enough how much Barbara is loved and honoured …'[17]

Following the 1869 Jardine-led massacre of Kaurareg for the killing of the crew of the *Sperwer*, violence and disease took a heavy toll on the people. In 1875 a severe measles epidemic swept through the islands, killing about one in four people. And while the Reverend McFarlane is curiously quiet on the epidemic in his writings – stating rather that the Islanders were being depleted by overwork on pearl-shellers and by alcohol – researcher Steve Mullins says that 'McFarlane was instrumental in spreading the 1875 measles epidemic through the Strait, and ... [it] is impossible to believe that he was unaware of the consequences of his actions'.[18]

Traders had also been increasingly coming to the Torres Strait Islands in search of pearl, tortoise and trochus shell, and by the 1860s several shore stations had been set up in the central and eastern islands. Elizabeth Osborne, in her comprehensive history *Throwing off the Cloak*, wrote that there was a collision of cultures when the Europeans started settling the islands in the nineteenth century.[19] This period has been described by Janine Peacock as 'a time of exploitation, with many documented abuses, including the forced labour of Aboriginal and Torres Strait Islander men and women to work in the fisheries, often without remuneration'.[20]

In 1879 all the Torres Strait Islands – and all the islanders – were annexed to Queensland. And with Federation they became a part of the state of Queensland.

By 1922 there were only about eighty Kaurareg left alive, and in that year they were taken off their traditional lands at gunpoint and forcibly removed to Moa Island. Even Thuined was ravaged by colonial settlers. In 1896 gold had been discovered there and mining continued for about a decade. Important sacred ground was destroyed. Today there are abandoned workings left on the island, including several mine shafts, one of which sits behind a memorial to Cook.

As the Reconciliation Australia report 'Recognising Community Truth-telling' says, 'The story of the Kaurareg, like that of many First Peoples in Australia, is one of enormous hardship, and dispossession, but also a remarkable story of survival and determination to preserve culture, identity and sovereignty, despite the depredations of colonialism.'[21]

Waubin Richard Aken, when asked what he felt whitefellas in Australia most needed to know, said, 'The truth. Coming from our people. Tell them the truth, that they don't be afraid of the truth. It will heal you. Once the country recognises the truth, it will heal you wherever you are.'

Notes

Quotations from the journals of James Cook, Joseph Banks and Sydney Parkinson are from:

- Cook, James & Wharton, W.J.L. (eds) (1893), *Captain Cook's Journal During His First Voyage Round the World Made in H.M. Bark Endeavour, 1768–71*, Libraries Board of South Australia.
- Banks, Joseph, (1997), *The Endeavour Journal of Sir Joseph Banks, 1768–1771*, University of Sydney Library, Scholarly Electronic Text and Image Service.
- Parkinson, S. & Kenrick, W. (1773), *A Journal of a Voyage to the South Seas, in His Majesty's Ship, the Endeavour: Faithfully Transcribed from the Papers of the Late Sydney Parkinson, Draughtsman to Joseph Banks, Esq. on His Late Expedition with Dr. Solander Around the World*, Stanfield Parkinson, London.

Munda Bubal/Tolywiarar (Point Hicks): Gunaikurnai & Bidwell Countries
1. Angove, A. (1994), *Kurnai Poems (Gunnai Wark)*, Ngarak Press, Ensay.
2. Gurnaikurnai Land and Waters Aboriginal Corporation, <www.gunaikurnai.org>.
3. Gunai/Kurnai Traditional Custodians (2015), *Nernila, 'Listen Continuously, Aboriginal Creation Stories of Victoria*, Creative Victoria.
4. Gurnaikurnai Land and Waters Aboriginal Corporation, <www.gunaikurnai.org>.
5. Fuller, L. (2019), *Our Land, Our Stories*, Australian Institute of Aboriginal and Torres Strait Islander Studies, Canberra.
6. Pepper, P. & De Araugo, T. (1985), *The Kurnai of Gippsland*, Hyland House, Melbourne.
7. Gammage, B. (2012), *The Biggest Estate on Earth: How Aborigines Made Australia*, Allen & Unwin, Sydney.
8. Gurnaikurnai Land and Waters Aboriginal Corporation <www.gunaikurnai.org>.
9. Thorpe, W. (2022), 'How a Young Fella Named Boondjil Noorook Discovered Captain Cook', *The Age*, 23 January.
10. MacDonald, J. (2001), 'Captain Cook ... the untold story!', *Signals 57*, Australian National Maritime Museum, Sydney.

11 Howitt, A.W. (1880), 'The Kurnai: Their Customs in Peace and War' in Fison, L. and Howitt, A.W., *Kamilaroi and Kurnai*, Anthropological Publications, Oosterhout.
12 George Dunderdale (1893), *The Book of the Bush, Containing Many Truthful Sketches of the Early Colonial Life of Squatters, Whalers, Convicts, Diggers, and Others Who Left Their Native Land and Never Returned*, War, Lock & Co, London.
13 Howitt, A.W. (1904), *The Native Tribes of South Eastern Australia*, Macmillan, London.
14 Darmangeat, C. (2019), 'Vanished Wars of Australia: The Archeological Invisibility of Aboriginal Collective Conflicts', *Journal of Archaeological Method and Theory*, vol. 26.
15 Gardner, P.D. (2001), *Gippsland Massacres: The Destruction of the Kurnai Tribes, 1800–1860*, Ngarak Press, Ensay.
16 Pascoe, B. (2014), *Dark Emu*, Magabala Books, Broome.
17 Gardner, *Gippsland Massacres*.
18 Rule, A. (2002), 'The Black Watch, a Verdict of History', *The Age*, 27 April.
19 Gardner, *Gippsland Massacres*.
20 Ibid.
21 McMillan, A. (1841), 'Sydney', *Port Phillip Patriot and Melbourne Advertiser*, 18 January.
22 Morey, S. & Gibson, J.M. (2018), 'Recovered Aboriginal Songs Offer Clues to 19th Century Mystery of the Shipwrecked "White Woman"', *The Conversation*, 11 December.
23 Grimshaw, P., Nelson, E. & Smith, S. (2002), *Letters from Aboriginal Women of Victoria, 1867–1926*, History Department, University of Melbourne.
24 Zafiris, A. (2017), 'Revealed: The Forgotten First Match Between a VFL Team and an Aboriginal Football Team, <www.Shootfarken.com.au> 25 May.

Gulaga (Mount Dromedary): Yuin Country
1 Perry, L.E. (2013), *Mission Impossible: Aboriginal Survival Before, During and After the Aboriginal Protection Era*, PhD thesis submitted to the Wollotuka Institute of Aboriginal Studies, University of Newcastle.
2 Harrison, M.D. (2023), *Gurawul the Whale*, Magabala books, Broome.
3 Harrison, M.D. (2009), *My People's Dreaming*, Finch Publishing, Sydney.
4 Roberts, A. (2010), *Aboriginal Women's Fishing in New South Wales: A Thematic History*, Department of Environment, Climate Change and Water NSW, Sydney.
5 Robinson, R. (1989), *The Nearest the White Man Gets: Aboriginal Narratives and Poems of New South Wales*, Hale & Iremonger Sydney; and (2022), *Yangary and Bhundoo: Aboriginal Places and Values around Batemans Bay*, Transport NSW, Sydney.

6   Gibbney, H.J. (1989), *Eurobodalla: History of the Moruya District, Sydney*, in association with the Shire of Eurobodalla.
7   Turner, J.W. (1996), *Thematic History of Eurbodalla Shire*, Hunter History Consultants, Newcastle.
8   Milne, E.O. (1916), 'The Passing of the Lithic People: A Story of the Coming of White Wings to Australia', *Life*, 1 April.

Kembla (Red Point): Dharawal Country
1   Author unnamed (undated), Dharug and Dharawal Resources, University of NSW <https://dharug.dalang.com.au/plugin_wiki/page/dharawal_welcome_to_country>.
2   Jodi Edwards, email correspondence, 10 December 2023. Organ, M.K. & Speechley, C. (1997), 'Illawarra Aborigines: An Introductory History', in Hagan, S. & Wells, A. (eds), *A History of Wollongong*, University of Wollongong Press. Unnamed (2005), *A History of Aboriginal People of the Illawarra 1770 to 1970*, NSW Department of the Environment and Conservation, Sydney.
3   Bursill, L., Donaldson, M. & Jacobs, M. (2015), *A History of Aboriginal Illawarra Volume 1: Before Colonisation*, Dharawal Publications, Yowie Bay.
4   Ibid.
5   Bursill, L, Jacobs, M, Lennis, D, Timbery-Beller, B & Ryan, M. (undated), *Dharawal: The Story of the Dharawal Speaking People of Southern Sydney*.
6   Bursill, L., Donaldson, M. & Jacobs, M., *A history of Aboriginal Illawarra Volume 1*.
7   Ibid.
8   Ibid.
9   Organ, M.K. & Speechley, C., 'Illawarra Aborigines'.
10 Organ, M.K. (1990), *Illawarra and South Coast Aborigines 1770–1850*, Aboriginal Education Unit, University of Wollongong.
11 Mitchell, W. & Sherington, G. (1984), *Growing up in the Illawarra*, University of Wollongong.
12 Organ, M.K. & Speechley, C., 'Illawarra Aborigines'.
13 Ibid.
14 Ibid.
15 Tyerman, D. & Bennett, G. (1840), *Voyages and Travel around the World*, John Snow, London.

Kamay (Botany Bay): Dharawal Country
1   Rose, D. (2001), 'The Saga of Captain Cook: Remembrance and Morality', in B. Attwood & F. Magowan (eds), *Telling Stories: Indigenous History and Memory in Australia and New Zealand*, Bridget Williams Books and Allen & Unwin, Sydney.

2   Donaldson, M., Bursill, L. & Jacobs, M. (2017), *A History of Aboriginal Illawarra, Volume 2: Colonisation*, University of Wollongong.
3   National Museum of Australia, Endeavour voyage <https://www.nma.gov.au/exhibitions/endeavour-voyage>.
4   State Library of NSW, 'Cook: It was Only Eight Days', <https://www.sl.nsw.gov.au/>.
5   Williams, S. (2020), *An Indigenous Australian Perspective on Cook's Arrival*, British Library.
6   Nugent, A. (2008), 'The Encounter Between Captain Cook and Indigenous People at Botany Bay in 1770 Reconsidered', in Veth, P., Sutton, P. & Neale, M. (eds) (2008), *Strangers on the Shore: Early Coastal Contacts in Australia*, National Museum of Australia Press, Canberra.
7   Nugent, A. & Scullthorpe, G. (2018), 'A Shield Loaded with History: Encounters, Objects and Exhibitions', *Australian Historical Studies*, 49:1.
8   McEncroe, J. (1863), 'The Cook Demonstration', *Sydney Morning Herald*, 27 April.
9   Flinders, M. (1814), *A Voyage to Terra Australis; Undertaken for the Purpose of Completing the Discovery of That Vast Country*, G. and W. Nicol, Pall-Mall.
10 Tench, W. (1789), *A Narrative of the Expedition to Botany Bay*, J. Debrett, London.

Warrane (Sydney Harbour): Dharug/Eora Country
1   Phillip, A. (1788), *Letter from Arthur Phillip to the Marquis of Lansdowne*, 3 July 1788, Mitchell Library, State Library of NSW.
2   Attenbrow, V. (2010), *Sydney's Aboriginal Past: Investigating the Archaeological and Historical Records*, UniNSW Press, Sydney.
3   Foley, D. & Read, P. (2020), *What the Colonists Never Knew*, National Museum of Australia, Canberra.
4   Author unnamed (undated), *Place Names Chart*, The Australia Museum. <https://australian.museum/learn/cultures/atsi-collection/sydney/place-names-chart/>.
5   Arthur, W.S. & Morphy, F. (eds) (2019), *Macquarie Atlas of Indigenous Australia*, Australian National University, Australian Bureau of Statistics, and Pan Macmillan Australia, Sydney.
6   Dawes, W. & Patyegarang (1791), *The Notebooks of William Dawes on the Aboriginal Language of Sydney*.
7   Collins, D. (1802), *Account of the English Colony in New South Wales*, W. Davies, London.
8   'Was the Didgeridoo a bit of Irish to the Aborigines?', *Sydney Morning Herald*, 23 June 2002.
9   State Library of NSW, <https://www.sl.nsw.gov.au/stories/eora>.
10 Raeburn, T., Doyle, K. & Saunders, P. (2022), 'How the Kidnapping of a First Nations Man on New Year's Eve in 1788 may Have Led to a Smallpox Epidemic', *The Conversation*, 11 January.

11 Tench, W. (1793), *A Complete Account of the Settlement at Port Jackson*, London.
12 Warren, C. (2014), 'Was Sydney's Smallpox Outbreak of 1789 an Act of Biological Warfare against Aboriginal tribes?' *Ockham's Razor*, ABC Radio National, 17 April.
13 Dowling, P. (1990), 'Violent Epidemics: Disease, Conflict and Aboriginal Population Collapse as a Result of European Contact in the Riverland of South Australia', thesis submitted for Master of Arts in Biological Anthropology, Australian National University.

Whibayganba (Nobbys Head): Awabakal & Worimi Countries
1 Tindale, N. (1974), *Aboriginal Tribes of Australia: Their Terrain, Environmental Controls, Distribution, Limits, and Proper Names*, ANU press, Canberra.
2 Ibid.
3 Arposio, A. (2020), *Nupaleyalaan Palii Awabakalkoba: Teach Yourself Awabakal*, Miromaa Aboriginal Language and Technology Centre.
4 Author unnamed (2015), *Filling a Void: History of Word 'Guringai'*, Aboriginal Heritage Office, Sydney.
5 Gunson, N. (ed) (1974), *Australian Reminiscences & Papers of L.E. Threlkeld, Missionary to the Aborigines, 1824–1859*, Australian Institute of Aboriginal Studies, Canberra.
6 Haslam, P. (1977–79), Percy Haslam Papers, University of Newcastle Archives. A5410 (i).
7 Perry, J.L. (2013), '"Mission Impossible": Aboriginal Survival Before, During and After the Aboriginal Protection', (PhD thesis submitted to Wollotuka Institute of Aboriginal Studies, University of Newcastle.
8 Author unnamed (undated), Worimi Conservation Lands, <https://worimiconservationlands.com/>.
9 Maynard. J. (2014), *True Light and Shade and Aboriginal Perspective of Joseph Lycett's Art*, National Library of Australia Publishing, Canberra.
10 'Aborigines of the Hunter' (1993), *Newcastle Morning Herald*, 11 May.
11 Maynard. J., *True Light and Shade and Aboriginal Perspective of Joseph Lycett's Art*.
12 Turner, J. & Blyton, G. (1995), 'The Aboriginals of Lake Macquarie, a Brief History', Lake Macquarie City Council.
13 Ibid.
14 Blyton, G. (2003) *Dispossession and Violence: A Brief Note on the Newcastle-Lake Macquarie Region in the 1920–1830s*, Awaba, University of Newcastle.
15 'Aboriginal History', <https://www.portstephens.org.au>.
16 Threlkeld, L. (1834), *An Australian Grammar Comprehending the Principles and Natural Rules of the Language, as Spoken by the Aborigines in the Vicinity of Hunter's River, Lake Macquarie &c. New South Wales*, Stephens and Stokes, Sydney.

Dooragan, Booragan & Mooragan (The Three Brothers): Birpai, Gumbaynggirr & Dunghutti Countries

1. Archibald-Simmons, H., Ballangarry, T., Lord, A., O'Reilly, K., Scott, E. (2011), *Birpai Yarns*, a Bago Community of Schools Project, coordinated & published by Andrew Lord.
2. Van Kempen, E. (2006), *The Birpai*, Kendall Community Centre.
3. King, Phillip Parker (1826), *Narrative of a Survey of the Intertropical and Western Coasts of Australia*, London.
4. Narelle Mathews (2005), *Her Story: Searching for the Lost Women of the two Rivers*, Hastings Council.
5. Ibid.
6. Aboriginal Interpretive Signage – Smoky Cape, Kempsey Council.
7. Morelli, S., Williams, G. & Walker, D. (2016), *Gumbaynggir Yuludarra Jandaygam: Gumbaynggir Dreaming Story Collection*, Muurrbay Aboriginal Language and Culture Cooperative, Nambucca Heads.
8. Undated and unnamed document provided by the Yarrawarra Aboriginal Cultural Centre, stating that the story is believed to have been recorded by anthropologist A.C. McDougall around 1900.
9. Morelli, S., Williams, G. & Walker, D., *Gumbaynggir Yuludarra Jandaygam*.
10. Watts, G. (2018), presentation regarding the Red Rock Massacre, Coffs Harbour City Libraries, accession number LS2023.87.1.
11. Archibald-Simmons, H., Ballangarry, T., Lord, A., O'Reilly, K., Scott, E. (2011), *Birpai Yarns*.
12. *The Sydney Gazette and New South Wales Advertiser*, 4 May 1816.
13. Wilson, H.L. (1889), 'The Early Days of Port Macquarie', republished by Dick, T. (1921), *The Port Macquarie News and Hastings River Advocate*, Feb 5.
14. Sati, W. (2021), 'Blackmans Point Massacre of Birpai People Could Soon be Formally Acknowledged', ABC Mid North Coast, 23 May.
15. Knowles, R. (2023), 'Aunty Rhonda Grew up Hearing About the Massacres at Blackman's Point. Now, This History Has Been Recognised', NITV, 5 May.
16. Anon. (1838), 'The Aborigines of Port Macquarie', *Sydney Gazette*, February 6.

Wollumbin (Mount Warning): Bundjalung Country

1. Wollumbin National Park, NSW Department of Planning and Environment, <www.environment.nsw.gov.au>, accessed 23 June 2023.
2. Steele J. (1984), *Aboriginal Pathways in Southeast Queensland and the Richmond River*, University of Queensland Press.
3. Fox, I. & Slabb, K. 'First People', in DeGood, M. (ed) (2016), *The Fragile Edge: A Natural History of the Tweed Coast*, Bogangar.
4. Information provided by the Tweed Regional Museum, Murwillumbah.
5. Fox, I. & Slabb, K. 'First People'.

6   Slabb, K., (undated), Tweed Regional Museum, Murwillumbah.
7   Fox, I. & Slabb, K. 'First People'.
8   Gannon, M. (2018), *Tweed Byron Local Aboriginal Land Council, Cultural Heritage Sites Inspection*, TBLALC Cultural Heritage Unit.
9   Mathews, R.H. (1898), 'Initiation Ceremonies of Australian Tribes. Appendix Nguttan Initiation Ceremony', *Proceedings of the American Philosophical Society*, 37:
10 Fox, I. & Slabb, K. 'First People'.
11 Boileau, J. (2004), 'Community-based Heritage Study, Thematic History', Tweed Shire Council, NSW Heritage Office.
12 Gannon, M. (2018), *Tweed Byron Local Aboriginal Land Council, Cultural Heritage Sites Inspection*.
13 Fox, I. & Slabb, K. 'First People'.
14 Oxley, J. (1825), *Narrative of Mr. Oxley's Expedition to Survey Port Curtis and Moreton Bay: With a View to Form Convict Establishments There*, John Uniacke.
15 Bostock, S. (2023), *Reaching Through Time: Finding My Family's Stories*, Allen & Unwin, Sydney.
16 Medcalf, R. (1993), 'Rivers of Blood, Massacres of the Northern Rivers Aborigines and Their Resistance to the White Occupation 1838–187', *Northern Star*.
17 Ainsworth, J. (1987), *Reminiscences 1847–1922: Ballina in the Early Days*, Beacon Print, Ballina.
18 'Living on the Frontier', NSW Environment & Heritage, <Environment.nsw.gov.au>.
19 Medcalf, R. 'Rivers of Blood, Massacres of the Northern Rivers Aborigines and Their Resistance to the White Occupation 1838–187'.
20 Fox, I. & Slabb, K., 'First People'.
21 Curr, E.M. (1887), *The Australian Race: Its Origin, Languages, Customs, Place of Landing in Australia and the Routes by which it Spread Itself Over the Continent*, J. Ferres.
22 Fox, I. & Slabb, K., 'First People'.
23 NSW Parks and Wildlife Service (2022), 'Wollumbin Aboriginal Place Management Plan', Environment and Heritage Group.
24 Bundock, M. (1835–98), 'Notes on the Richmond River Blacks', in Papers of the Bundock Family of Wyangarie Station, Richmond River, Mitchell Library, State Library of New South Wales, cited in Bostock, S. (2023), 'From Colonisation to My Generation: An Aboriginal Historian's Family History Research Past to Present', PhD thesis submitted to Australian National University, Canberra.
25 Bostock, S. (2023), *Reaching Through Time*.
26 Bostock, S., 'From Colonisation to My Generation'.
27 Census (2016), Language spoken at home by sex, <stat.data.abs.gov.au>.

Beerwah & Tibrogargan (The Glass House Mountains): Kabi Kabi & Jinibara Countries

1. Ford, R. & Blake, T. (1998), *Indigenous Peoples of Southeast Queensland: An Annotated Guide to Ethno-historical Sources*, FAIRA Aboriginal Corporation, Woolloongabba.
2. *The Daily Mail*, 21 July 2019.
3. Glass House Mountains Visitors Centre.
4. Story collected by Gwen Trundle, mid-1800s, Gwen Trundle papers, John Oxley Library South Brisbane, cited in Northage, I. (2017), *The National Heritage Listed Glasshouse Mountains*, Celebrate Glasshouse Country Inc.
5. Jacques, O. (2019), 'Ten Times More Glass House Mountain Rescues than any Other Queensland Climbing Spot', ABC Sunshine Coast.
6. Steele, J.G. (1972), *The Explorers of the Moreton Bay District, 1770–1830*, University of Queensland Press, St. Lucia.
7. Tucker, A. (1999), *Side by Side*, Omnibus Books, Adelaide.
8. Kerkhove, R.C. (2014), 'Aboriginal "Resistance War" Tactics: "The Black War" of Southern Queensland', *Cosmopolitan Civil Societies Journal*, Vol. 6, No. 3.
9. 'Something that must be Enquired Into', *Sydney Morning Herald*, 5 December 1842.
10. Gibbney, H.J. (2006), entry for Sir Evan Mackenzie (1816–1883) in the *Australian Dictionary of Biography*, <https://adb.anu.edu.au/biography/mackenzie-sir-evan-4108>.
11. Murphy, K., Lillis, J., Gall, B. (2017), *Jinibara Traditional Inputs for the Sunshine Coast Heritage Study, For Sunshine Coast Regional Council*, Australian Heritage Specialists.
12. Mackenzie-Smith, J. (2000), *Moreton Bay Scots 1841–59*, Church Archivists' Press, Nudgee.
13. Jolly, L. (1994), *Gureng Gureng: A Language Program Feasibility Study*, University of Queensland Press, St Lucia.
14. Kerkhove, R. (2023), *How They Fought: Indigenous Tactics and Weaponry of Australia's Frontier Wars*, Boolarong Press, Tingalpa.
15. Connors, L. (2006), 'Traditional Law and Indigenous Resistance at Moreton Bay 1842–1855', *ANZLH E-Journal*, University of Southern Queensland.
16. Kerkhove, R. (2018), *Kabi Kabi Sites and History of the Legendary Mount Coolum*, Keperra, Queensland.
17. Murphy, K., Lillis, J., Gall, B., *Jinibara Traditional Inputs for the Sunshine Coast Heritage Study, For Sunshine Coast Regional Council*.
18. Ibid.

K'gari (Fraser Island): Butchulla Country

1. Burns, M. & Bonner, N.J. (2023), 'Traditional Owners, Butchulla People, K'gari, Great Sandy National Park', Queensland Government Parks and Forests, Department of Environment and Science.
2. Miller, O. (1994), *Legends of Fraser Island*, Rigby Heinemann, Port Melbourne.
3. Armitage, E. (1923), 'Corroborees of the Aborigines of Great Sandy Island', *Journal of the Royal Geographical Society* (Queensland Branch), vol. 48.
4. Cronin, G., transl. in Chandler, L. (2014), *East Coast Encounter*, One Day Hill, Melbourne.
5. Curtis, J. (1838,) *Shipwreck of the Stirling Castle: Containing a Faithful Narrative of the Dreadful Sufferings of The Crew And The Cruel Murder Of Captain Fraser By The Savages: Also, The Horrible Barbarity Of The Cannibals Inflicted Upon the Captain's Widow Whose Unparalleled Sufferings are Stated by Herself, and Corroborated by the Other Survivors*, George Virtue, London.
6. Behrendt, L. (2016), *Finding Eliza: Power and Colonial Storytelling*, University of Queensland Press, St Lucia.
7. Dawson, B. (2014), *In the Eye of the Beholder: What Six Nineteenth-century Women Tell Us About Indigenous Authority and Identity*, ANU Press, Canberra.
8. Youlden, H. (1853), 'Shipwreck in Australia', *The Knickerbocker*, No. 4.
9. Evans, R. & Walker, J. (1978), '"These strangers, Where are They Going?": Aboriginal–European Relations in the Fraser Island and Wide Bay Region 1770–1905', *Aboriginal History*, Vol. 2, No. 1:2.
10. Ibid.
11. Ibid.
12. Barrowcliffe, R. (2021), 'Celebrating K'gari: Why the Renaming of Fraser Island is About so Much More than a Name, *The Conversation*, September 28.
13. Behrendt, L., *Finding Eliza*.
14. Matthews, T. (1995), *River of Dreams: A History of Maryborough and District*, Maryborough City Council Maryborough, Qld.
15. Fairlie, J. (1932), Early Maryborough, *Maryborough Chronicle*, 9 July.
16. Richards, J. (2008), *The Secret War: A True History of Queensland's Native Police*, University of Queensland Press.
17. Foley, F. (2020), 'The People of Fraser Island: Working Through 250 Years of Racial Double Coding', *Genealogy*, 4(3), 74.
18. Evans, R. (2020), *Passionate Histories: Myth, Memory and Indigenous Australia*, ANU Press, Canberra.
19. Evans, R. & Orsted-Jensen, R. (2014), '"I Cannot Say the Numbers that Were Killed": Assessing Violent Mortality on the Queensland Frontier', SSRN, 19 July. Wallis, L., Burke, H. & Meston, T. (2023), 'Our Mapping Project Shows How Extensive Frontier Violence was in Queensland. This Is Why Truth-Telling Matters', *The Conversation*, 14 November.

Gooragang (Bustard Bay): Gooreng Gooreng Country

1. Gladstone Ports Corporation (2009), *Place of Water Koongo, Place of Shells Yallarm, Book 1, the Dreaming to 1934*, Gladstone Ports Corporation, Gladstone.
2. Macarthur, A. (1997), *His Majesty's Bark Endeavour: The Story of the Ship and Her People*, Angus & Robertson, Sydney.
3. Brennan, C. (2019), 'The Physical "Endeavour": How a Wooden Ship Shaped Cook's First Circumnavigation', *Journal of the Royal Australian Historical Society*, 105(2).
4. Author unnamed (undated), Agnes Waters Museum.
5. Gladstone Ports Corporation, *Place of Water Koongo, Place of Shells Yallarm, Book 1, the Dreaming to 1934*.
6. Curr, E.M. (1887), *The Australian Race*, Government Printer, Melbourne.
7. Laurie, A. (1959), 'The Black War in Queensland', *Journal of the Royal Historical Society of Queensland*.
8. Behrendt, L. (2018), *Indigenous Australia for Dummies*, Wiley, Brisbane.
9. Quoted in Reynolds, H. (1996) *Frontier: Reports from the Edge of White Settlement*, Allen & Unwin, Sydney.
10. Jolly, L., *Gureng Gureng*.
11. Woolford, N. (2013), *Gooreng Gooreng Country: Language*, <GoorengGooreng blogsport.com>.
12. Spelitis, H. (2015), 'Indigenous Elder Pushes to Preserve Local Language', *Courier Mail*, 24 March.

Ngari (Hook Island, Whitsundays): Ngaro Country

1. Dickson, F. (2009), 'The Ngaro People of the Whitsundays', ABC Local, <http://www.abc.net>.
2. Briggs, V. (2023), *Seafaring: Canoeing Ancient Songlines*, Magabala Books, Broome.
3. Rowland, M.J. (1986), 'The Whitsunday Islands: Initial Historical and Archaeological Observations and Implications for Future Research', *Queensland Archaeological Research*, 3.
4. Barker, B. (2004), *The Sea People: Late Holocene Maritime Specialisation in the Whitsunday Islands, Central Queensland*, Pandanus Books, Research School of Pacific and Asian Studies, Australian National University.
5. Dickson, F., 'The Ngaro People of the Whitsundays'.
6. Rowland, M.J., 'The Whitsunday Islands'.
7. Reynolds, H., cited in Burke, H., Barker, B., Cole, N., Wallis, L. A., Hatte, E., Davidson, I., & Lowe, K. (2018), 'The Queensland Native Police and Strategies of Recruitment on the Queensland Frontier, 1849–1901', *Journal of Australian Studies*, 42(3).
8. Dickson, F., 'The Ngaro People of the Whitsundays'.

9 Foley, F. (2020), *Biting the Clouds: A Badtjala Perspective on the Aboriginals Protection and Restriction of the Sale of Opium Act, 1897*, University of Queensland Press, St Lucia, Queensland.

Thul Garrie Waja (Cleveland Bay): Bindal & Wulgurukaba Countries

1 Morrill, J. (1864), *Sketch of a Residence Among the Aboriginals of Northern Queensland for Seventeen Years; Being a Narrative of my Life, Shipwreck, Landing on the Coast, Residence Among the Aboriginals With an Account of Their Manners and Customs and Mode of Living, Together With Notices of Many of the Natural Production and of the Nature of the Country*, Newcomb's Steam Printing Office, Boston.
2 Ibid.
3 Tindale, N., *Aboriginal Tribes of Australia*.
4 Jukes, J.B. (1847), *Narrative of the Surveying Voyage of H.M.S. Fly: Commanded by Captain F.P. Blackwood, R.N., in Torres Strait, New Guinea, and otherIislands of the Eastern Archipelago, During the Year 1842–1846; Together with an Excursion into the Interior of the Eastern Part of Java*, London, T. & W. Boone.
5 Smith, J.W. & Dalrymple, G.E. (1860), *Report of the Proceedings of the Queensland Government Schooner "Spitfire" in Search of the Mouth of the River Burdekin, on the North Eastern Coast of Australia*, T.P. Pugh Printing Office, Sydney.
6 Bell, P. (2000), *A Short History of Thuringowa*, City of Thuringowa.
7 Breslin, B. (2023), *Exterminate with Pride: Aboriginal–European Relations in the Townsville-Bowen Region to 1869*, Australian Scholarly Publishing.
8 Loos, N. (1986), *Invasion and Resistance: Aboriginal–European Relations on the North Queensland frontier 1861–1897*, Australian National University Press, Canberra.
9 Breslin, B., *Exterminate with Pride*.
10 Magnetic Island's Resident Scientific Community (2004), *Magnetic Island's World Heritage Values: A Preliminary Assessment*, Magnetic Island Community Development Association and Magnetic Island Nature Care Association.
11 Burnum Burnum & Stewart, D. (1988), *Burnum Burnum's Aboriginal Australia: A Traveller's Guide*, Angus & Robertson, Sydney.
12 Layland, P. (1998), 'Captive Lives, Moving Stories', *National Library of Australia News*, Canberra.
13 *Townsville Daily Bulletin*, 3 March 1930.
14 Watson, J. (2006), entry for Robert Henry (Bob) Curry, Australian Dictionary of Biography, <https://adb.anu.edu.au/biography/curry-robert-henry-bob-12874>.
15 Prior, R. (1993), *Straight from the Yudaman's Mouth: The Life Story of Peter Prior Before, During and After the Robert Curry Days, Never Told Before*, James Cook University of North Queensland.
16 Hooper, C. (2008), 'Under the Rainshadow', *The Monthly*, September.

Munamudanamy (Hinchinbrook Island): Bandjin & Girramay Countries

1. Cambell, J.B. (1979), 'Settlement Patterns on Offshore Islands in Northeastern Queensland', *Australian Archaeology*, no. 9.
2. Pike, G. (1954), *The Kennedy Expedition*, Historical Society of Queensland, 22 April.
3. Cambell, J.B., 'Settlement Patterns on Offshore Islands in Northeastern Queensland'.
4. Author unnamed (1861), Native Police Report, Legislative Assembly of Queensland.
5. Marr, D. (2023), *Killing for Country*, Black Inc, Melbourne.
6. 'The Abandonment of Gilberton', *The Queenslander*, 4 April 1874.
7. <www.Frontierconflict.org>.
8. *Brisbane Courier*, 19 November 1867.
9. Heydon, C., *Brisbane Courier*, 9 February 1874.
10. Wallis, L., Burke, H. & Meston, T. (2023), 'Our Mapping Project Shows How Extensive Frontier Violence was in Queensland. This is Why Truth-Telling Matters', *The Conversation*, 14 November.
11. Australian War Memorial, (2023), *Deaths as a Result of Service with Australian Units*, Australian War Memorial, Canberra.
12. Richards, J. (2008), 'The Native Police of Queensland', *History Compass*, 6/4.
13. Burke, H., Barker, B., Cole, N., Wallis. L.A., Hatte, E., Davidson, H. & Lowe, K. (2018): 'The Queensland Native Police and Strategies of Recruitment on the Queensland Frontier, 1849–1901', *Journal of Australian Studies*.
14. Rosser, B. (1990) *Up Rode the Troopers: The Black Police in Queensland*, University of Queensland Press, St Lucia.
15. Burke, H., Barker, B., Cole, N., Wallis. L.A., Hatte, E., Davidson, H. & Lowe, K., 'The Queensland Native Police and Strategies of Recruitment on the Queensland Frontier, 1849–1901'.
16. Bottoms, T. (2013), *Conspiracy of Silence: Queensland's Frontier Killing Times*, Allen & Unwin, Sydney.

Djilibirri (Cape Grafton): Gunggandji, Mandingalbay, Yidinji & Irukandji Countries

1. Gunggandji PBC Aboriginal Corporation (2013), 'Gunggandji Land and Sea Country Plan', Great Barrier Reef Marine Park Authority.
2. Ibid.
3. Buluwai Indigenous Corporation (2018), *In Brief: Cairns Regional Claim Native Title Tribes': Aboriginal Rainforest People's History Project*, Buluwai Indigenous Corporation.
4. Author unnamed (2018), 'Embracing Our Stories: Cairns Indigenous Interpretive Signage Trail', Cairns Regional Council.
5. <https://www.youtube.com/watch?v=nDZj1P-LkWM>.

6 'Embracing Our Stories'.
7 Lounsbury, L., & Watson, B. (2021), 'Marriage and Relationships' in Watson, B. (ed.), *Remembering Mona Mona: The Mission in the Rainforest*, Signs.
8 Dawul Wuru Aboriginal Corporation and Yirrganydji People (2014), *Yirrgandji Kulpul-Wu, Mamingal, Looking after Yirrganydji Sea Country Plan*, Queensland government.
9 International Research Group on Wood Protection (2023), 'Location and History', IRG54, <https://www.irg-wp.com/IRG54/location.html>.
10 'Embracing Our Stories', Signage Trail, Cairns Regional Council, Queensland government.
11 Pannell, S. (2008), 'Aboriginal Cultures in the Wet Tropics', in Stork, N.E. & Turton, S.M. (2008), *Living in a Dynamic Tropical Forest Landscape*, Blackwell Publishing.
12 Roth, W.E. (1898), 'Cooktown to Home Secretary's Office', 4 February, Queensland State Archives, COL/139.
13 Author unnamed (1861), 'Report of the Select Committee on the Native Police', Queensland Legislative Assembly.
14 Mann. J.F. (1885), *Notes on the Aborigines in Australia*, Geographical Society of Australasia, NSW and Victorian Branches, 1st session, vol.1.
15 Buluwai Indigenous Corporation (2018), *In Brief: Cairns Regional Claim Native Title Tribes, Aboriginal Rainforest People's history Project*, Buluwai Indigenous Corporation.
16 Foley, F., *Biting the Clouds*.
17 Burnum Burnum, & Stewart, D. (1988), *Burnum Burnum's Aboriginal Australia: A Traveller's Guide*, Angus & Robertson, North Ryde.
18 Williams, C. & Nimmo, J. (2023), 'Overcrowding Contributes to People Dying Young in Yarrabah: Residents Hoped a Voice to Parliament Should Help', *ABC*, 24 October.

Kulki (Cape Tribulation): Kuku Yalanji Country
1 Yalanji Warra People, Jabalbina Yalanji Aboriginal Corporation (2016), *Nganjinanga Bubu, Nganjinanga Jalun, Nganjinanga Bama Plan: Our Land, Our Sea, Our People Plan. Eastern Kuku Yalanji Indigenous Protected Area Management Plan Stage 3*, Jabalbina Yalanji Aboriginal Corporation, Mossman.
2 Anderson, C. (1996), *Traditional Material Culture of the Kuku Yalanji of Bloomfield River, North Queensland*, Records of the South Australian Museum 29.
3 Voyages Indigenous Tourism Australia (2023), *Meet the Kuku Yalanji People*, Mossman Gorge Cultural Centre. <https://www.mossmangorge.com.au/our-community/kuku-yalanji-people>.
4 King, P.P., (1826), *Narrative of a Survey of the Intertropical and Western Coasts of Australia Performed between the years 1818 and 1822*, John Murray, London.

5 Unnamed author, (1874), 'Inquiry into the Deaths of Aborigines at the Normanby River, "The Palmer"', *Brisbane Telegraph*, 23 January.
6 Loos, N., *Invasion and Resistance*.
7 Steffensen, V. (2020), *Fire Country*, Hardie Grant, Melbourne.
8 Anderson, C, (2022), 'A Case Study in Failure: Kuku-Yalanji and the Lutherans at Bloomfield River, 1887–1902', in Swain, T. & Rose, D.B. (eds), *Aboriginal Australians and Christian Missions*, Australian Association for the Study of Religions, Adelaide.

Whalumbal Birri (Endeavour River): Gugu Yimidhirr Country
1 Cormick, C. & Ludwick, H. (2020), *On a Barbarous Coast*, Allen & Unwin, Sydney.
2 Ibid.
3 Deeral, E. (2001), James Cook Museum, Cooktown.
4 Kirkman, N. (1978), 'A Snider is a Splendid Civilizer: European Attitudes to Aborigines on the Palmer', in Kennedy, K.H. (ed.), *Race Relations in North Queensland*, James Cook University, Townsville.
5 Hughes, I. (1975), 'A State of Open Warfare: Frontier Conflict in the Cooktown Area', in Dalton, B.J. (ed.), *Lectures on North Queensland History*, second series, James Cook University, Townsville.
6 Hill, W. (1938), *The Palmer Gold Field, Early Day Experiences*, Cummins and Cambell.
7 Kirkman, N.S. (1984), 'The Palmer Goldfields, 1873–1883', honours thesis, James Cook University, Townsville.
8 Author unnamed (undated), *The Missions*, James Cook Museum Cooktown.

Pajinka (Cape York Peninsula): Gudang-Yadhaykenu Country
1 Moore, D.R. (1979), *Islanders and Aborigines at Cape York*, Australian Institute of Aboriginal Studies, Canberra.
2 Carron, W. (1849), *Narrative of an Expedition Undertaken under the Direction of the Late Surveyor E.B. Kennedy for the Exploration of the Country Lying between Rockingham Bay and Cape York*, Kemp and Fairfax, Sydney.
3 Nugent, M. (1979), 'Jacky Jacky and the Politics of Aboriginal Testimony', in Konishi, S., Nugent, M. & Shellam, T.S.B (1979), *Indigenous Intermediaries: New Perspectives on Exploration Archives*, ANU Press, Canberra.
4 Ibid.
5 Barolsky, V., Berger, K. & Close, K. (2023), *Recognising Community Truth-telling: An Exploration of Local Truth-telling in Australia*, Alfred Deakin Institute for Citizenship and Globalisation, Centre for Inclusive and Resilient Societies and Reconciliation Australia.
6 Austin, C.G. (1949), *Early History of Somerset and Thursday Island*, Historical Society of Queensland.

7   Sharp, N. (1992), *Footprints along the Cape York Sandbeaches*, Aboriginal Studies Press, Canberra.
8   Ibid.
9   Jardine, F. (1871), 'The Settlement at Cape York', *The Queenslander*, 20 May.
10 Sharp, N., *Footprints along the Cape York Sandbeaches*.
11 Ibid.
12 Barolsky, V., Berger, K. & Close, K., *Recognising Community Truth-telling*.
13 Author unnamed (2016), *Abandoned: The incredible Tale of a French Castaway*, Queensland State Archives 2 November.
14 Maynard, M. & Haskins, V. (2018), 'Narcisse Pelletier or "Anco"', *Speaking Out*, 13 May.
15 'The Narrative of Narcisse Pelletier, *The Capricornian*, 5 June 1875.
16 Pelletier, N. (1876), *Dix-sept ans chez les sauvages: aventures de Narcisse Pelletier*, Constant Merland, Paris.
17 Sharp, N., *Footprints along the Cape York Sandbeaches*.

Thuined (Possession Island): Kaurareg Country
1   The rightful language of the Kaurareg is Oomee, but after the removal of Kaurareg people in 1922, they adopted Kala Lagaw Ya languages.
2   Author unnamed (2019), *Possession Island*, Naval Historical Society of Australia. https://navyhistory.au/possession-island/.
3   Taylor, G. (undated), '"Over Cooked": Is Captain Cook the Source of British sovereignty in Australia?' *Sovereign* Union, http://nationalunitygovernment.org/.
4   Cook, J., (undated), Log of H.M.S. *Endeavour*, 1768–1770.
5   Collins, D. (1798), *An Account of the English Colony of NSW Vol 1*, T. Cadell Jr & W. Davies.
6   Lawrie, M. (1970), *Myths and Legends of the Torres Strait*, Taplinger Publishing Company, New York.
7   Roberts, S. & Carter, C. (2021), 'Native Title: Protecting Culturally Significant Sites from Development', *Law Society Journal online*, 1 May.
8   Smith, A. (2018), 'The "Forgotten People": When Death Came to the Torres Strait', *CNN*, May 25.
9   Flinders, M. (1814), *A Voyage to Terra Australis, Volume 1*, G and W Nicol, London.
10 McNiven, I.J. (2020), *Torres Strait Islanders: The 9000-year History of a Maritime People, Awakening: Stories from the Torres Strait*, Queensland Museum.
11 McNiven, I. (2018), 'Ritual Mutilation of Europeans on the Torres Strait Maritime Frontier', *The Journal of Pacific History*, 22 August.
12 Peacock, J. (2000), 'Inner Weavings: Cultural Appropriateness for a Torres Strait Island Woman Artist of Today', PhD submitted to Griffith University.

13 Haddon, A.C., & Ray, S.H. (2011), *Reports of the Cambridge Anthropological Expedition to Torres Straits: Volume 3: Linguistics*, Cambridge University Press, Cambridge.
14 Peacock, J., 'Inner Weavings'.
15 Lack, C. (1939), 'The Story of Barbara Thomson: Tragedy and Adventure on the Queensland Coast, number 10', *The Sunday Mail*, 26 November.
16 Moore, D.R. (1979), *Islanders and Aborigines at Cape York*, Australian Institute of Aboriginal Studies, Canberra.
17 Barolsky, V., Berger, K. & Close, K., *Recognising Community Truth-telling*.
18 Mullins, S. (1993), 'Torres Straits Pre-colonial Population: The Historical Evidence Reconsidered', *Queensland Archaeological research*, vol. 9.
19 Osborne, E. (2009), *Throwing off the Cloak: Reclaiming Self-reliance in Torres Strait*, Aboriginal Studies Press, Canberra.
20 Peacock, J., *Inner Weavings*.
21 Barolsky, V., Berger, K. & Close, K., *Recognising Community Truth-telling*.

Acknowledgements

Thank you in many, many different languages to all the people we talked to for this book, and in particular those who shared their knowledge and experiences with us. It was the greatest honour to be entrusted with your stories:

Aara Welz, Adele Hyslop, Aunty Alberta Hornsby, Alex Friday, Alex Wisniowiecka, Alex Wymarra, Alfred 'Touche' Grey, Alison Page, Alison Williams, Amber Rogers, Andrew Malloch, Asmi Wood, Boe Spearim, Brent McLellan, Aunty Catherine Prior, Chelsea Purcell, Chenica Saltner, Chris Matthews, Clayton Harrison, Clifford Prior, David Watts, Dale Johnson, Darren McKenny, David Barnett, Aunty Dorothy Hellyer, Aunty Dorothy Savage, Dwayne 'Bob' Broome, Eddie Savage, Fiona Foley, Uncle Gavi Duncan, Galiina Ellwood, Harry Van Issum, Helen Tait, Aunty Hope O'Chin, Aunty Jacqueline Johnson, Jacqueline Wright, Jan McLucas, Aunty Jeanette Singleton, Jess Shapiro, Jodi Edwards, Joe Perry, John Maynard, Kerry Blackman, Kerry Neill, Lisa Fuller, Aunty Lorraine Brown, Luke Barrowcliffe, Lyndall Ryan, Maekeira Hellyer, Marcus Arvidson, Margaret Johnson, Margot Neal, Marie Shipton, Mary Jacobs, Aunty Melinda Holden, Michael Bell, Uncle Michael Mansell, Michael Organ, Aunty Minne Johnson, Nardja Carter, Aunty Narelle Thomas, Uncle Neville Johnson, Ngawi Armstrong, Nicholas Wymarra, Uncle Noel Butler, Peter Read, Peter White, Phil Rist, Ray Kelly, Rhonda Radley, Richard Campbell, Rita Metzenrath, Rob Hudson, Rose Barrowcliffe, Samantha Faulkner, Sharon Mason, Shauna Bostok, Uncle Shayne Williams, Shona Coyne, Uncle Tais K'Reala Randanpi, Terry Olsen, Therese Ardler, Thomas Holden, Tim Appo, Tina Pidcock, Trevor Prior, Aunty Vivian Mason, Uncle Warren Foster, Waubin Richard Aken, Wayne Shipp, Uncle Wayne Thorpe, Aunty Zeitha Jalmala Murphy.

Everybody we interviewed and quoted in the manuscript was consulted on the draft texts and had the final say on their text. For the very small handful who we were unable to reconnect with, despite multiple attempts, we have taken advice from others and trust we have been faithful to your stories.

Thank you to our agent Tom and publisher Ben for believing in us and the book, and to our editor Meredith for her invaluable input, and also to our eagle-eyed cultural reader and proofreader Casey Mulder.

We also want to acknowledge our long-suffering wives, Rachel and Sharon, for putting up with our endless jaunts away, and especially Craig's wife Sharon for letting us raid the family mortgage to pay for much of the travel and community consultations needed to research this book when our generous publisher's advance had run out.

Twenty-five per cent of royalties on the sale of this book will be donated to the Indigenous Literacy Foundation. To help out, go to indigenousliteracyfoundation.org.au.

Image Credits

Text

All text images not credited in this list are by Craig Cormick. Cook's charts are sourced from the American Geographical Society Library Digital Map Collection.

PAGE IX: chart created by William Whitchurch, reproduced courtesy of the State Library of NSW.

PAGE 12: photo by Laura Ferguson.

PAGE 39: photo supplied by Uncle Noel Butler.

PAGE 76: sketch of gadi plant, 1790s, courtesy of the State Library of New South Wales.

PAGE 111: photo supplied by Aunty Rhonda Radley.

PAGE 139: sketch of English-style glass house by Denis Diderot.

PAGE 142: photo by Sarah Neill.

PAGE 143: photo supplied by Aunty Zeitha Jalamala Murphy.

PAGE 154: sketch of Indigenous Australian resistance leader Dundalli shortly before his execution, by Silvester Diggles, 1855, courtesy of the State Library of Queensland.

PAGE 173: photo courtesy of John Oxley Library, State Library of Queensland, negative number 31352, reproduced with the permission of Galiina Ellwood.

PAGE 232: sketch of Djilibirri (Cape Grafton), courtesy of the State Library of Queensland.

PAGE 252: photo of man with a woomera and shield at the Bloomfield River Mission, ca. 1884, courtesy of the State Library of Queensland.

Insert

PAGE 1: *Gulaga* © Cheryl Davidson, reproduced with the permission of the artist; *The Arrival of Captain Cook* © Kevin Butler, reproduced with the permission of the artist; *Twelve Turtles* © Wanda Gibson/Copyright Agency, 2024, reproduced with permission of the National Museum of Australia.

IMAGE CREDITS

PAGES 2–3: *Terra Nullius* © Gordon Bennett, reproduced with the permission of Leanne Bennett.

PAGE 4: Both photos by Craig Cormick.

PAGE 5: Mary Ann Cowan photographed in 1873 by J.W. Lindt; 'Portrait of a Gudang woman wearing a shell necklace' photographed by William Kennett.

PAGE 6: 'Portrait of James Morrill lost for 17 years among the Blacks near Port Denison, found close of 1862'/John Ness/PIC Box PIC/8270 #PIC/8270, kindly provided by the National Library of Australia.

PAGES 8–9: All photos by Craig Cormick.

PAGE 10: Photo of Queensland native police courtesy of the State Library of Queensland.

PAGE 11: *Auntie Dot* © Julie Dowling//Copyright Agency, 2024; *Eyes of Innocence* © Colina Wymarra, reproduced with permission of the artist and NPARC (Northern Peninsula Area Regional Council), and of the National Museum of Australia.

PAGE 12: Both photos by Craig Cormick.

About the authors

Darren Rix is Gunditjmara-GunaiKurnai man with Ngarigo bloodlines. He grew up in the tin huts and tents of 'Silver City', South Nowra, with his mother, stepfather and eleven siblings, largely living off the land and the sea. His family got their first house in the Bega Valley some years later, through Gunya Aboriginal Housing. At fourteen years of age he moved to Ngunnawal Country – Canberra. He has worked as a radio reporter for the Brisbane Indigenous Media Association and as a culture sites officer. Darren is also an accomplished musician, something he has in common with his uncle, Archie Roach. He has six children and twelve grandchildren.

According to Craig, Darren is one of the nicest blokes you'd ever hope to meet and end up travelling with.

Dr Craig Cormick OAM is an award-winning author and science communicator. He has published more books than he can count on his fingers and toes. He was born on Dharawal Country – Wollongong – and currently lives on Ngunnawal land in Canberra. He trained as a journalist and social scientist and has worked for many different agencies, including the CSIRO and Questacon. He is drawn to stories of people whose voices have been hidden from history – as he was drawn to this project. He has four children and three grandchildren.

According to Darren, Craig is a kind-hearted fulla – and it's been a great journey to be a part of doing this book with him, and the people we met on the way.